THE HEALING LAND

THE HEALING LAND

THE BUSHMEN AND
THE KALAHARI DESERT

Rupert Isaacson

GROVE PRESS
New York

First published in Great Britain in 2001 by
Fourth Estate, London, England

Printed in the United States of America

FIRST AMERICAN EDITION

Library of Congress Cataloging-in-Publication Data
Isaacson, Rupert.
    The healing land : the Bushmen and the Kalahari Desert / Rupert
Isaacson.
        p. cm.
    Originally published: London : Fourth Estate, 2001.
    ISBN 0-8021-1739-2
    1. San (African people)—Africa, Southern—Social life and customs.
    2. San (African people)—Kalahari Desert—Social life and customs.
    3. Isaacson, Rupert—Journeys—Africa, Southern. 4. Isaacson, Rupert—
Journeys—Kalahari Desert. 5. Africa, Southern—Description and travel.
    6. Kalahari Desert—Description and travel. I. Title.

DT1058.S36 I83 2003
306'.089'961—dc21   2002029728

Grove Press
841 Broadway
New York, NY 10003

03 04 05 06 07   10 9 8 7 6 5 4 3 2 1

For the Ancestors
And to my son, Rowan Besa Isaacson

Circling, circling . . .
I have entered the airy, dancing lightness of love.

Rumi

Contents

Acknowledgements

First and foremost I have to thank my wife, Kristin, for her unlimited patience during my long absences in the Kalahari, as well as for her reading of endless drafts and for acting as an unpaid copy editor. It could not have been done without her. Thanks are due to Charles Norwood and Merrigan Turner at Safari Drive, for supplying me with vehicles out of sheer goodwill. Also to Rian Malan for putting up with me more times than he needed to in Johannesburg and to Tessa Boase, for publishing the initial piece in the *Daily Telegraph* that made the idea of the book a possibility. John Mitchinson helped me put the book proposal into a coherent form so that my agent, David Godwin, could make it happen. Thank you to Nicholas Pearson at Fourth Estate for being brave enough to commission the book, Jane Robertson for making the text leaner and Bela Cunha for making it stronger.

As for those who helped me on the ground: Jackie at the Chameleon, Windhoek; Bulanda Thamae in Ghanzi; Cait Andrews, Roger Chennels, Chris Walker and Belinda Mathee in South Africa; my cousins Frank and Michael Taylor as well as Andrea Kennagh and Tom Hardbattle in Botswana; my cousins Gert and Cynthia Loxton in Keimoes; Karnells – without whom we'd never have made it through the Central Kalahari; Benjamin Xishe in Nyae Nyae; Tom Parsons, Greg Packard and Mondi Leombruno for the company and cost sharing; Rikki Schwartz, Regopstaan (Vetkat), Kabuis, Izak, Bukse and Dawid Kruiper; Katherine and Xwa Hardbattle and above all – and from all of us – thanks to Besa.

Glossary

badimo	gods
bakkie	pick-up truck
Bliksem	lightning; also means to hit someone
bloed	blood
Boesman	Bushman
Boesmantaal	Bushman tongue or 'speak'
braai	barbecue
braai vleis	meat cooked on an open fire
Broederbond	secret brotherhood of white Afrikaners
bruin mense	brown people, coloured
dagga	marijuana
doek	scarf
Donner	thunder; also to hit someone
inganga	witch doctor
kak	shit
kaptein	leader
kaross	fur blanket
kerrie	club; short for knobkerrie
kgotla	BaTswana tribal council. The word can mean both the council itself and the fenced-off circle in the village where the council meets.
khadi	a liquor made from *moretlwa* berries
Kraal	corral
ledang	a kind of root good for menstrual problems

lekker	nice
moikero meetsa	root good for treating kidneys and bad periods in women
mokalane	tree whose roots and bark are used to build strength and immune systems of livestock
muti	medicine, also votive or magical object
n/um	strength that begets wisdom; also marijuana
naai	'fuck' – can also mean to sew with a needle
nxole	paste made from a root
nyore	village in Ju'/Hoansi language
xai	small skin loincloth
zol	joint

THE HEALING LAND

PART ONE

ANCESTRAL VOICES

I

Stories and Myths

In the beginning, so my mother told me, were the Bushmen — peaceful, golden-skinned hunters whom people also called KhoiSan or San. They had lived in Africa longer than anyone else. Africa was also where we were from; my South African mother and Rhodesian father were always clear on that. Though we lived in London, my sister Hannah and I inhabited a childhood world filled with images and objects from the vast southern sub-continent. Little Bushman hand-axes adorned our walls; skin blankets, called karosses and made from the pelts of rock hyraxes,★ hung over the sofa; Bushman thumb pianos, made from soft, incense-scented wood, with metal keys that went 'plink' when you pressed down and then released them, sat on the bookshelves next to my mother's endless volumes of Africana. There were paintings by my maternal grandmother Barbara: South African village scenes of round thatched huts where black men robed in blankets stood about like Greek heroes. Next to them hung pictures by my own mother, of black children playing in dusty mission schoolyards, of yellow grass and thorn trees. In my earliest memory, these objects and my mother's stories forged a strong connection in my mind between our London family and the immense African landscapes the family had left behind.

I remember my mother playing an ancient, cracked recording of a Zulu massed choir and trying to show me how they danced. 'Like this, Rupert,' she said, lifting one leg in the air and stamping it on the floor several times in quick succession. 'They spin as they

---

★Also known as rock rabbits, they are small creatures similar in appearance to the guinea pig. Curiously, their closest known relative is the elephant.

jump, so it looks as if they're hanging in the air for a second before they come down, like this, watch.' She and I would stamp, wheel and jump, a small blonde woman and a smaller blond boy trying to imitate the lithe warriors of her memory.

When I was about five or six years old, my cousin Harold, a tall, bearded, Namibian-born contemporary of my father's who had settled in London as a doctor, gave me a small grey stone scraper – a sharply whittled tool that sat comfortably in my child's hand. It had been found in a cave in the Namib Desert. 'This', he told me, 'might have been made thousands of years ago. But it could also be just a few hundred years old, or perhaps even more recent than that; there are Stone Age people living in Africa right now who still use tools like this.' I closed my hand around the scraper, marvelling at its smooth, cool surface. 'Is it worth a lot of money?' I asked. The big man laughed. 'Perhaps,' he said, 'but maybe it's more valuable even than money.'

He showed me a glossy coffee-table book, illustrated with colour photographs of Bushmen. They were small and slender, naked but for skin loincloths, and carried bows, chasing antelope and giraffes across a flat landscape covered with waist-high grass. They had slanted, Oriental-looking eyes, and whip-thin bodies the colour of ochre. The women, bare-breasted, wore bright, beaded headbands and necklaces of intricate geometric patterns. According to my cousin, they were a people who lived at peace with nature and each other, whose hunting and tracking skills were legendary and who survived in the driest parts of the desert.

I put the scraper among my treasures – a fox's skull, a dried lizard, the companies of little lead soldiers, a display of pinned butterflies. Occasionally, in quiet moments, I would take it out, hold it and imagine scraping the fat from a newly flayed animal skin.

I remember, too, my mother reciting this hymn, written down in the nineteenth century, recorded from Bushmen on the banks of South Africa's Orange River. 'Xkoagu', my mother read, pronouncing the 'Xk' as a soft click:

Xkoagu, hunting star,
Blind with your light the springbok's eyes
Give me your right arm
and take my arm from me
The arm that does not kill
I am hungry

My mother knew the power of language and made sure that, though we lived in England and knew and loved its knights and castles, green woods and Robin Hoods, we also felt her birthplace moving in us just as she did.

Around this time another cousin came to stay, Frank Taylor, a childhood playmate of my mother's. He lived, she told us, on the edge of the great Kalahari, where the Bushmen lived. He had brought a small bow and arrow, which I was encouraged to try. I set one of the pointed shafts to the taut sinew of the bowstring and, at a nod from the grown-ups, let fly at the stairs. The arrow stuck, quivering in the wood. With my head full of longbows and Agincourts, I was impressed by its potentially lethal power. But this bow and arrow, said my mother, was not a weapon of war. It was for hunting the great herds of antelope that thronged the Kalahari grasslands.

Kalahari – what a beautiful word. It rolled off the tongue with satisfying ease, seeming to imply distance. A great wilderness of waving grasses, humming with grasshopper song under a hot wind and a sky of vibrant blue.

My father was less reverent about Africa than my mother. Born in Rhodesia (now Zimbabwe), he had been an asthmatic Jewish intellectual growing up among tough, bellicose Anglo and Afrikaans boys. He had been bullied right through his childhood, and had quit Africa for Europe at the first opportunity. He would imitate, for our amusement, the buttock-swinging swagger of his old school's rugby First Fifteen as they marched out onto the field, arranging his moustachioed, black-eyebrows-and-spectacles face into a parody of their arrogant insouciance. All his stories tended to the ridiculous. There was the MaShona foreman of the night-soil collectors, who came round each day on a horse and cart to empty the thunder-boxes of the wealthy whites and called himself 'Boss Boy Shit'; the adolescent house-boy whose balls and penis used to hang, fruit-like, from a hole in his ragged shorts and who, when asked by my father what the fruit was for, demonstrated by upending the bemused house cat and attempting to jam his penis into its impossibly small anus. The cat had twisted and sunk in its claws: deep, causing the house-boy to run off howling.

My father's tales, like my mother's myths, contrasted tantalisingly with the overwhelming ordinariness of our London life. My sister and I, avid listeners, tried to learn the Afrikaans rugger songs like '*Bobbejaan klim die Berg*' ('The Baboon climbed up the mountain'), which we quickly corrupted into 'Old baba kindi bear'. The song's chorus – '*Want die Stellenbos se boois kom weer*' ('the boys of Stellenbosch will come back again' – a reference to the Boer War) became 'for the smelly, bossy boys, come here'. Who, we wondered, were these smelly, bossy boys? What was a kindi bear? How strange and mysterious was this land that our parents came from.

At Christmas my father's father, Robbie, would visit from Rhodesia where he ranched cattle and farmed tobacco – a feudal baron in a still feudal world. He brought us small gifts – leopards and spiral-horned kudus carved from red African hardwoods. My grandfather presented Africa as somewhere real, a place where actual lives were lived. I would listen to him and my parents argue across the dinner table, bringing the continent into sharper focus. The talk, back then, was mostly of the war of independence then raging in Rhodesia; my grandfather told how the Munts* had attacked his farm and shot his farm manager, burning crops, rustling cattle into the night. When he spoke, Africa came across as a hard, violent place and, with his stern voice, lined face and disapproving stare, he seemed to carry something of this with him as he moved about our London house.

An endless succession of white Africans passed through our lives. They talked incessantly of the land of their birth. There were stories

*A corruption of the Shona word *muntu*, meaning 'people'.

about the barren, blasted Karoo, where only dry shrubs grew, stunted by summer drought and bone-cracking winter frost. And the jungly, mosquito-ridden forests of the Zambezi River where lions and buffaloes, hippos and elephants, crocodiles and poisonous snakes lurked around every corner. Up in the high, cold mountains of Lesotho, the landscape resembled Scotland and was inhabited by proud people who wore conical straw hats, robed themselves in bright, patterned blankets and rode horses between their stony, cliff-top villages. I learned of the rolling grasslands around Johannesburg, known as the 'highveld', which stretched to a sudden escarpment that fell away to the game-rich thorn-scrub, the 'lowveld' or 'bushveld'. Long before I ever went to southern Africa, its names and regions had been described to me so many times that I could picture them in my mind's eye, the landscapes flowing one into the other across the great sub-continent, each more beautiful than the last.

I later came to realise that these eulogies to Africa's natural beauty arose partly from guilt: the speakers came from families whose forebears had, almost without exception, carved out their wealth in blood. Many of these educated descendants of the colonial pioneers were haunted by the feeling that their ancestors should somehow have known better. Yet they also feared the black peoples whose freedom they so longed for, whose oppression by their own kind caused them such shame. They knew that black resentment of white drew little distinction. They were all too familiar with the violent warrior traditions endemic to most black African cultures, and lived in terror of the great uprisings that must one day inevitably come. For them, the myth of a pure, uncomplicated Africa contrasted favourably with the Africa they actually knew. It was a sense of this that they, no doubt unconsciously, imparted to us as wide-eyed London children, and which resonated deeply in my magic-starved mind. Only years later did I realise that, with the exception of cousin Frank, most of these white African visitors knew little or nothing of the bush, let alone the Bushmen. For the most part, they were urbanites much more at home in European cities than out on the dry, primordial veld.

★   ★   ★

When I was eight and Hannah eleven, our parents took us to Rhodesia to visit my grandfather Robbie. From the moment we stepped off the plane I found the place as seductively, intensely exciting as all the stories had led me to expect. 'Take off your shoes,' my mother said, as we pulled up at Robbie's house, set in a landscaped garden in a white suburb of the capital Salisbury (now Harare). 'You're in Africa now and kids go barefoot.' Hannah and I did as she bid, despite a dubious look at the green, irrigated lawn, which was crawling with insect life. When my grandfather's manservant, Lucius, opened the front door, a small, cream-coloured scorpion dropped from the lintel. Lucius whipped off his shoe and killed it, then presented me with the corpse as a trophy. I was thrilled. That night the chorus of frogs in the garden was deafening. My father took us out into the darkness with a torch and at the edge of one of my grandfather's ornamental ponds showed us frogs the size of kittens.

The war for independence was still being fought at that time. Out at Robbie's farm a high-security fence ran all the way around the homestead, and the white men carried handguns on their hips (things were later to get so bad that my grandfather hired AK-47-wielding guards and an armoured car to patrol his vast territory). We saw his herds of black Brangus cattle, his tobacco fields and drying houses. At night the drums in the farmworkers' compound thundered till dawn, while my sister and I lay in our beds and tried not to think about the big spiders that sat on the walls above our sleepless heads.

On a bright, hot morning, after a particularly loud night of drumming, two *ingangas* (witch doctors) performed a ceremony in the compound. Despite having been born in Africa, none of my family could tell us quite what was going on, but there was frightening power in the singing of the assembled black crowd, in the maniacal dancing of the *ingangas*, whose faces were hidden by fearsome, nightmare masks. It made me shiver.

At a game reserve near the ruins of Great Zimbabwe,* we visited

---

*A walled city, dating from the thirteenth century, founded by the ancestors of today's MaShona people.

a friend of the family, a zoologist studying crocodiles in the Kyle River. He had caught four big specimens – between twelve and fifteen feet long – and had penned them in a special enclosure built out into the muddy river. Having asked if we'd like to see them, he guided us into the pen, telling us to stay close to the fence and not approach the great, murderous lizards where they lay half in, half out of the shallows.

For some reason I did not listen and, as the man was explaining something about crocodile behaviour to my parents, I walked towards the beasts for a closer look. There was a quick, low movement from the water and suddenly I was being dragged backwards by my shirt collar, loud shouting all around. 'He almost got you!' panted the zoologist, who had saved me by a whisker. Forever afterwards, my mother would tell the story of how she almost lost her son to a crocodile.

Sometime towards the end of that month-long trip, we went to look at a cave whose walls were painted with faded animals and men – exquisitely executed in red, cream and ochre-coloured silhouettes. The animal forms were instantly recognisable, perfectly representing the creatures we had just seen in great numbers in the game reserves. Standing there in the cool gloom, I picked out lyre-horned impala, jumping high in front of little stickmen with bows and arrows, kudu with great spiralled horns and striped flanks, giraffes cantering on legs so long they had seemed – when we had seen them in real life – to gallop in slow motion. Paintings like these, my mother told us, could be found in caves all over southern Africa. Some were tens of thousands years old. Others were painted as recently as a hundred years ago. But no one, she said, painted any more.

'Why not?' I asked.

'Because the people were all killed,' answered my mother. 'And those not killed fled into the Kalahari Desert.'

She told us how, sometime in the middle of the last century, a party of white farmers in the Drakensberg mountains of South Africa had gone to hunt down the last group of Bushmen living in their area. Having seen all the game on which they had traditionally relied shot out, the Bushmen had resorted to hunting cattle and the farmers

9

had organised a commando, or punitive raid against them. After the inevitable massacre up in the high passes, a body was found with several hollowed-out springbok horns full of pigment strapped to a belt around his waist. 'He was the last Bushman painter,' said my mother.

Laurens van der Post, whose writings in the 1950s established him as a Bushman guru, included this poignant story in his *Lost World of the Kalahari*. In his version it is one of his own forebears who went out on a similar raid, sometime in the late nineteenth century, in the 'hills of the Great River'. Someone in his own grandfather's family (van der Post's words), having taken part in the massacre, discovers the body of the dead artist. Over the years I have encountered this story again and again, from the mouths of liberal-minded whites and in books, each time with a different location and twist. Perhaps all of them are true. Like so much that concerns the Bushmen and the great, wide land that used to be theirs, the story has become myth – intangible, impossible to pin down. Irresistible to a small boy of eight.

Back in the grey, drearily ordinary city of my birth, I found that the bright continent had worked its magic on me. I became more curious about our origins, about the dynastic lines going down the generations, and began to quiz my parents on more detail.

Though from vastly different origins and cultures, both sides of the family had gone at the great continent like terriers; yapping, biting and worrying away at it until they had established themselves and become white Africans. On my father's side were the Isaacsons and Schapiros, poverty-stricken Lithuanian Jews who had emigrated from the small villages of Pojnewitz and Dochschitz (pronounced Dog-Shits) in the early 1900s. They had gone first to Germany, then to the emerging colony of German Southwest Africa, now Namibia, where my grandfather Robbie had been born in 1908. He grew up poor; his father worked at a low-paying job as a fitter on the railways while his mother kept a boarding house in the small capital Windhoek (though one family rumour has it that she was sometimes a little more than a landlady to her male guests).

The German colony was too rigidly anti-Semitic to allow Jews to make easy fortunes. So, on reaching his twenties, my grandfather crossed the great Kalahari, travelling through British Bechuanaland (now Botswana) to Rhodesia, where, after a brief spell selling shoes, he managed to land a job as a trainee auctioneer in a firm owned by another Litvak Jew – one Herschel (known as Harry) Schapiro. There followed a Machiavellian rise to fortune: my grandfather courted and married Freda, daughter of this man Schapiro, became head auctioneer, began slowly buying up farms that came to the company cheap and, eventually, took over the firm.

Harry Schapiro himself had a more romantic story. While still a young man in Lithuania he had abandoned his wife Minnie (a notoriously difficult woman, according to my father) and set off into the world to make his fortune. He took a ship to England, intending to go from there to America, but – owing to his lack of English – got on the wrong boat and ended up in Port Elizabeth, just as the Boer War broke out.★ With characteristic opportunism, he enlisted in the Johannesburg Mounted Infantry believing that once the war was over they would be demobbed in the Transvaal – where the gold mines were. Harry spent three years tramping up and down central South Africa without seeing a shot fired. Then, when the Armistice came, the regiment was demobbed not in the mine fields as promised, but back in Port Elizabeth where Harry had started from.

Undaunted, he set out for the Transvaal anyway, only to end up, not a mining magnate as he had hoped, but a butcher in the mine kitchens, where his wife Minnie managed to track him down, having travelled all the way from Lithuania to do so. Harry stayed with her just long enough to sire Freda (Robbie's wife and my father's mother, who died from Alzheimer's while my sister and I were still small), before running away again, this time to Rhodesia, where he graduated from butcher to cattle trader to wealthy owner of a livestock auctioneering house. Minnie, no less resourceful, tracked him down

★The Second Anglo-Boer War (1899–1902) resulted in the British annexation of the whole of South Africa outside the Cape colony. The first war, won by the Boers, was in 1880.

a second time, whereupon he capitulated, though she of course never forgave him.

My father remembered Minnie – by then an old woman – drinking champagne by the gallon and forcing Harry to buy her a neverending stream of expensive gifts – Persian rugs, Chinese vases and the like – which she would then sell, banking the money. Because, she claimed, she never knew when her husband might take it into his head to disappear again. During these latter years she developed delusions of grandeur and used to tell my father that she had married beneath her, having spent her girlhood in a Lithuanian palace. 'Rubbish, Minnie,' Harry would harrumph from his armchair, 'you were born in a hovel.'

My father's side was successful financially, my mother's side less so. But the Loxtons were made of epic stuff. My mother's father Allen, for example, after spending an idyllic boyhood riding his horse Starlight across the rolling green hills of Natal, became a journalist, then a tank soldier in the 8th Army during the war in North Africa. He escaped his burning tank at Tobruk and jumped onto an abandoned motorbike just as the Afrika Korps came running over the dunes. On his return from the war, Allen resumed his career as a journalist, roving all over southern Africa as a feature writer for the *Sunday Times* and *Johannesburg Star*. My mother showed us great fat binders full of his cuttings – stories of travels with crocodile hunters, with witch doctors, with Bushmen; the black and white pictures and *Boys' Own* language (at which he excelled) conjuring a world of adventure that stood out in stark contrast to the world I knew in London.

No less intrepid, his wife – my grandmother Barbara – also went to the war, putting my mother (then aged six) and aunt (aged eight) into a children's home and roaming the Western Front as a freelance war artist for the South African papers. As with Allen's cuttings, my mother would show us Barbara's paintings, which were kept in a big leather trunk in our sitting room. Barbara had painted everything she saw: London families sleeping in the Underground during the Blitz; the Battle of the Bulge, with the American dead lying in the snow of the Ardennes, cut down like wheat by the German Tiger tanks; the blood-spattered agony of the military hospitals; civilians starving on the streets of the Hague. Shortly after Berlin fell, she and a group of other journalists were allowed into Hitler's eyrie, high in the Bavarian Alps, literally days after the great dictator and his mistress Eva Braun had committed suicide. Barbara rifled the desk drawers and brought back a few of Hitler's personal effects — minor things like photographs, an Iron Cross or two, and some official documents — to pass on to the children. My sister and I felt proud that my mother's parents had taken part in this great story.

But the Loxtons paid for their adventurous spirit by being heavy drinkers, prone to irrational rages, and subsequent wallowing remorse. Allen was no exception, and drove Barbara to leave him a few years after their return from the war. The effect on my mother and her sister Lindsay was far-reaching. Once she left Allen, Barbara (who seems to have been kind, but emotionally cool) never had her children to live with her again. Having been put into boarding schools as near infants while their parents went adventuring, they experienced but a brief couple of years of family life before being shunted off once more, to grow up in institutions until they reached university age.

My petite, blonde, bespectacled mother grew up a true Loxton, becoming involved, while at university, in anti-apartheid campaigns. Her old photograph albums show pictures of the time: my mother (a platinum perm atop a Jane Mansfield bust) and a black male student symbolically burning the government's separate education bill; my mother speaking on podiums; brawls between Afrikaans students loyal to the system and my mother's leftist crowd; pictures of more serious attacks by policemen. One in particular stands out: a march by black domestic maids, protesting for better working conditions, charged with batons and dogs. In the foreground, a woman is on the ground, a police-dog savaging her abdomen, the handler's truncheon raised high, about to deliver a skull-cracking blow to the woman's head.

By this time Barbara had remarried, and she and her new husband (a politically active, left-wing lawyer named George Findlay) decided it would be best if my mother left the country before the inevitable arrest that must follow such activities. She was glad to get out and go adventuring in the world as her parents had and took the boat to England along with her sister, Lindsay. In England my mother flirted with the ANC, but became diverted – by art school, by meeting my father, himself an African émigré – and settled down to produce my sister and I while embarking on a career as a sculptor and artist. But when I was eighteen months old, and my sister four, my mother took us back to Africa and presented us to Barbara and Allen (who, though as much of an alcoholic as ever, had moved to Johannesburg and started another family).

A year later, both Allen and Barbara were dead. And in a sad postscript to their failed relationship, though they lived at opposite ends of the country they died within hours of each other. One day while at work in the *Sunday Times* office, Allen collapsed from emphysema (he had been a heavy smoker), and never regained consciousness. A telegram was sent to Barbara. According to her husband, she went quiet, and retired to have a think and be alone with her memories. When he knocked at the door a short time later to see if she was all right, there was no response. He opened the door and found her lying dead from a stroke.

My mother went almost mad with grief. She had at last begun to know her parents, and now suddenly they had been snatched away. Throughout our childhood, she would be prone to periodic depressions, and the sense of being an exile never left her. Unlike my father, who fitted happily into London (he later told me that even in his Rhodesian childhood he had longed for cities: 'The first time I went to Johannesburg and smelled the car fumes and saw all that concrete around me, I felt an almost sensual thrill of excitement and pleasure'), my mother missed Africa keenly. She expressed it in her sculpture, her painting, almost all of which featured African people, African scenes.

It was perhaps to make up for the loss of her parents, and of all that she had hoped we children would have learned from them, that she became such a willing story-teller. She told us of the four Loxton brothers – Jesse, Samuel, Jasper and Henry – who in 1830 had come to South Africa from the Somerset village of Loxton and immediately dispersed into the wide spaces of the dry north, the area known as the Great Karoo.

Like all the other early Karoo settlers, the Loxtons lived, at first, by pastoral nomadism learned from the Khoi, a people who looked like Bushmen and spoke a similar clicking language, but who lived by herding rather than hunting. Having shown the whites how to follow the rains and where to find water in this unendingly arid land, the Khoi soon found themselves dispossessed, along with the local Bushman clans. By the time the Loxton brothers arrived, the Khoi had been reduced to working for the whites, and the last remaining Karoo Bushman had retreated to mountain strongholds, from where they watched the white men carve out farms by the land's few natural springs and kill off the game.

For the whites, it was a slow, monotonous existence, enlivened only by hunting, mostly for wild animals, but sometimes also for Bushmen, who would, as their situation became more and more desperate, occasionally materialise from nowhere to raid livestock. For many Karoo settlers, hunting Bushmen became a well-known, if little talked about, sport. I can only speculate that my family must have done as others did.

Eventually, the Loxton brothers bought land and settled down. Henry, the youngest (my great-great-grandfather) trekked over the Drakensberg mountains into Natal – Zulu Country – where he ended up a wagon-maker, wedded to an Afrikaner woman named Agathe-Celeste (my great-great-grandmother), who had been abandoned as an infant in the court of the Zulu king Mpande by her ivory-hunting father. She had spent her girlhood there, re-entering white society only when she became a young woman and married my great-great-grandfather.

There are many stories about Agathe-Celeste. The best was included in a book of African reminiscences (*Thirty Years in Africa*), written by a bluff old Africa hand called Major Tudor Trevor, who knew my great-great-grandparents well. It concerned her two pet lions – Saul and Deborah. According to the major, these two lions, which Henry Loxton had given to his wife as cubs, had a game. They would wait at the garden hedge, which ran along the pavement and around the street corner, until someone came walking by. When the walker was halfway along the hedge, one of the cubs would slip through the foliage, drop onto the pavement and silently trail the unwitting pedestrian until he or she turned the corner. There the other cub, who had previously slipped through the hedge on that side, would be waiting. It would let out a kittenish roar in the face of the astonished walker, who would then turn and find the other cub behind, roaring too. While the cubs were still small, and could be run off with a shout, the burghers of the town tolerated their game as a charming, harmless local eccentricity.

Around the time that Saul and Deborah were half-grown ('as big as mastiffs', wrote Trevor Tudor), a new predikant, or Minister of the Dutch Reformed Church, arrived in town. One Sunday after church, while sitting on the porch with the Loxtons, the major saw this new priest coming up the road, formally turned out in frock coat, black topper and gloves, with a Bible under his arm. 'At that moment,' he wrote, 'out from behind sprang Deborah. She crouched low. The parson heard the thud of her landing and turned round as if to greet a parishioner . . . then we heard a kind of drawn out sob, his hat fell off, his Bible dropped, and in a flash he turned and ran off down the street . . .'

Deborah caught up with him in a few easy bounds and, first with one swipe, then another, ripped off his flying coat tails. The predikant put on a spurt, rounded the corner at a gallop, whereupon out jumped Saul, roaring. With a squeal like the air being squeezed from a bagpipe, the predikant crumpled to the ground. Saul climbed onto his chest and began licking his face, intermittently snarling at Deborah to leave off what he considered his kill. The major, meanwhile, was running to the rescue. Coming up on Saul where he lay, pinning the priest to the road, he fetched the half-grown lion a vicious kick in the ribs. But instead of backing off as expected, Saul turned, slashed at the major's leg and made ready to spring. It was my great-great-grandmother who saved the day, arriving seconds later with a heavy *sjambok* (giraffe- or hippo-hide whip), 'at the first stroke of which', wrote Trevor Tudor, 'and a stream of abuse in Dutch, the cubs went flying.' The major remained, ever after, in awe of my great-great-grandmother, referring to her always as 'that magnificent woman'.

But Henry Loxton could match his wife's legendary feats. Fording the Komaati River on his horse one night (the river lies at the southern end of what is now the Kruger National Park), he was attacked by a large crocodile but, so the story goes, managed to beat it off with his stirrup iron. Arriving at the little town on the other side, he stamped angrily into the bar of its one, small hotel, and demanded to know what the devil they meant by allowing such a dangerous beast to infest the ford. For answer the barman told him, apologetically, that nobody in town had a rifle of sufficient calibre to tackle the croc. The only big gun was owned by a German tailor who was short-sighted, could barely shoot, and was holding the weapon as a debt for unpaid services. Hearing this, Henry Loxton rushed over to the tailor's house and demanded that he accompany him to the river.

Once at the ford, Henry got straight down to business: 'I'll go and stand in the middle, and when the croc comes I want you to shoot it.'

'But I can't shoot,' protested the unfortunate tailor. 'What if I hit you? What if I miss?'

Henry considered a moment, then took the man by the shoulders and frog-marched him into the water. 'Stay there,' he said menacingly: 'If you move before the croc comes I'll shoot *you*.' So the tailor waited, trembling, until sure enough, the croc came gliding silently out from the shore. The gun went off, the croc reared up, then collapsed back into the water with an almighty splash, and the tailor sprinted, howling, for the bank. The great reptile was dead. Thanking his reluctant assistant, Henry Loxton gave him back the rifle and continued on his way. Legend has it that, next morning, the tailor's hair turned white.

Henry and Agathe-Celeste had four sons, all of whom grew up to fight on opposite sides of the Anglo-Boer War (one of them even mustered his own irregular cavalry unit, known as Loxton's Horse). And it was into this line that Allen, my mother's father, was born in 1906.

Before the war however, Jesse, one of Henry and Agathe-Celeste's elder sons, had gone back to the Karoo and founded a small, dusty town which, predictably, he had named Loxton. He married and had a son, Frederick, who, being a chip off the old block, resolved to mark out a private domain for himself, just as his father had done. Frederick set off first for the Eastern Cape, where he married, had children, and tried to settle. But the lure of the wild, empty north where he had been born proved too strong. Soon enough, he abandoned his young family and rode away to the Orange River country, southernmost border of the Kalahari, then the absolute frontier of civilisation.

But even then, in the 1880s, this part of South Africa (still known today as Bushmanland) was fast being tamed, not by whites but by people of mixed white and Khoi blood – the Griqua, Koranna and Baster★ – who had trekked away from their white masters some decades earlier. Skilled riders and marksmen, these coloured pioneers had claimed the river's fertile flood-plain, a corridor of green winding through the vast dryness on either side, making fortresses of the many river islands, from which they raided each other's camps and enslaved the local Bushmen, occasionally attacking the Dutch and British settlements to the south. By the time Frederick Loxton arrived mission stations had been set up and the old raiding culture was giving way to a more settled farm life. But for a white man with a little money, a good horse and a repeating rifle, there remained a free, frontier possibility to the Orange River country. Ignoring the fact that he already had a family back in the Cape, he met and fell in love with Anna Booysens, the striking daughter of one of the Baster *kapteins* (leaders). When, some years later, news came of the first wife's death, Frederick married this woman, and was given a dowry of flood-plain land near the present-day town of Keimoes.

On his death in 1894, Frederick left his farms to his three Baster children and they, when they died, left them to theirs. 'We have coloured cousins?' I remembered asking my mother. Indeed we did. But where they were now no one in the family knew. Through the decades that preceded and paved the way for apartheid, the white and the coloured Loxtons had drifted irrevocably apart. Cousins

★'Baster' means 'bastard' literally; a term used for people of mixed race.

with KhoiSan blood. Almost Bushmen. I pictured them as lean, wild-looking people in a barren landscape of red and brown rock cut through by an immense, muddy river.

As childhood turned to adolescence, it became less comfortable to be caught between cultures, to be part English, part African. The stories, artifacts, white African friends and relatives that constituted my life at home began to clash more and more with the reality of living and going to school in England. I didn't fit in. Was our family English or African, I would be asked? Neither and both, it seemed.

I was restless in London, and began to long for the open air. We had a great-aunt with a farm in Leicestershire, a horsewoman, who spotted the horse gene in me and taught me to hunt and ride across the Midlands turf on an old thoroughbred that she let me keep there.

Though I made friends with some of the other Pony Club children, I continued to feel like an outsider. Still, it was oddly consoling to think of that great network of ancestors and relatives. Somehow the Kalahari, the dry heart of the sub-continent, seemed central to that inheritance and identity that I was – however unconsciously – trying to find.

So, when I was nineteen, I told my grandfather Robbie over Christmas lunch that I wanted to go to Africa again. The following summer, he sent me a plane ticket.

2

Lessons in Reality

It was the African winter: dry, cool, dusty. As the plane touched down in Harare, Zimbabwe, in June 1985, I saw that the grass by the runway was yellow-brown and burnt in places, the trees bare and parched-looking. Walking to the customs building, the early morning air was chilly despite the cloudless blue sky. A faint smell of wood smoke, dust and cow dung was borne in on the bone-dry breeze.

I made my way westward across the grassy Zimbabwe Midlands and into the dry, wooded country of southeastern Botswana, hitch-hiking and taking buses and trains. On the third day in the freezing dawn I arrived at Gaborone, Botswana's dusty, sleepy capital. Cousin Frank Taylor picked me up and drove me out to his place in the red ironstone hills west of town, weaving his beat-up car between teams of donkey-drawn carts made from pick-up trucks sawn in half, driven Ben Hur-style by young BaTswana men. Once out of town, the landscape was barren; red, dry and sandy without a single blade of grass (this was in the height of the terrible droughts that afflicted southern Africa from the 1980s right into the mid '90s) and the tree branches bare of leaves. I had never seen a landscape so desolate and unforgiving. I sneaked a look at cousin Frank. He matched the landscape: tall, spare, with the capable, practical air of a man used to fixing things himself. Sitting in the passenger seat next to him I felt soft and frivolous and stupid.

I had come to expect that all white Africans lived in big houses surrounded by manicured gardens, where soft-footed black servants produced tea and biscuits punctually at eleven, discreetly rang little bells to call one to lunch, and generally devoted all their energy and ingenuity to surrounding one with understated luxury. Frank

Taylor's house – built with his own hands on a stretch of rocky hillside granted him by the local *kgotla*★ – was austere: one long room like a dusty Viking's hall, little furniture and no water, unless you drove down to a communal tap in the village below.

Frank, his wife Margaret and his three sons were all fervent Christians. That evening, the initial exchanges of family news done, Frank fixed his grey seer's gaze on me and asked: 'So, at what stage of your spiritual odyssey are you?'

I did not know how to answer, but hid my discomfort behind a façade of chatty, light-hearted banter. Later, not knowing quite what to do with me, Frank enlisted my help in the new house he was building down on the valley floor. I was not handy with tools, knew nothing about mixing cement, dropping plumb lines, fixing car engines, laying pipes, nor even how to change a flat tyre. I began to realise how unrealistic I had been to dream of just floating into the Kalahari of my childhood stories.

Frank had been in Botswana just over twenty years, having left a prosperous family farm in South Africa to come – missionary-like – and devote himself to improving the lot of Botswana's rural poor. Foremost among these were the country's Bushmen, most of whom, I learned, had lately been reduced to pauperdom through a sudden upsurge in cattle ranching. During the 1970s, Frank told me, foreign aid money had come pouring into Botswana, and the cattle-owning elite of the ruling BaTswana tribe had used it to carve roads into previously unreachable areas, and to put up wire fences and sink boreholes. The result, for the Bushmen, was disastrous. The game on which they had traditionally relied was killed if it approached the new boreholes, and prevented by the new fences from following the rains. The animals died along the wire in their hundreds of thousands. With the exception of a few clans still living outside the grasp of the ranchers, most of the Bushmen had found themselves, within a few years, enclosed by wire, their age-old food source gone, reduced to serfs looking after other people's cattle on land that had once been their own.

★Village council.

21

In the first few years after his arrival in Botswana, Frank had set up several non-profit-making businesses: textile printing, handicrafts, small-scale poultry farms and the like. But these had been mere preliminaries to his real mission. It seemed to him that for the Remote Area Dwellers (as the Botswana government called the Kalahari peoples, Bushman or otherwise), the real way out of destitution lay not in learning to be Westerners, but in marketing the wild foods and medicines that they had been gathering in the bush since time immemorial. It seems a simple enough idea – agro-forestry – but back then it was revolutionary. At that time, most NGOs (non-governmental organisations) were trying to turn indigenous people into farmers or small businessmen. The eco-terms that we now take for granted had yet to be coined. Frank was ahead of his time.

Frank borrowed money and established a small nursery of wild, fruit or medicine-producing shrubs and trees beside his house. He had found that these indigenous plants bore fruit even in drought years, and did not exhaust the dry Botswana soil if planted and harvested year to year, as maize and livestock did. He was convinced that the Kalahari peoples could take these traditional plants beyond mere subsistence, that they could be cultivated for both survival and cash, and that there might even be a market abroad for them. The problem was funding.

Listening to Frank explaining all this convinced me that he was the man to take me into the Kalahari. I tried a tactful approach – perhaps I could accompany him on one of his forays into the heart-land? But no, came the answer, he was too busy for the next month or two to take any trips into the interior. However, one night his two elder boys (Michael and Peter, already experienced and bushwise at ten and twelve years old) took me up to sleep out on the wild ridge top. Sitting around the fire – which they could kindle, and I could not – they told me stories about the journeys they had made with their father into that interior. I listened intrigued, intimidated and envious that these boys, not yet in their teens, should have experienced so much of what I longed to experience. At dawn, I got up and went by myself to look out over the vast, wild flat lands that yawned away below – the emptiness, the reds and browns and angry dark burnt umber of the rocks and bare trees. I raised my arms in greeting to that harsh land – the land of my fathers.

I bid the Taylors goodbye and went back eastward into Zimbabwe, where my grandfather had arranged for me to stay on a ranch some hours north of Harare. There I was in heaven: I rode horses, handled guns, shot and killed an antelope and felt a surge of genuine bloodlust as I did so. I swam and fished, drank beer and laughed at jokes about blacks and women. I began to understand how my forebears had reinvented themselves, from Litvak Jew to rich auctioneer, from Somerset peasant to empire builder. Then, one hot morning while I was in the swimming pool, reality returned with a bump. Hearing shouting, I surfaced just in time to see my white rancher host land first one fist, then another, in the face of one of his Shona farm-workers who, it turned out, had been AWOL on a drunken binge and had now shown up for work again, useless and reeking.

Later, the ranch's black foreman and I were sent to round up a steer for slaughter. We cut a half-grown calf out of the herd and drove it into a corral, where a ring of farmworkers lined the outside of the fence, waiting to see the *baas* make the kill. The big red-faced man wandered into the corral with a rifle and took aim, pointing the barrel at the flat space between the steer's eyes. What would happen, I wondered, if the bullet missed and hit one of the farm-workers? But his aim was true. He fired, and a fountain of bright blood erupted from the beast's head. It did not fall down however; instead it stood, staring through the crimson blood that now pumped from the round hole between its eyes. The rancher shot again, still the steer stood there. He shot a third time. Again the beast did not fall, but kept its feet, swaying, its face a stunned mask of gore. Quickly the foreman reappeared, ducked through the bars of the corral with a huge butcher's knife in his hand, walked briskly up to the dazed, wounded beast and slit its throat. Blood poured out as if emptied from a bucket, the steer letting out a long death-bellow as the life drained out of the jagged cut. It remained standing until the blood stopped flowing, then crashed onto its side, dead at last.

Realising that I was too squeamish for life on an African farm, I left the guns in their locked cabinet and took long walks with the farm boys, who would show me animals and birds and tell me their names in Shona.

The following year, I travelled to Africa again, and this time went ranging over the great sub-continent, visiting all the places of the family stories, before taking a truck up into East Africa to witness the great wildebeest migration of the Serengeti.

But then I left Africa alone for a while, spending a couple of years adventuring in North America and then trying to establish myself as a freelance journalist in London. The need to identify with the land of my fathers seemed to diminish, become less pressing. A constant presence, but no longer an urgent one.

Then one day, out of the blue, a distant Loxton cousin from Australia wrote to my mother, saying that he had spent ten years researching the family and now wanted to put all the clan back in touch with each other. Among his researches, he had traced the Baster Loxtons, the coloured branch of the family, to a wine farm outside a small town called Keimos, at the southern edge of the Kalahari.

It seemed that they had prospered, and had, against the odds, managed to hold onto their land all through the apartheid years despite several attempts by the white government to dispossess them. Their farm, Loxtonvale, extended along several islands of the great river, where the original Baster *kapteins* had established their station-ary pirate strongholds. Gert and Cynthia Loxton had transformed the islands into vineyards and orchards where they produced Chardonnay and sultana grapes and fruit. They also had a cattle ranch up in the southern fringe of the Kalahari.

My mother got the necessary addresses and flew out that year. When she returned, the link between the two sides of the family had been restored. And between these coloured Loxtons and the Taylors (my mother also visited Frank Taylor on that trip and reported that his Veld Products Research organisation was thriving), it seemed that the door to the Kalahari had finally opened a crack.

In 1992, I returned once more, having landed a contract to write a guidebook to South Africa. During my first week back in the country, I visited the Cultural History Museum in Cape Town, where eerie life-like casts of Bushmen (taken from real people, said the plaque) stood on display behind glass as if living people had been frozen in time. As I travelled I read, learning for the first time the proper history of these, the first people of southern Africa, whom academics called 'KhoiSan', but whom others called 'Hottentots' or 'Bushmen'.

Many geneticists and anthropologists, I learned, considered the KhoiSan to be the oldest human culture on earth, possibly ancestors to us all. What was certain was that for thirty thousand years, perhaps longer, they had populated the whole sub-continent, pursuing a lifestyle that included hunting, gathering, painting, dancing, but not, it seemed, war (no warrior folk-tales, weaponry or battle sites exist from this time). Then, sometime around the first century AD, the warriors had arrived – black Africans, whom the academics called 'Bantu peoples' – migrating down from west and central Africa with livestock acquired, it is thought, from Arab traders in the Horn and the north of Africa. By the Middle Ages these ancestors of the modern nations of MaShona, Zulu, Ndebele, Xhosa, BaTswana and Sotho had pushed the Bushmen out of most of southern Africa's lushest areas – what is now Zimbabwe and eastern South Africa. They kept Bushman girls as concubines and adopted some of the distinctive clicks that punctuated the KhoiSan languages. Rain-making ceremonies and healing practices were also absorbed into the new dominant culture. By the time the first whites settled the Cape in the mid-seventeenth century, the Bushmen had vanished from almost everywhere except for the more rugged mountain ranges and the dry Karoo and Kalahari regions.

Some Bushmen clans, however, took on the culture of the invaders, adopting warrior traditions alongside the herds of cattle and fat-tailed sheep. These peoples – the Khoi or Hottentots – first traded with, then fought, the white settlers, confining the colony to a small settled area around modern-day Cape Town for a generation until successive waves of smallpox in the early eighteenth century so reduced the Khoi that they became absorbed into a general mixed-race underclass known today as 'coloureds'. Only one group of Khoi survived into modern times – the Nama of northwestern South Africa and southern Namibia.

Having colonised the Cape, the white settlers began pushing north into the Karoo. Extermination and genocide followed, until by the twentieth century Bushmen survived only in the Kalahari. Now even these remote people, as I already knew from Frank, were under threat from the steady encroachment of black cattle ranchers.

As the year drew to a close, I travelled up to the southernmost edge of the Kalahari, where it reaches down into South Africa in a dunescape of red sands tufted with golden grass, and dry riverbeds shaded by tall camel-thorn trees. Even here, I was told, no Bushmen had been seen since the 1960s, maybe earlier. The crisply khakied reception staff at the Kalahari Gemsbok National Park – a narrow tongue of South Africa that makes a wedge between Namibia and Botswana – pointed vaguely northwards into the shimmering, heat-stricken immensity beyond the reception building and told me that I would have to go 'deep Kalahari', beyond the park even, if I wanted to see Bushmen.

Once again, it seemed, the gentle hunters of my childhood stories were going to remain just that – fictional characters. Instead, Africa had another kind of experience lined up for me. The year from 1992 to 1993 saw the lead-up to the elections that would change South Africa for ever. Anger that had been seething for generations was starting to erupt. I was researching the Transkei region, down in South Africa's Eastern Cape Province, at this time still one of the 'tribal homelands', a region set aside for rural blacks – in this case the Xhosa – to live their traditional lives far away from white eyes. Overcrowding, overgrazing and therefore poverty were the pre-dominant facts of life. Resentment was rife everywhere, but especially so in the Transkei: between the late eighteenth and the late nine-teenth centuries, the Xhosa people fought and lost no fewer than nine consecutive wars against the Dutch and the British, forfeiting almost their entire territory in the process. Finally, in despair, all but three clans of the great tribe slaughtered their herds and destroyed their stores of grain, hoping that by this sacrifice their warrior ancestors would rise from the grave and drive the hated white men into the sea. But the ancestors did not come.

This humiliation only whetted the Xhosa's determination to ultimately win out and beat the white man at his own game – politics. Many black South African leaders, including Nelson Mandela, came from the Transkei. During that pre-election year the region became a focus of anti-white feeling. One night, while in a beach-side rondavel* down on the 'Wild Coast', Transkei's two hundred kilometres of beautiful, sparsely inhabited strands, I woke with a start to see a man coming through the window holding a large kitchen knife. As if in a dream, almost without registering that I was doing it, I was out of my sleeping bag and pushing the intruder backwards, so that he fell the few feet to the ground outside with a muffled thud. Still in my dreamlike state, I put my head out of the window to see what was happening. There was a flicker of movement from the left – I jerked back just in time. His friend, who had been pressed against the wall, swung a knobkerrie, missing my head but hitting my shoulder hard. In an instant the mattress was off the bunk and pressed against the window, and the bunk frame was against the door. The bandits thumped and stabbed at both, but there was no way they could get in.

A few days after the attack, I headed back to the Transkei capital, Umtata. Coming out of the store, both hands laden down with shopping bags, I found my way blocked by a large crowd. It was the end of the day and the city's workers were thronging the main streets, waiting for the minibus taxis that would take them home to their houses on the edge of town. While I was walking through the mass of people, a man approached me, asking the time and, before I could react, had me around the neck while several other hands grabbed me from behind. It was a nasty mugging, the frightened onlookers standing by, pretending nothing was happening, while the fists bloodied my face and mouth and the attackers shouted 'White shit!'

A week after that, in Pietermaritzburg, Natal – a small, handsome city of red-brick and wrought-iron colonial buildings – I found

*Traditional African round, thatched hut.

myself in the midst of a riot. Chris Hani, the head of the South African Communist Party, which had strong links to the ANC, had been shot dead a few days before by a white supremacist. A nation-wide series of 'mourning and protest marches' was planned and, though I had seen the warnings on television, I forgot and ended up driving downtown on the scheduled day, intent on picking up my poste restante mail. The streets, usually jammed with commuter traffic, were strangely empty. Turning into Longmarket Street, I felt a little glow of satisfaction at being able to park directly outside the ornate, pedimented entrance to the post office. I stopped the car and got out, slamming the door. Then I heard it. '*HAAAA!*'

I looked around and saw, some two hundred yards up the wide street, a wall of armed Zulu youth approaching at a run. Smoke and licks of flame billowed out from the buildings as they came. '*HAAAA!*', the shout went up again, and in a flash I remembered the news warning. How could I have been so stupid? I had about thirty seconds in which to make a decision. The car, as bad luck would have it, was having battery problems, so I set off down the street at a sprint, but after just a few paces a door opened on my right and a hand beckoned. It was a bakery-cum-takeaway-shop whose staff had for some reason decided to ignore the news warning and open for business. There was no time for explanations, only to duck down with my saviours behind the counter. The first wave of the crowd swept by, roaring. I risked a look over the top of the counter, just in time to see the shop's large, plate-glass window explode inwards. Shattered glass, stones, bricks and broken wood flew everywhere. Something sharp hit me on the shoulder, tearing my shirt and leaving a light gash on the skin. I ducked down again, then thought of the car with my laptop in the boot. I got up tenta-tively from behind the counter and walked out into the crowd of young men, all in their late teens and early twenties, who were milling about, as if deciding what to do. This was the second wave; few of them were armed, as the first, most destructive rank of rioters had been. These second-rankers were less angry, more bent on mis-chief. It showed in their smiles and the alert, slow-walking set of their bodies. A small group of young men with more initiative than the rest were looting a clothing store on the other side of the street, and that drew most of the crowd's attention. However, standing around my car was a small knot of youths. Walking up to them I had the odd sensation of watching myself from outside my own body. 'Morning, morning,' I said, cheerily, stepping between two gangly teenagers dressed in expensive-looking sweatshirts. They did nothing, merely stood by as I unlocked the door, got in and fired up the engine first time. Waving jauntily, I slipped the clutch, rolled slowly forward and – to my amazement, and probably theirs – the youths stepped aside to let me go.

The volume of people, however, forced me to follow the direction of the crowd. After a couple of minutes, I was back among the first wave of rioters. Here, the street was in mayhem. Most of the youths were brandishing spears, ox-hide shields and kerries and shouting and smashing shop windows – some of them were throwing molotovs into the interiors. I was noticed almost immediately. A tall youth, holding a large rock in both hands, was staring around, looking for something to do with it. When he heard the car engine and turned to see a whitey sitting right in front of him in a car, his eyes opened wide and he made ready to smash the rock through the windscreen on top of me. I looked up at him, making pleading gestures with my hands. The car was still. We locked eyes for a couple of seconds, then abruptly he lowered the rock and gestured with his thumb down the street, shouting 'Go!'

I sped off, a couple of rocks bouncing loudly but harmlessly off the car roof, but the end of the street was blocked by a wall of young men, making a human chain, presumably waiting for the riot police (and news cameras) to arrive. A shower of rocks greeted my approach, though only one connected, hitting the car bonnet and rolling off. I slowed down, searched for someone to make eye contact with, found a gaze in the human chain and held it with my own, taking my hands off the wheel and making the same pleading gestures as before. It worked. After a moment's hesitation, in which another two rocks hit the car, the man – who was older than the others, perhaps in his mid-thirties – slipped his arm from the man next to him, made a space in the line and gestured for me to go through.

I saw him mouth the words, 'Quickly, quickly'. The ranks behind grudgingly made way, striking the car with hands, weapons and shouting 'Kill the Boer! One Settler One Bullet!' But they let me through. Once on the other side I floored it until I was out of the town centre and making for the suburb where I was staying, listening to the noise of police sirens and helicopters heading back towards the trouble. Later that day, I learned that several people had been killed by the mob.

So many violent incidents followed that year of 1993 that they began to blur into one another. By the time my year was up I had not only failed, for the third time now, to get to the Kalahari, I had not even managed to make contact with my coloured Loxton relatives. Instead, I returned home to London exhausted, feeling that I had run out of luck, doubtful if I would ever return to the land of my fathers.

Eighteen months later, however, I was back, this time to write a guidebook covering the three countries just to the north of South Africa: Zimbabwe, Botswana and Namibia. By then, 1995, the memory of those violent times in South Africa had faded a little, and my determination to find the Bushmen had reasserted itself. After all, the three countries I had to cover encompassed most of the Kalahari.

This time I was not travelling alone, but with my girlfriend, Kristin, a Californian. By a happy accident we managed to borrow a Land-Rover, the vehicle necessary for penetrating Bushman country. There were to be no detours this time. We picked up the vehicle in Windhoek, the Namibian capital, just around the corner from the Ausspanplatz, the town square where, as a boy, my grandfather Robbie had earned pennies by holding the horses of the farmers when they came to town. Two sweaty driving days later, we arrived at the tiny outpost town of Tsumkwe in Eastern Bushmanland, gateway to the 'deep Kalahari'.

I had been told, during that previous trip to South Africa, that if you drove about fifteen kilometres from Tsumkwe, you would see some big baobabs rising above the thorns to the south. A track would then appear, leading off towards them. And somewhere at the end of that track were villages of the Ju'/Hoansi Bushmen, who still lived almost entirely the traditional way, by hunting and gathering. We drove through Tsumkwe and out to the east, following these instructions. Sure enough, after twenty minutes or so, several great baobabs rose above the bush away to the right; vast, grey, building-sized trees topped with strangely foreshortened branches. The track appeared. We turned down it. The bush crowded in on either side of the vehicle, wild and lushly green from a season of good rain, swallowing us instantaneously.

We made camp under the largest of the great baobabs, an obese monster almost a hundred feet high, got a fire going and put some water on to boil. Looking around at the surrounding bush, which hereabouts was open woodland, we saw the grass standing tall and green in the little glades and clearings. Everything was in leaf, in flower. Fleshy blooms drifted down from the stunted branches of the baobab, making a faint plop as they landed on the sandy ground below. The blossoms had a strong scent, like over-ripe melon. And then there was a crunch of feet on dead leaves. We turned. Two Bushmen had walked into the clearing.

3

Under the Big Tree

In front walked a lean young man, wearing jeans and a torn white T-shirt, and whose sharp, finely drawn features made one think of a little hawk. Behind him came a shorter, grizzle-headed grandfather with a small, patchy goatee, dressed only in a skin loincloth. Above this curved a rounded belly – though not of fat. Rather it was as if the stomach, under its hard abdominal wall, had been stretched and trained to accommodate great feasts when times were good, as they seemed to be now, with the bush green and abundant with wild fruits. Both men had the golden, honey-coloured skin of full-blooded Bushmen. They stood facing us under the vast tree, silent, as if waiting for us to acknowledge their arrival. 'Hi,' I said. Kristin smiled.

Smiling shyly, the younger man stepped closer, into conversational range, and said in slow, perfect English: 'I am Benjamin. And this is /Kaece [he pronounced it 'Kashay'], the leader of Makuri village. You are welcome here.'

I had assumed that I would have to get by with signs and gesticulation, so it was startling to be addressed in my own language. Kristin and I got up, told the man Benjamin our names and offered him and /Kaece some coffee, which they accepted. Benjamin squatted down by our fire, while the older man took a seat on a buttress-like bit of baobab trunk, which jutted out from the main body of the tree like a small, solid table, and watched with frank, open curiosity, his eyes round like an owl's.

'Where did you learn English?' I asked, trying to open a conversation, and hoping it wouldn't sound rude, too direct.

'Mission School,' answered Benjamin, holding his coffee cup in both hands and sipping gently. 'In Botswana,' and he gestured to the east.

'Perhaps you have some sugar?' he added. 'We like our coffee sweet.' He smiled. Only when four spoonfuls had been deposited into each mug did he give a thumbs-up sign, turn to me again and repeat: 'So, you are welcome.'

I looked at this young, articulate man with his perfect English and his good, if slightly frayed, clothes. I noticed that he was wearing Reeboks. 'Are you from Makuri too?' I said, gesturing back towards where he and the old man had come from.

'No,' said Benjamin. 'I live at Baraka.'

'Baraka?'

'Yes. The field headquarters for the Nyae Nyae Farmer's Co-operative.' He pronounced the official-sounding words slowly, as if they did not sit easily on his tongue, using the monotone of one who must mentally translate the words before speaking. 'Maybe twenty kilometres from here ... I am a field officer, an interpreter.'

'The Nyae Nyae what? What's that?' I asked, never having heard of it before.

'An organisation, you know, an NGO, non-government organisation, aid and development.' His voice was sleepy, hypnotic. 'But it's a problem there. Many problems. Sometimes these people say they want us to be farmers. Then another one comes and says no, we should be hunters. Too many foreign people always telling, telling, telling ... They don't ask us what we want.' Benjamin's tone became more vehement: 'We the Ju'/Hoansi'; pronouncing the name 'jun-kwasi', with a loud wet click on the 'k'.

'The people round here,' I ventured, 'are they farmers then? Do they still hunt?'

'Oh yes, they are hunting. There is a lot of game here – kudus, you know, wildebeests, gemsboks, everything ...' He took a sip of coffee. Dusk was falling and the birds had ceased their song. He was waiting for me to speak again.

'Do you still have those skills? I mean, do you still hunt?' I eyed his Western clothes apprehensively.

Benjamin smiled, inclined his head. 'Yes, even me, I still have the skills.'

33

'Tomorrow . . .' I said, suddenly emboldened. 'Would you take us hunting?'

Benjamin smiled again, a smile that seemed to say he knew that this question had been coming. Perhaps I wasn't the first to ask. 'Yes,' he said. 'Tomorrow at dawn we will come for you. We will walk far. Do you have water bottles?'

I looked over at Kristin, whose slim, black-eyed face, tanned dark beneath her freckles, was as excited as my own. 'Yes,' she said, 'Yes, we'll bring everything we need . . .'

Ten minutes later the two men had walked off into the dusk, the low murmur of their voices carried back to us on the breeze.

It was a hot night, full of flying insects. Small beetles, whirring into the firelight, committed suicide in our cooking pot. Occasionally, while eating our rice stew, we would crunch down on a hard-boiled wing-case. We didn't care, so elated were we, but turned in early so as to be up before dawn, ready for the hunt. Hunting with the Bushmen. It was finally going to happen.

In the dim pre-dawn the bush came alive with the rustlings of small animals and strange chirruping sounds. The earth smelled greenly alive. It was just cool enough to raise a faint gooseflesh on the arms – a luxury when one thought of the heat to come. We made up the fire and brewed coffee, nursing our excitement, and listening to the chatter and whistle of the waking bush.

Imperceptibly, the blue darkness paled, and there came a lull in the birdsong. The pale light in the clearing blushed slowly from blue to rose, from rose to pink, with here and there a wisp of shining, gilded cloud, reflecting the still unrisen sun. Then, with sudden, astonishing speed, the sky became a vast roof of hammered gold and the sun itself came rising above the black boughs of the eastern bush.

But no one appeared in the clearing. We got the fire going again, made more coffee. Still no one came. Half an hour later, buzzing with the strong camp-brew, we could contain ourselves no longer, but picked up our day-packs, water bottles and cameras and went to find the *nyore* (village), which we knew lay a half-mile or so through the thick scrub.

We found Makuri village still sleeping. As we entered the circle of tiny, beehive huts, only the *nyore*'s pack of weaselly, starveling dogs were up to greet our arrival. They rushed towards us, barking. But despite the noise, no one appeared from the huts. We stood sheepishly in the centre of the village, throwing small stones at the dogs to keep them off. It was long past dawn now. The first heat was in the sun. Already some animals would be slinking into shady cover for the day. Were we too late? Had the hunters forgotten us and left already?

The rib-thin dogs began to fight among themselves – one had found a bloody section of tortoise-shell and the others wanted it. They chased and fought around the huts, yapping louder and louder until at last a flap in the low doorway of one of the little huts opened, and a wrinkled face appeared. Old man /Kaece crawled out, straightened stiffly, shouted at the animals to shut up and threw a tin mug at the nearest. He stretched luxuriously, raising his hands above his head, sticking out his hard belly and closing his eyes with the bliss of it. He yawned, then looked our way and, as if noticing us for the first time, nodded to us while energetically scratching his balls inside his *xai* and hawking up a great gob of phlegm. He spat it out, leant forward to examine the colour, and nodded, as if pleased with what he saw. Then, his morning ritual done, he shuffled over to the next-door hut and banged on the side.

There was a muffled noise from within and Benjamin's head appeared, his sharp, handsome features bleared with sleep and, I realised later when near enough to smell his breath, with liquor. He crawled out, his good, store-bought clothes rumpled from being slept in. He yawned, looked at us vaguely, as if surprised to find us there. Then a pretty young woman with seductive almond eyes, and an ostrich-eggshell necklace draped over her breasts, ducked out of the opening in the beehive hut behind him, saw us, giggled, and darted away out of sight. Benjamin watched her go, stretching his lower back and obviously making an effort to collect his thoughts.

He nodded at us, looking irritated: 'OK, yes. I'll be with you now, now.' He went to a tree at the edge of the huts and hidden by the thick trunk, urinated in a loud, splashing stream before returning and ducking back inside the hut's low doorway to reappear a few moments later with his hunting kit. A bow of light-coloured wood, a quiver of arrows made from a hollowed-out root, a digging stick and a short spear, all hanging conveniently over his right shoulder in a bag made from a whole steenbok skin. He went over to another hut, banged on it, and roused a smaller, even slighter-built young man, similarly bleary and clad in T-shirt, jeans and running shoes. This, said Benjamin, was his co-hunter Xau; he turned to the smaller man and said something in Ju/'Hoansi, then looked back at us: 'Let's go.'

A moment later we were trotting awkwardly behind the two fit, fleet men, out of the village and into the tall grasses. Despite having just been roused from drunken sleep, they moved fast and fluidly, in deceptively small steps, seeming almost to glide above the ground, so smooth was their stride. Benjamin and Xau cast what seemed only the most cursory glances at the ground as they walked. Every few yards we would come upon a narrow track of red or yellow dust criss-crossed with hoof and paw prints. 'See,' Benjamin stopped and pointed. 'That steenbok, we want him.' Following his gaze I nodded sagely, though I couldn't distinguish one track from the next. 'This morning,' I said hesitatingly, 'I'm sorry – I didn't mean to take you away from your wife. I know you've been away in Baraka . . .'

Benjamin looked at me blankly, then away, stifling a grin. 'That', he said, 'was not my wife.' He turned quickly and walked on.

A moment later he stopped short, crouched and turned his head, motioning for us to get down too. 'See', he whispered, pointing ahead. Through a gap in the thicket I saw a small antelope head turn in our direction for a brief second – all flickering ears, limpid, deep brown eyes and little, straight horns – then, reassured that there was no danger, it dipped to graze again. It was a steenbok, a notoriously shy, alert, nervous antelope and we were very close, not twenty yards away.

Xau crept noiselessly up to Benjamin and, using a fluent, silent language of the hands, enquired what he should do. Benjamin replied in the same way, the fingers of one hand making precise gestures

36

against the palm of the other, and Xau crawled off to the left, making a slight noise that caused the antelope to look his way – away from us.

Slowly, so slowly it almost hurt to watch, Benjamin reached back into his shoulder bag for the bow and quiver. Unscrewing the quiver's cap of stiffened hide he noiselessly shook out an arrow – sticky and dark below its small steel tip with a poison made from mashed beetle larvae mixed with saliva. He fitted the arrow to his bow string and rose to a half-standing position. One swift movement lifted the bow and poised the arrow to eye level. Leaning forward from the hips, Benjamin looked directly down the shaft at the antelope, who still grazed blithe and unaware. Up arced the arrow, soundlessly covering the intervening yards between us and the steenbok to hiss into the grass behind it. The head and neck flew up, making – for a brief second – a frozen, alarmed silhouette. Then it took off, disappearing into the trees in three great bounds. Benjamin shrugged, smiling a little sheepishly, and went to retrieve his arrow.

Much later, as the morning heated up towards humid noon, we sighted a group of red hartebeest in a glade of sour plum trees. Large, the size of horses, they are one of Africa's oddest-looking antelope. Their extremely narrow faces taper to barely two inches across at the muzzle. Their eyes stick out and their short horns jut forward in a strange, double-kink. At Benjamin's whispered order, we crouched down a second time. 'They'll come this way. We must wait.' Next to us, a large, talcum-powder white mushroom was growing from a red termite mound. Benjamin reached out and picked it, breaking the white flesh into long sections which he silently offered us. They tasted of lightly smoked cheese, and we munched for a minute or two in happy silence. Then the hunters' faces registered sudden alarm, and with curt gestures they told us to lie flat. Hoofbeats, growing louder. I raised my head and saw the heads and horns of two hartebeest rising and dipping at a canter straight down the trail on which we were crouched.

The first animal burst through the grasses right on top of us and, seeing us, plunged to a halt and reared. Benjamin leapt to his feet and let fly his arrow. There was a blur of hooves, red-coloured hide and dust; the beasts wheeled and were gone. 'Did you hit it?' I was shouting with excitement. Benjamin leant down in the grass and came up with the arrow in his hand. He put his hand over his mouth and giggled. Xau let fly a torrent of abuse. Laughing, Benjamin translated: 'He says I am shit!'

By now the heat was mounting – the animals would start lying up in the shade. To continue hunting would probably be fruitless. Benjamin turned us north, back to Makuri. After a few minutes, I asked, 'So how often do you manage a kill?'

He sighed. 'A big animal, with bows and arrows like this? Maybe one time in a month.'

'So what do you live on the rest of the time?'

'Roots, berries, wild fruits . . .' Benjamin's voice trailed off, then became suddenly vehement. 'We need money – not just for food. There are many problems here, man, many. There are cattle herders from Botswana – the Herero – coming in here, and nothing to stop them because we have no power, no money. And the young people going to the town to drink and not learning the skills because they say that this life is finished. Yes, we need money.' He paused. 'Maybe people like you – tourists – might come here and see our life. There is money in this, I think?'

So, as we walked, we hatched a plan. When I returned to Windhoek and after that to London, I would try to find a safari company that would be prepared to work with the Ju'/Hoansi, bringing clients to experience what we had just experienced – but who would offer the Bushmen a share of the profits rather than just pay them to work as trackers and guides. I knew a company called Footprints, in Windhoek, who sometimes took people up to this region – Benjamin had himself mentioned them earlier, as if planting the seed in my mind. When I got back to the city I would go and talk to them, I promised. Then, for the contact in Britain, I thought of Safari Drive, the company who had lent us the vehicle. They had the contacts, moved in the circles that could attract moneyed clients, and were good people. Walking back along the trail I agreed with Benjamin that next summer – the Namibian winter – we would try and set up a prototype trip, get Safari Drive to organise some clients from England, and together we concocted a happy future.

Back at Makuri, we found a big white Toyota Land Cruiser parked outside the circle of huts. Three white people – a young, dark-haired man and two women in their later thirties – stood talking to old man /Kaece. They looked irritated. As we walked up the narrow trail in the now stifling late-morning heat, the young white man turned, saw us and said half-angrily, half-jokingly, in an accent that sounded American or Canadian: 'Benjamin! Where the fuck have you been? We've been looking for you for hours. Get in the car!'

Without a word Benjamin left us, went off to his hut, came out with a small holdall, and got into the car where the three whites were now waiting, gunning the engine impatiently. They hadn't introduced themselves, but I guessed that they must be from Baraka – the Nyae Nyae Farmer's Co-operative field headquarters where Benjamin had told us he worked. A few minutes later they were gone, Benjamin giving us a quick wave from the back seat as the Land Cruiser disappeared round a bend in the rutted track.

Immediately old man /Kaece and young Xau turned on us and began demanding money, thrusting out their hands and jutting their chins aggressively. The two men – one old, one young – shared a clear family resemblance: the same sharp neat nose, the same eyes that were half mischievous, half soulful. Benjamin, though taller, had also shared this look. Were they all related? I reached into the pocket of my shorts, took out some notes and counted out into the old man's hand the price I had agreed with Benjamin the evening before – ten Namibian dollars for the night's camping, ten for Xau and ten for Benjamin. I hoped Xau would give Benjamin his share.

Placated, the younger man drifted back to his hut, but /Kaece took my arm and led me to his hut where his wife sat, scraping the flesh from the inside of a tortoise shell. Seeing us, she rose, a tiny frail figure, with an old *doek** round her head, several strings of white ostrich-eggshell beads around her wattled old neck, and a beaded steenbok skin knotted at one shoulder. A small dark nipple peeked

*Scarf.

cheekily out of a tear in the hide. She took off one of the necklaces and offered it to Kristin, while /Kaece said 'Twenty, twenty', in Afrikaans. A few minutes later we had bought not only the necklace, but the tortoise shell, a beautiful hunting bow with a set of poison arrows in a quiver, a digging stick, a skin bag to put game in, two sticks for making fire, and a short stabbing spear. A small crowd gathered, each with something to sell. Unable to resist, we saw our roll of notes shrink and vanish. When there was no money left, the people lost interest and melted away among the huts again, leaving us alone.

Standing there with all our newly-bought artifacts, Kristin and I felt suddenly self-conscious, glutted, almost ashamed. We turned and began the walk back to camp. The hunt had been the true fulfilment of a dream. Benjamin had made us feel accepted, respected, welcome. Yet his sudden disappearance and our subsequent fleecing had revealed, with brutal honesty, what we actually represented here: money.

We lay the rest of the day under the great baobab, watching the heavy, sweet-smelling blossoms glide earthward from the high, misshapen branches, plotting how to carry out the promise I had made. As evening fell we heard voices again, and a flurry of children broke upon the camp in a small, joyous wave. Their parents followed, led by old man /Kaece: about twenty adults in all, the men mostly in ragged shop-bought clothes, the women more traditional and neater in a mixture of skins, head scarves and Western dresses with Bushman touches; a fringe of coloured beads tagged onto the hem, or necklaces of ostrich eggshell, black porcupine quills or red wood draped round their necks and hanging over their printed cotton dresses. Most had babies, either slung around their back in a hide sling or a piece of old cloth, or else balanced at the hip, the nipple of a free-hanging breast plugged firmly in their mouths. The children flew back from us in a little flock, and formed a bright-eyed phalanx in the twilight under the great tree.

Using gestures, old man /Kaece told us that we should build another fire to the right of the tree, where the clearing was wider. We did so, lit the wood and sat down with the people in a circle, the adults talking

40

casually among themselves, pulling out little pipes made of bone or hollowed-out rifle bullets. After first asking us through sign language if we had any tobacco, they disappointedly stuffed the pipes from their own small hoards, before relaxing again, laughing and joking. The children snuggled in close to their parents, staring in silence at the rising flames, whose heat, on that summer evening, was enough to raise a sweat even from several yards away.

Old man /Kaece's wife began to sing. Her first, quavering alto note pierced the air above the fire's crackle and silenced the happy chatter. She began to clap, alone at first, then slowly being joined by the other women around the fire. One moment there was a sporadic melody, a few hand-claps among the general talk, the next the night was alive with rhythm and song, the fire roofed with sound. As the song swelled, old man /Kaece rose stiffly to his feet and, in the flickering circle between the singers and the fire began, slowly, to dance. A shuffling forward step, a stamp, a pause, a sudden crouch, knees bent, like a hunter surprised by the sudden sight of his quarry. And then, through subtle shifts of posture and expression, he *became* the quarry. Tossing his head, stamping a foot that, through movement and shadow-light, was transformed into a hoof. Snorting once, twice, as if blowing flies away from his nose, /Kaece was – in that flickering firelight – unmistakably a gemsbok.* A dignified, powerful bull, wary yet confident of his physical power, veteran of fights against other bulls and against those predators unwise enough to try and hunt him. One by one, the other men rose and followed /Kaece's circular progress, each man becoming beast as the dance took him.

As the song changed, the men transformed themselves into other creatures – ostriches, giraffes, lions. Sometimes /Kaece or one of the other men sat down to rest while the others danced on. Sometimes the children would rise and try a few steps or the youngest women would lay their infants aside and dance opposite each other, bobbing their bodies, dipping their heads, rolling their eyes and looking at each other sideways on – like doves courting on the ground. Hours

*A big antelope of the Kalahari – also known as the South African oryx.

passed, until our palms became sore from clapping and, on a final downbeat everyone brought their hands spontaneously together, and the dance was done.

'Ah, so you've been at Makuri?', asked Nigel, the white ranger in charge of Tsumkwe's Nature Conservation Department office, when we dropped in there on our way back to civilisation. Thin, sunburnt, and gnarled by the harsh Namibian climate, his gruff exterior was belied by the kindly twinkle to his eye. In his shorts he looked like a lanky, overgrown schoolboy.

'How's /Kaece doing, the old *skelm* [rascal]? Did he get all your money? Benjamin took you hunting, eh? Now that's a treat, man. Real bow and arrow stuff, eh? *Jasus*, I wish I got time to do that.'

I told him about the tourism plan Benjamin and I had dreamt up. Would he – or at least, his department – support such a venture?

'Eco-tourism with the Bushmen, eh? You won't be the first to try it, I'm telling you. Bet Benjamin didn't tell you that, did he? Well, good luck to you. Something has to work, eh? *Ja*,' he grinned, 'I can see you've got the Bushman bug. You can always tell when the Bushies have got hold of someone. You're finished, man. Toast. Done. Hey, do you like painting?'

To our surprise he took us home to his shabby government-issue house, gave us cups of tea and showed us a collection of surprisingly good, if unfinished, wildlife paintings: a hook-beaked, grey-feathered goshawk; a brooding, hungry leopard; sketches of a spiral-horned kudu. '*Ja*, once the Bushmen get into you man, that's it. I should know. Spend half my time trying to keep them out of jail. Maybe I should give you some background. Do you like Baroque music?'

So, as Vivaldi's lute and mandolin concertos poured out of his dusty stereo speakers, and the Namibian sun beat down outside, Nigel filled us in. The situation with the Ju'/Hoansi was complicated. Their area – officially known as Eastern Bushmanland – was the last place in Namibia where Bushmen could hunt and gather at will. But as Benjamin had told us, an aggressive cattle-owning tribe called the Herero was moving in. They were not Namibian Hereros, as most people in that tribe were, but had arrived a few years back from Botswana. They were the descendants of warriors who had fought the Germans back in the 1900s, when Namibia was still a fledgling colony, and who had, after their inevitable defeat, been driven out into the waterless Kalahari to die. A small number had made it to the natural springs near Ghanzi in Botswana and established a Herero population there. The present German government, anxious to atone for its century-old war crime, had now repatriated five thousand of these Botswana Herero in Namibia.

But, said Nigel, slurping his tea, they had not been welcomed by their fellow tribespeople, whose grazing was already over-stretched and who felt they could not accommodate the cattle that the new-comers had brought with them over the border. So the Botswana lot had been placed in a refugee camp at Gam, south of Bushmanland, there to wait while the Namibian government decided what to do with them. It was from Gam that the Herero families were filtering into the Ju'/Hoansi territory. 'You can hardly blame them,' admitted Nigel; 'They're desperate for land, poor sods. But they kill all the game as they come and they treat the Bushmen like shit. No, man, it's a bad scene. You get your tourism thing working if you can. The Bushmen need all the help they can get. And not just here – it's the same story right across the Kalahari.'

Back in Windhoek we found that, by some fortuitous coincidence, Charles Norwood, one of the Safari Drive owners, had flown in unexpectedly on business. We went straight down to his hotel, told him all that had happened and he, infected by our excitement, accompanied us next day to a meeting at the Footprints office, and from there to the Nyae Nyae Foundation (the headquarters, despite its confusingly different name, of the Nyae Nyae Farmer's Co-op, for whom Benjamin worked). Hearing our proposal, Wendy Viall, the good-hearted South African lady in charge, agreed, in principle, to the plan. We would come back the following year, to make the prototype trip. Footprints would act as the local operator and, assuming the idea caught on, they would then continue to bring clients in, giving /Kaece and his people at Makuri a proper profit-share. Allan, the Footprints guy, talked about giving them as much as 60 per cent.

★   ★   ★

The following year, I found myself and a friend, Tom, driving hard for two days to rendezvous with Benjamin at Baraka, the Windhoek office of the Nyae Nyae Foundation having radioed him to say that we were coming. When we arrived at the remote, dusty field headquarters, a collection of outsize rondavels and workshops surrounded by an endlessness of dry wilderness, Benjamin seemed impressed that we had made it, and happy to see me. Sadly, he could not get away from his work in order to accompany us, as he had hoped, but he had arranged for three of Makuri's best hunters to take us out: Bo, a fiftyish, stick-thin man; another in his mid-thirties called Fanzi; and Xau, a lad of eighteen or so who Bo was training as a hunter. Bo, said Benjamin, was known as the finest hunter in the whole district and Fanzi was not far off in skill. There would be a language barrier but, as Benjamin reassured us: 'They will make sure you don't die. Just follow them and you'll be OK.'

It was the dry season again, and the bush was parched and waterless. Elephants had moved into the area, and were hanging around the waterholes that the villagers used. We had encountered a small group of them a quarter-mile or so from the big baobab when we bumped in down the slow dirt track. Elephant spoor was all round the house-sized tree. For this reason, as the stars came out and the temperature began to plummet towards zero, the three hunters told Benjamin that it would be best to hunt eastward, away from the waterholes. It was too dangerous to risk an encounter with the elephants on foot. As Benjamin translated this to me, a question formed in my mind. What about other dangerous game like lions? The previous year, Nigel, the wildlife officer in Tsumkwe, had told me that there were several prides in the area. How did the hunters propose to make sure we avoided them, and what should we do if we ran into one by chance?

'You won't,' said Benjamin.

'How do you know?'

'The healers, doctors in the village, ask the lions where they are and then they tell the hunters not to go that way.'

'What do you mean they ask the lions? How can they ask the lions?'

Benjamin looked down, appearing not to want to answer. Tom stirred the pot full of pasta and soya mince, looking on. At last Benjamin spoke, sounding uncomfortable. 'Sometimes they can ask the lions.'

With that he turned back to the three hunters, veering the conversation away to talk about a number of kudu that had moved into the area between Makuri and Baraka. But the enigmatic words lingered, tantalisingly, in the night air. Healers that talked to lions.

The next day we followed the three hard, athletic men as they made several unsuccessful stalks at the kudu herd that were – just as they had predicted – browsing the bush east of Makuri. Then they abruptly changed spoor, and brought us, after another long walk, upon the corpse of a wildebeest. How had they known it was there? Had this been what we had been searching for all along – maybe a beast they had shot with a poison arrow the day before★?

Fanzi, Bo and Xau walked straight up to the swollen, cow-sized carcass and, grabbing it by the horns and tail, wrestled its stiff, bloated form out into the open and onto its back. They stripped to the waist and produced small, home-made knives from their game bags. With a surgeon's precision, Bo slit the belly, releasing a belch of rotting gas that made Tom and I gag even where we sat a few yards off. Out spilled yellow-white, reeking intestines heavy with dung, which Fanzi rolled away to one side. Then, using his knife, Bo severed the great muscles, tendons and ligaments of haunch and shoulder, rotating the four great joints so that they dislocated neatly and easily from their bright, white sockets. Fanzi, meanwhile, squeezed the dung from the intestines, and placed these, along with the large, feathery tripes, on the lower branches of a sapling, where they hung like a line of soiled laundry drying in the sun. Xau, equally busy, hefted the heavy joints away and placed them on the lower branches of a sturdy thorn, so that they should not be dirtied with sand.

Next came the liver. As soon as it had been cut out, the three

★Bushmen use slow-acting poisons, made from certain roots mixed with a crushed beetle larva, to bring down big animals. The lethal poison can take up to twenty-four hours to finally kill, during which time the hunter must either track it or make sure that he can return next day and find the carcass. The poison is rendered harmless when the flesh is cooked.

men stopped work, made a quick fire by rubbing two sticks together on a wad of dry grass and, grinning and chatting happily, ate this, the hunter's portion. Then, the liver consumed, the three hunters produced their hollowed-out bone and old rifle-shell pipes and we all settled down to a serious smoke.

Our small gift of tobacco had closed the gap between us a little. Until now the hunters had communicated with us only insofar as to occasionally look back and check we were still with them. At no point had any of them looked us in the eye. Now, after that first smoke, every few minutes, one of the three hunters would glance up from his bloody work and give us a shy smile. After half an hour, Xau looked up enquiringly and ran a reddened finger along the blade of his knife, followed by a dismissive gesture. Tom, quick to understand, grabbed his bag, rooted inside for a moment and handed over his own pen-knife. Snapping it open, Xau began to cut the flesh, hanging it next to the other meat on the branches in long, festive-looking red strips, letting them dry in the desiccated air. They blackened, shrivelled and shrank with incredible speed, the moisture in them evaporating almost as one watched.

The wildebeest had long ceased to be recognisable as an animal. Even the horned head, split open with little hand-axes like the ones that had adorned the walls of my parents' London house, now lay in pieces, the brains and the tongue drying alongside the shredded muscles and organs. The hide had been left lying in the sun, little pools of blood in its folds attracting dainty blue butterflies who drifted down to drink. They flew upwards in a cloud as the three men grabbed the hide and cut it into strips and sections and fashioned it, ingeniously, into three knapsacks, sewn together with the stripped fibres of a dry, green reed-like plant (sansevieria) that grew nearby. The half-dried, much-reduced, meat strips were then stuffed into the newly made bags – the wildebeest would be taken back to Makuri in its own hide.

The haunches and forequarters, too heavy to carry back this time, were stashed in the spiky branches of a thorn tree, out of reach of predators and scavengers, to be collected later. Then Bo squatted down and made a small depression in the sand, filling it with two inches of water from my canteen. He washed the knives in it quickly, handing Tom's back cleaner than it had been before. And after a quick rub-down with sand, the three men, up to their elbows in blood and dung for the past two hours, had shed all trace of their work. Shouldering the hide knapsacks and impaling the racks of ribs on their digging sticks, they set off, single file, on the trek home, leaving only a pile of dung, already drying into fibres, where the wildebeest had lain.

It was a long walk, and hot. The hunters stopped often to ease their shoulders from the weight and their faces from the flies that buzzed incessantly around the bloody loads. Tom and I offered tobacco and water around until both ran out. At the next stop Fanzi, pointing to a small, leafless twig poking up from the cracked earth, began hacking at the soil with his digging stick. A minute later he had unearthed a large, round tuber which, when cut, revealed white flesh dripping with water.

As we sat there, eating the succulent tuber, letting the moisture drip down our throats, there came a sharp, shrill cry from above. We looked up: two eagles were chasing a white goshawk out of their section of sky. Lighter and more agile, the goshawk spiralled up and out of reach into the dazzling blue, the heavier eagles flapping below in slow but unrelenting pursuit. We watched, silent, until all three had dwindled to mere dots, their fading, high-pitched cries floating down to where we sat on the dry earth. Bo, hefting his heavy, fly-blown load once more, creaked to his feet, and caught my eye. He smiled – his mouth turned down ironically at the corners – and pointed to himself, 'Boesman,' he said in Afrikaans, and shook his head, laughing.

That night, and the two that followed, the village feasted but still there was plenty of meat left over. The hunters, having provided food for the month, rested. We spent the remaining days playing with the children who turned up shyly each morning beneath our tree, or going out with the women to forage for wild foods. They showed us how well-stocked the Kalahari is with edibles, even in the parched dry season, leading us through the seemingly barren bush, and stooping every few minutes to pluck, dig, pick up foods

47

until their skin aprons and ragged cotton skirts were filled with sweet *moretlwa* berries, tart, lemony baobab fruit, wild onions, tubers that looked like sweet potatoes, even nuts encased in dried piles of last year's elephant dung. Sometimes they would make Tom and I climb on each other's shoulders to pick caramel-tasting acacia gum from where it had bubbled out and dried between the forked branches of the thorn trees.

Back home, I published a piece on the trip in the *Daily Telegraph*, but the anticipated reaction did not come. No tourists rang up, anxious to book their own Bushman adventure. In fact, over the course of that year, 1996, things became decidedly worse for Bushmen right across the Kalahari. The Herero cattle herders trickled steadily into Nyae Nyae unopposed, slowly dispossessing the Ju'/Hoansi as they came. In Botswana, the government began a campaign of forcibly removing Bushmen from the vast Central Kalahari Game Reserve – an area the size of Switzerland that had been set aside specifically for the Bushmen in the early 1960s – and herding them into permanent settlements outside the reserve's borders. Meanwhile, in central northern Namibia, the Hai//om Bushmen, who had been ejected from the vast Etosha National Park back in the 1970s, became so desperate at their landless state that they staged a demonstration outside the gates of the national park and were tear-gassed and put in jail.

A fledgling Bushman political organisation – called, aptly enough, First People of the Kalahari – emerged in Botswana and began attracting some press attention that year. But after a brief flare of publicity, the leader, John Hardbattle (the mixed-race son of a Nharo Bushman woman and an English rancher), died suddenly from stomach cancer, leaving the organisation leaderless and floundering. I had, it seemed, satisfied my childhood desire to meet and hunt with the Bushmen of my mother's stories just as they were about to cease to exist.

That year I moved to the USA. While there I stumbled across a recent *National Geographic* which had a picture of two leopards on the cover and the title 'A Place for Parks in the New South Africa'.

Inside was a picture that stopped me in my tracks. It showed two Bushmen kneeling in the red sand beside the recumbent body of their father, an ancient man, toothless and obviously dying. According to the caption this was Regopstaan, patriarch of South Africa's Xhomani Bushmen, the last remaining clan of traditionally living Bushmen left in the whole country. This clan, the caption explained, had lodged a land claim with the South African government, both for access to their old hunting grounds in that country's Kalahari Gemsbok National Park, and to receive compensatory ground to live on outside the park fence.

I recalled how, three years before, I had driven to the Kalahari Gemsbok National Park, hoping to find Bushmen, and had been told by the park staff that no Bushmen had existed in the region for decades. Now, looking at this picture in the *National Geographic*, I realised I had been misled. Not only had there been Bushmen in the region, but they had been ejected from the very park whose staff had denied their existence to me. Moreover, concluded the photograph's caption, the park's authorities were resisting the Bushman land claim. I rang the magazine's editorial offices, and was put in touch with Roger Chennels, the South African human rights lawyer who had taken on the case. And he in *his* turn put me in touch with a woman called Cait Andrews in Cape Town who was the person who had first alerted him to the Xhomani cause. She confirmed that the staff at the park had indeed misled me. Bushmen had always lived in the area. In fact the official literature that accompanied the park's declaration, back in the 1930s, had stated that its main aim was to protect the Bushman way of life as well as the game on which they relied – in fact classifying the Bushmen as game to be protected along with the rest of the wildlife. But that, she said, had changed with apartheid, which had reclassified the Bushmen as human (but the wrong kind of human) and had evicted them from the park in the 1970s. Under apartheid national parks were for whites only.

So the Xhomani had been surviving in the dunes outside the fence ever since, living in a state of near beggary, suffering every form of abuse, and falling victim to the inevitable by-products of despair, alcoholism and violence, as well as an almost complete break-down of their culture. No longer able to forage at will, they lived by making crafts for tourists whose cars they waved down as they drove along the road to the park. Half the clan had gone to live in a private game reserve far to the south, where they existed as inmates in a human zoo, posing in their skins for tourists' cameras. They had even lost their language and only a few of the older generation were still able to remember the Xhomani tongue. The rest spoke mostly in Nama or Afrikaans, the language of those who had dispos-sessed them.

Under Mandela's New South Africa, the clan had at last come above ground, and had been persuaded to file this new land claim. For the first time, they were being taken seriously by a government. Old 'Madiba' (the popular name for Mandela) had even invited Dawid Kruiper, the leader of the Xhomani since old Regopstaan had died, to present his case personally over tea at the presidential residence in Cape Town. Theoretically, there was every chance that they might win. But there was stiff opposition from the old order, in the person of the park's chief warden and the National Parks Board as a whole (which was, Cait Andrews confided, still an enclave of entrenched Afrikanerdom). On top of this, the Xhomani land claim was being opposed from another quarter, entirely unconnected with the national park. A group of local coloured farmers, known as the Mier, were claiming that, back in the 1960s, a large tract of *their* traditional land had been appropriated by the Kalahari Gemsbok National Park. If the Xhomani had a land claim, they said, then so had they. To complicate matters further, it seemed that much of the land which the lawyers said should be given to the Xhomani in compensation for what they had lost to the park, actually belonged to these Mier farmers, and stood to be forcibly purchased from them should the Bushmen win the claim. Land is everything in South Africa: the thought of giving up land to Bushmen, even with due compensation, was, said Cait, pure anathema to the Mier. They had resolved to fight the Xhomani land claim to the last.

But should the Xhomani win, however long that took to happen, they would set a political precedent for the other countries of the

Kalahari, where Bushmen were still being dispossessed on a grand scale. She and the lawyer Roger Chennels were part of a growing movement to reverse this. That year for example, a new, Namibian-based Bushman NGO called WIMSA★ had been formed with German and Scandinavian donor money. This organisation was paying the legal fees for the Xhomani land claim and financing a smaller NGO called SASI (South African San Institute) which now represented the Bushmen in South Africa. WIMSA had also announced its intention to campaign on behalf of Bushmen everywhere – South Africa, Botswana, Namibia, even Angola, Zambia and Zimbabwe. But it was the Xhomani land claim that needed to be won in order to set the necessary precedent. The tide of history – the centuries of dispossession and oppression – was finally turning. If ever there was a time to be chronicling events on the Kalahari, Cait assured me, it was now.

★Working Group for Indigenous Minorities in Southern Africa.

PART TWO

THE MANTIS, THE MOUSE
AND THE BIRD

4

Regopstaan's Prophecy

Late the following year – October 1997 – I arrived at the Red House, or *Rooi Huis* as the Xhomani called it, with notebook, camera and recording equipment, accompanied by Cait Andrews, Chris, a film-maker friend who wanted to make a documentary about the land claim, and a truck full of gifts with which to buy goodwill. We even had a driver – Andrew, a tall, bearded white South African, to pitch our tents, cook our food and ferry us around while we conducted our research among the Xhomani, who lived on the outskirts of Welkom, a bedraggled settlement of poor coloured farming folk some ten kilometres south of the Kalahari Gemsbok National Park. 'We're here,' said Cait, as we pulled up outside a red-daubed, open-fronted shack – the Red House. A barrage of yelling, runny-nosed, grinning children, some naked, some in ragged shorts, ran up shouting and laughing, as we got out, stiff from the long drive, and began to look about us. Chris went to the back of the Toyota to fetch his camera. Cait and I looked down at the kids. A small, greying man with a squashed nose and eyes lost behind deep, mischievous wrinkles, came hobbling over from the house with a spryness that seemed at odds with his pronounced limp. He wore a bizarre mixture of clothing: a blue jacket striped with spangly gold lamé, above a *xai*, or loincloth of animal skin, his legs, chest and stomach all bare. 'This,' announced Cait, 'is Dawid Kruiper, head of the Xhomani clan.' He shook my hand and hers, squinting ingratiatingly, and said, *'Ja, Ja Mama'*.

Some ten or so adults pushed through the staring wall of children, also proffering hands. Cait made the introductions. There was Jakob, a handsome man with a beard and slightly dreadlocked hair, clad only in a *xai*, his lined face betraying an age of perhaps fifty, though his body was that of a twenty-year-old. Leana, his wife, had obviously been a beauty with features as regular as a model's under a cream-coloured scarf wrapped stylishly around her head. Her skin, darker than her husband's, glowed, despite its scars and stretch marks. A tiny, slender and very pretty girl with the widest cheekbones I had ever seen, and a gap where her two front teeth should have been, turned out to be Oulet, Dawid's daughter. Next to her stood her husband Rikki, dressed in torn old jeans, and a stained black T-shirt with 'Chicago Bulls' printed on it in red. Lean, wiry, his eyes deep-set and staring, he radiated a mad, haunted strength which contrasted directly with the gentle, good-looking slender youth standing next to him, whom Cait called Vetkat ('fat cat').

Cait took charge, detailing the men to unload the goods we had brought. Sacks of mealie meal (maize flour), boxes of rough tobacco, fresh red meat in bags of ice, boxes of tinned vegetables and, on Cait's advice, a sizeable bag of *dagga* (marijuana): we had not come empty-handed. As the supplies were being stacked in a corner of the Red House, Dawid led us into its shady interior and motioned for us to sit around the cooled ashes of the central hearth. Here sat two others: Sanna, Dawid's wife, whose face was a stiller, older version of the young woman Oulet's, and Bukse, Dawid's younger brother, who was small but very muscular, with a quick-looking, snub-nosed face. The rest of the clan followed us in and squatted around us in a circle, looking on with detached, polite interest, waiting for us to say why we had come.

Cait explained in Afrikaans. Chris and I were journalists, she said, her tone portentous, come to tell the world that the Bushmen were at last going to fight for what was theirs. As she spoke, Dawid looked at the ground, stealing occasional glances – at once shrewd and polite – at Chris and I. We were by no means the first journalists he had met. Many had come, asked questions, taken photographs, scribbled notes and pushed microphones and camera lenses into his tired old face. Yet here Dawid and his people still sat, landless squatters on the edge of a poor coloured village, most of whose inhabitants, though little more than paupers themselves, looked down on their Bushmen neighbours and regarded them as little better than dogs.

And what difference did I think I could make? I now had a commission, having managed to persuade a publisher to let me write a book on the Xhomani land claim and the plight of the other groups across the Kalahari. But it would be years in the writing, and even when it was published, it might not be of any help to them. In the meantime, there was no guarantee that any articles I wrote would see the light of day, let alone provoke some action. It seemed to me that Dawid, this shrewd, tough old Bushman who sat watching us, could sense all this, yet he said nothing, only nodded as Cait spoke, gazing at the ashes in the hearth while the other members of the clan looked on in silence. Feeling a fraud, I looked away from him and let my eyes wander around the interior of the hut, to a long shelf which ran along the smoke-blackened back wall. A number of objects were stored on it: folded animal hides, a row of battered, blackened pots, a pile of long, straight gemsbok horns and a large, framed photograph from the *National Geographic*, the picture which had brought me here to the Red House at the edge of the dunes. I now recognised the figures tending the ancient, ailing man – they were Dawid and his brother Bukse.

As Cait finished her speech, Dawid said something to Sanna, his wife. She got up and went into one of the shadowed corners, returning with a small skin pouch. Dawid reached in, pulled out a pinch of rough tobacco, a dried bud of marijuana, some torn newspaper, and rolled a joint. Lighting it, he passed it around once so that we all had a hit, then rose and asked us to stand at the entrance to the Red House, where it looked out over the dunes, northwards towards the park. In the middle distance stood a tall camel-thorn tree, its great tap-root presumably stretching deep down through the sand and rock below to some deep, underground water source. The feathered green of its leaves shone bright against the orange-red dune. 'There is buried old Regopstaan,' said Dawid, 'where he can look one way and see us, and the other way to see our land, the park.'

In Afrikaans the word 'Regopstaan' means 'stand up straight'. It is also a name for the meerkat, or suricate, a kind of small mongoose that lives in colonies and packs up together to fight off predators. An appropriate name for the old leader. During the drive Cait had told me that, shortly before his death, Regopstaan had bequeathed a prophecy to his people: '*When the strangers come, then will come the big rains. And the Little People will dance. And when the Little People in the Kalahari dance, then the Little People around the world shall dance too.*'

Cait, Dawid, Chris and Andrew sat silent and awkward in the dark interior of the Red House. Most of the people that had followed us in – Jakob, Leana, Rikki, Vetkat and the rest – began to drift away, back to their own huts. I got up to clear my head and walked outside, around the Red House's crimson-coloured walls. In two places the red mud-daub was disrupted by the sculpted heads of gemsbok, painted – as in real life – with white faces striped black from eyes to muzzle and topped by long, rapier-like horns. One of the heads was life-size and had real horns. The other was a giant, the head alone measuring about three feet long and the horns made of wooden poles that stuck up towards the roof. It jutted out from the red wall like a buttress. Benjamin had told me that the gemsbok was a symbol of strength for the Bushmen. Perfectly adapted to desert life, they can go a month without water. They could also be vicious when provoked; safari guides are full of stories of gemsbok killing predators, and sometimes even people. Once, in the Etosha National Park in Namibia (which, like South Africa's Kalahari Gemsbok National Park, had been a Bushman hunting ground until the 1970s), I saw a game warden try to rescue a gemsbok that had become stuck in the deep mud around a waterhole. Whenever he approached, the animal swiped its long horns in challenge, never letting him get closer than a few feet. After a few minutes it became so incensed by the warden's presence that it heaved itself bodily from the mud and chased the man back into the cab of the truck, which it then raked and slashed with its horns. It seemed fitting that gemsbok heads should be mounted on the Red House – a symbol of the Bushmen's defiance and endurance.

From one of the further shacks came the sound of quiet singing. An elderly woman, wearing only a skin kilt, was weaving her thin, ancient body to and fro in a dance. She swayed past me, dry aged breasts flapping against her bony chest, and stepped into the sheltered entrance of the Red House, whose roof was supported on wooden poles, like the extended front of a marquee. 'Cait,' she said quietly, 'my mother.' Cait looked up from the fire where she had been talking with Dawid and Chris: 'Antas!' she said, smiling, and got up. 'My mother,' repeated the old lady, though she must have been at least thirty years Cait's senior. She took Cait's hand and, still dancing and quietly singing, led her outside, to sit down on the sand. She then pushed the thin white woman gently back, until she lay stretched out, and began to move her hands in a circular motion in the air an inch above Cait's lower belly. For perhaps ten minutes, Antas moved her hands above Cait's stomach, singing all the while, then abruptly she stood up, ceased her song, and motioned for Cait to rise. When she was back on her feet, Antas hugged her around her middle, repeating the words 'My mother, my mother' and swayed off in the direction from which she had come. Cait looked over at me: 'Time to go, I think.'

We made our good-byes. Dawid looked at Chris and I and made the gesture of a film camera in motion, holding one hand in front of his eyes to suggest the lens and rotating the other, before erupting into gently mocking, violently coughing mirth. We started up the Toyota and headed back out to the main dirt road that led to the national park, where we were camping.

'What was that old woman doing, making you lie down and singing like that?' I asked Cait.

Cait said nothing for a while. Then, as if having made a decision, told us quietly: 'Just before you came out,' she said, 'I went to the doctor to see about some pains in my stomach. It turns out I've got a cancer. Nothing serious yet, but cancer all the same. You're the first one outside the family I've told.'

'I'm sorry,' I said, embarrassed. 'So that old woman, Antas, I mean, nobody could have told her about it before she came over and did that thing on you, right?'

'No,' replied Cait, staring back at the road. 'Nobody told her.'

We drove on in silence. I had heard before of the Bushmen's

reputation as great healers. Until now, this had not fascinated me as much as their wildness, their elusiveness.

Arriving back at our camp site, we found that ground squirrels had broken into our tents, and devoured the extra sacks of mealie meal that we were saving to give away on our departure. As we unzipped the tent and looked in, one of the creatures paddled its little legs through the white drifts of spilled meal and flopped through the hole it had made, so distended it could barely move. As we cleaned up the mess and the sun finally set, Andrew got a fire going, and the sickle moon rose over four steaks, grilling nicely.

We opened a bottle of wine and Cait took up the conversation we had let lapse in the car: 'You just have to get used to strange things happening when you're around Bushmen. When Regopstaan was alive, for instance, he used to tell me to watch out for praying mantises in my house down in Cape Town. If one appeared – and they didn't very often – then I'd know he wanted to talk to me. I'd ring the national park office or the Kagga Kama reception – that's the reserve half of them live on now – and someone would send a message down to him. When he eventually came on the line he'd say "What took you so long? I've been trying to get your attention for days."' Even the way she had stumbled into the story had been strange, Cait went on. She had been told all her life that there were no Bushmen left in South Africa. She had only found out about the Xhomani back in 1990 when the clan had ended up in court after being lured onto a ranch by a local entrepreneur called Lockie Henning, who had intended to set up a private game reserve and display the Xhomani as 'show Bushmen'. The venture had failed and the entrepreneur had done a runner, leaving the Bushmen liable for the rent. The magistrate had let them off, seeing that they had been swindled themselves, but a news crew had then got hold of the story and driven up to interview the Xhomani. The resulting short documentary – which Cait had seen only by chance – had detailed their plight, how they had been expelled from the park that had once been their home and were now destitute, but had left it at that.

Another white farmer, Pieter de Waal, a wealthy wine grower from the vineyards near Cape Town – had also seen the documentary, and had been similarly inspired by the idea of creating a Bushman reserve. De Waal contacted the Xhomani and offered them jobs on a game farm he owned down in the mountains of the Karoo, midway between Cape Town and the Kalahari. There were old Bushman paintings in a cave on the property, he told Regopstaan, then still alive. It would be like a homecoming, Bushmen reclaiming an area from which their ancestors had disappeared. Feeling that any opportunity was better than none, the Xhomani had agreed, arranging to go there in shifts; half their number staying up in the Kalahari, the rest going down to Kagga Kama, and swapping over every few months, with De Waal providing the transport.

Cait went on. 'By the time I managed to make contact with the Xhomani, most of them had already moved down to Kagga Kama. So I went there, met Regospstaan – who was very old by then, and Dawid, who wasn't yet the leader – and asked if I could at least record their language, which I understood was dying out. I hoped that I could archive it for posterity.' Cait paused, took a sip of wine. 'Regopstaan told me to ask Dawid for a decision – as he was close to death and his son would soon be the leader. I did as he asked, and Dawid said yes, that would be fine, but I must do something in return. He said he wanted "a school, a lawyer, and a land to walk around in." Just that. So that's what's been done. I organised the school with Pieter de Waal – though I hear it's not functioning right now. The lawyer was less of a problem; I already knew Roger Chennels – who's now representing their land claim – from way back, from the days of the Struggle. He agreed to take it on, as you know. And now we're working on the "land to walk around in" part.'

This was how the land claim had been conceived: the Xhomani were to demand the restoration of their hunting and gathering rights inside the park, as well as the right to visit ancestral graves there. In addition, they demanded that they be given land outside the park that they could live on. But then the problems started: not just opposition from the park, and from the local Mier farmers. The

Xhomani were also having trouble being recognised as Bushmen. When they had been kicked out of the park back in the 1970s, Cait explained, they had had to obtain Pass Books – identification documents that defined people by race (all non-whites were required to have these). When the race officials in Upington, the nearest administration centre, had asked them what race they were, the Xhomani had said 'Bushman'. Not possible, the officials had replied; there were no Bushmen left in South Africa. 'So, they had to register as coloured, and it's haunted them ever since. It's one of the justifications that the parks people use for not letting them back in – they say that they aren't real Bushmen and that therefore their claim can't be legal.'

There was a further irony to this. By being registered as coloured the Xhomani had been lumped in with the Mier, the group that represented the largest obstacle to the Xhomani's land claim after the National Parks Board. The Mier leader, said Cait, was a guy called Piet Smith, who was also the Nationalist Party MP for the region. According to Cait, he had stated that Bushmen would receive Mier land only over his dead body.

While Cait had been speaking, a young woman had come and joined our circle. A friend of Andrew's, Belinda, we had met her briefly the night before, as we were driving in: Andrew had stopped the vehicle and introduced us. She had been on her way back from a visit to the Bushmen, she had told us, shaking hands through the car window. Andrew had told us a little about her, that she was the first coloured manager that the park had ever employed – an attempt by the Afrikaner parks management to embrace the New South Africa.

She took a seat next to me and I asked her if she had been spending much time with the Bushmen.

'Not really, no. I only met them for the first time a few days ago. But what about you? What are you doing in the Kalahari?'

Taking a deep breath I told her. By the time I'd finished my story it was after midnight and Cait, Andrew and Chris had all sought their tents. Belinda stood up to go. 'These Bushmen,' she said, stretching. 'I don't know what it is. I came here for peace and quiet, and already I can see how political the whole thing is. Well, goodnight. Come and say howzit to me tomorrow when you're back from the Bushmen – my house is just through the gate beyond the administration building. Anyone can show you the way. I'd like to know how it went.'

Next day we awoke to an oven-hot dawn, too stifling to linger in the tent or sleeping bag for more than a few moments. Outside, a white-hot sky presaged a day of pounding discomfort: perhaps building up for a rain.

Before driving out of the park to visit the Bushmen again, we took a pass along one of the dry riverbeds inside the National Park, the old Xhomani hunting ground. Now, at the parched, dead end of the dry season, only the drought-proof creatures were in evidence. Springbok – slender gazelles with short, lyre-shaped horns, a red-brown stripe on their flanks and huge, liquid eyes fringed with luxuriant black lashes that seemed heavily daubed with mascara – drifted along the roadside. From afar, their colours and delicate shapes blended perfectly with the yellow grasses and shimmering haze above the sand. Seen closer to they seemed to glide across the land, so fluid was their gait. Every now and then one of them would leap six feet into the air, arch its back so that the white hairs along its spine raised themselves like a crest, and touch all four hooves together before landing back on the ground. Known as 'pronking', this was apparently a response to predators – though we could not see any.

Alongside the springbok were smaller groups of more massive gemsbok, inelegant, gawky blue-black wildebeest and large, reddish-coloured hartebeest, all goggling brown eyes and crumpled, strangely foreshortened horns. They stood still in the heat, seemingly stunned by the hammering sun, not even foraging for the patches of yellow grass that stood here and there along the riverbeds. As we neared the park gate, we came upon a lone male wildebeest standing stock still at the edge of a flat, white piece of bare ground surrounding a small waterhole. Only his tail moved, flicking at the flies that buzzed around its hindquarters. Three lions lay at the waterhole – two lionesses and a young male just entering his prime. All three had coats bleached almost white by the fierce sun. Their eyes were fixed on the wildebeest, and his on them. The lions looked relaxed, but ready to spring into lethal action at any moment. The wildebeest could not move forward towards the water he needed, nor could he turn and go, in case the big cats pursued him; in his weakened, dehydrated state, he might not outrun them. The lions, lying just too far off for a successful sprint, also could not move, for that might trigger a flight that they in their turn might not outrun. So predators and prey waited, immobile, patient, the sun beating savagely upon them while the flies buzzed and bit. A contest of patience and endurance.

Back at the Red House, when we told Dawid what we had seen, he laughed, gestured towards the fences that surrounded the little settlement and shrugged. Next to him *Ou* Anna, his ancient, wrinkled aunt (and the late Regopstaan's sister), chimed in: 'Life here is still good. We have the sand, the sunshine. Sometimes the white people come and help us. But there in the park – that, that is life.'

Chris and I wanted to know if it would be possible to organise a hunting and gathering foray for the Xhomani, which we could perhaps film, maybe on one of the surrounding farms, which were still semi-wild. Cait said that there was an old coloured farmer some kilometres to the south who was known to be better disposed towards the Bushmen than others in the area and who sometimes allowed them on his land. She consulted Dawid, who said he thought the man might be persuaded, for a fee, to let them try their luck across his dunes. After a brief, shouted exchange with the rest of the clan, the senior men, Dawid and Jakob, along with Dawid's youngest son Pien, a tautly muscled youth in his early twenties, squeezed themselves into the back of the Toyota, along with Sanna, Leana, Dawid's daughter Oulet and assorted kids. The men brought bows and the women digging sticks and skin bags. The back of the vehicle was stifling hot, but everyone squashed themselves in cheerily, elated at the prospect of an unexpected outing, laughing and joking in rapid-fire Afrikaans and clicking Nama.

The farmer, who lived in a two-roomed concrete block cottage with a battered old car and donkey cart parked in the yard, turned out to be amenable: for two hundred rand, he said, Dawid and his people could spend the afternoon on his land, and catch or gather whatever they could find, as long as it wasn't a sheep. We paid, then drove up into the dunes. Around us the veld had been reduced to bare sand. Goats and sheep had stripped every low-growing bush almost to the ground. Clumps of desiccated grass and leafless thorn clung to the few sheltered hollows between the dunes. Yet still there was life – from one of these hollows a small steenbok went skipping away in front of us to the accompaniment of shouts and howls from the back. Did Dawid want to stop and hunt, we asked. 'No,' he said. 'Drive on.'

We sighted a shack standing by itself in the hot dunes; a strange, crumpled construction, consisting of a sawn-in-half truck supporting a large tent of woven grasses. Outside, in its scant shade, squatted two Mier shepherds: middle-aged, sun-shrivelled men with bodies lean and gnarled as *biltong*★ inside loose-fitting blue overalls, battered felt hats pulled down over their eyes. They showed no surprise at our approach, nor when Dawid told us to stop and we pulled up outside their shack.

Getting out of the suffocating vehicle was sweet relief – though the outside air was hardly cool. The two shepherds greeted Dawid familiarly. He squatted down in the shade next to them, pulled his tobacco pouch from his little skin shoulder-bag, and rolled up a cigarette with a torn piece of newspaper, making a perfectly symmetrical, fat cone that he licked smooth with one long stroke of the tongue before lighting it from a match offered wordlessly by one of the shepherds. Then, as we whites hovered in the background, the three men began to talk, asking each other how they were, how their families were, how the sheep had been. Was there still grazing? Were jackals or leopards stealing the stock?

This was obviously going to take some time, so I drifted over to the shade of a small thorn tree where two gaunt, droop-headed horses, a grey and a dark bay, stood swishing and stamping at the flies. Above my head, hanging from one of the spiky branches, I suddenly noticed

★Dried meat.

the freshly skinned body of a young goat, dead eyes staring from a peeled face down which dripped blood and clear fluid. It gave off the rich, sickly smell of meat left out too long in the sun. Flies crawled up and down it, clustering at the eyes and nostrils. I left the tree and wandered back towards Dawid and the two shepherds, who were still conversing quietly. Cait, Andrew and Chris had also gravitated towards the trio. It looked as though they had finished their smoke. Abruptly, Dawid got up, and bid a quick, curt good-bye.

Driving away, Cait leaned back to shout through the glass partition – why had we stopped there? Dawid replied angrily, then spat. 'He says he wanted to buy a sheep or a goat from them,' translated Cait. 'But they were asking too much. He's annoyed, says the coloureds always try and rob the Bushmen.' So this was no hunt, but a shopping expedition. If the National Park management were claiming that the Xhomani were no longer 'real Bushmen', that they had lost their ancient skills and their place in the Kalahari's delicate ecological balance, Dawid seemed to be proving them right. When he next asked Andrew to stop the vehicle – by a particularly large dune – it was again neither to hunt nor gather but just to have another smoke. This time all the men and women – looking Bushmanlike enough with their *xais*, bare torsos and bows carried over the shoulder in the traditional way – climbed the dune, obviously relieved to be out of the truck, and sat up on the ridge, where there was a breeze, rolling newspaper *zols* (joints) and chatting quietly, completely ignoring us and seemingly impervious to the searing sun.

We got out of the car too. Cait caught my sour expression and smiled wryly: 'There's always another agenda with the Bushmen. It always happens like this – you arrange to do something and then the next thing you know you're driving up and down the road giving this person a lift, waiting while that person goes off to buy some dope, then going back to pick up somebody else's stuff and take it to some other place, until eventually you forget what it was you originally set out to do. They don't often get a chance to be driven around, so when it comes they make the most of it. We're just the taxi drivers. They tell you whatever you want to hear, then take total advantage.'

Andrew, the driver, lit a cigarette and chuckled. I looked over at Chris. If he was frustrated at having nothing to film, he wasn't showing it, but sat, enjoying the shade, eyes closed behind his sunglasses, just relaxing.

Some time later, tinkling down the breeze, there came a light sound of children's laughter. I got up, went to the cab of the Toyota and fetched my camera. Up on the dune, which had turned a vibrant orange-red in the early evening light, the children were playing under the quiet, smiling eyes of their elders. Taking turns, one naked child would lie flat on his or her back while another grabbed the legs and pulled them down the dune. Then, with a shout, the puller would dart sideways and the other child would sit up, pitch forward and somersault down to the bottom of the dune, before running back up to repeat the process once more, laughing all the while. The game seemed to have no logic, no object, no way to win or lose. The game just *was*, and that was all.

As the light mellowed and deepened, Dawid said a few words to Jakob, and he and the rest of the clan came back down the dune. We should do our thing now, he said; this was the right time for filming, now that the light was *lekker* (nice). Surprised that Bushmen knew about light and filming we followed Dawid and Jakob to a flat space where a patch of dry grasses waved in the light wind, golden with evening, sparkling against the deep blood of the sand. What followed was a masterfully choreographed re-creation of Bushmanness. When I looked at the slides some weeks later there was no telling that everything had been staged, so natural were the expressions, the movements, the placing of hands and bodies and arms to suggest action. There was a beautiful picture of Dawid leading the clan in single file through the dunes, as if travelling from one camping place to another, the men shouldering their bows, the women slinging skin bags and babies expertly on their hips. Another slide showed Dawid and Jakob crouching in the dunes, bows ready, arrows on the string, as if they had just sighted game and were lining up for the bow-shot. On the same dune, Chris filmed an interview with Dawid, sitting there in his *xai*, telling the camera, through Cait, about his people's plight; how they had been ejected from the park, how now they had decided to fight for the return of their land, of their hunting grounds, how he invited Mr Mandela to come and witness the injustice of their position.

Doubts began to nag at me again. Did Dawid and Jakob still possess the skills they had imitated for the benefit of our cameras? Did Sanna and Leana and Oulet still know how to look for the wild roots and tubers hidden under the sand? Were they able to pass on any such knowledge to the children we had watched playing on the dune? Did the younger men, like Pien, Vetkat or Rikki, who had grown up since the Xhomani had left the park, know anything of the old culture?

As we drove back to Welkom in the failing light, Cait told us more about Rikki. 'Now there's a story. He tends to keep himself to himself at the moment – the clan only recently decided to let him live and he's sort of keeping his head down . . .'

'What d'you mean – decided to let him live?'

'Rikki is – *was* – a healer,' Cait explained. 'But last year he went completely mad, turned to drink, became dangerously violent.' It had happened like this, she said: two BaTswanas from across the border had come to Welkom to get a healing from the Bushmen for a mental problem and Rikki had ended up doing the healing. Somehow in his trance, the Xhomani had told her, the disease had left the BaTswana's brain and entered Rikki's. 'They say that's a real danger,' Cait explained. 'Sometimes the sickness can transfer itself into the healer.

'One day he even went for me,' she went on. 'He was fighting drunk and trying to hit one of the older guys. I got between them, which made him so angry that he ran to his house, came back with a bow and arrow and threatened to shoot me. I thought he really might; it took a long time before I could make him put the bow down. And right after that, do you know what the rest of the clan said? "Don't worry Cait, if he'd killed you we would have avenged your death within three minutes."' She paused to laugh. 'Within three minutes! Like that was supposed to make me feel better! Anyway, eventually Rikki got so bad that the clan decided to kill him. Jakob actually cut Rikki's throat about eight months ago, but he

68

survived. He's much calmer now – says the demons went out of him with the bleeding. But the clan are still keeping an eye on him – he's on parole, as it were.'

I didn't like what I was hearing. The Bushmen were the gentle people, the only Africans without a warrior tradition, the ones who did not resort to violence to settle conflicts. Again the myth was being cast into doubt. 'What about Oulet,' I asked, 'Didn't she mind Jakob trying to kill her husband?'

'I think she was probably all for it,' laughed Cait. 'She was probably at the end of her tether with the beatings . . .'

'But hold on,' I said, 'I didn't see any scar on Rikki's throat. How could it have healed so quickly and not left a mark?'

'Ah,' said Cait, enigmatically, 'He's a Bushman.'*

Arriving back at the Red House we heard music drifting across the sand: the sound of a Hammond organ played at full vibrato, and over that the sound of a man singing a hymn. The Red House had been taken over by missionaries, two thin men in polyester white shirts and ties, and a large woman in a pink flowery dress, a wide-brimmed straw hat on her head. Those Bushmen who had not come with us that day sat around them, quietly watching.

'*Je-esus!*' they sang, sharing a mike that had been wired up to a car battery. '*Je-e-sus*, is my Lord . . .'

Dawid hobbled into his house, and said a few words in Nama. The singing stopped, the organ died away, and the mike was switched off with a fuzzy click. I caught Cait's eye, she indicated with a flick of her scarf-bound head that we should leave the old man to it. So we walked away across the sand to Jakob's hut, which stood a little apart from the others at the far end of the settlement where the big dunes began. A desiccated gemsbok head, complete with horns, was mounted on a pole outside the grass and corrugated iron shack, near a donkey cart, its shaft and traces lying unused in the sand. Jakob,

---

*When I got to know him better, I asked Rikki (who did have a small scar on his throat) if this story were true. He said it was, and that Antas had healed him with songs, as well as roots and a mixture of fats and vegetable juices to minimise the scar.

who had gone straight up to his house the moment he had heard the sound of missionaries, sat stringing beads of reddish-coloured wood onto a hide string. He looked furious.

'Do you mind the missionaries being here?' I asked. It was an obvious question, but I wanted to record his response. As if guessing my motive, Jakob's bearded face suddenly closed. 'I'm just going on with my work, here, at my house,' he replied, nodding down at the unfinished necklace in his hands. 'Just sitting here, doing my work, in my own house,' he repeated, between his teeth.

We took the hint. Back at the Red House the missionaries were packing up, preparing to carry their equipment back to their vehicle. They nodded to us as they left. Dawid sat, looking at a new fire that Sanna was busy kindling. 'You see', he said, as Cait and I came over, 'Everything belongs to somebody else – the dunes, the veld, even the Red House – anyone can just come when they like. We need a place. I don't want to kick anyone out of their place. I don't want to do to the park what they did to us. But we just need a place.'

When we got back to camp, I asked Cait: 'Why doesn't the park want the Bushmen back in? I mean, it's the New South Africa and everything, Mandela's even said he supports the Bushmen. Surely it'd be a real *coup* for the park to have the Bushmen hunting and gathering inside again? Tourists would come from all over the world if they knew there were Bushmen in the park and that they could go walking with them and visit them and stuff. Private game reserves are doing it – look at Kagga Kama. The park could make millions. Why don't they want them?'

Cait shook her head. 'Why don't you ask them?'

A yellow gravel road led from the camp site up to the park's administration building. Inside, a young brunette in crisp khakis, her hair curled in a light perm, smiled brightly at me and asked if she could help. Her smile faded a little when she saw my tape-recorder, headphones and mike.

'I was wondering if I could have an interview with Mr Engelbrecht, the chief warden?'

The girl looked alarmed, but recovered quickly and said: 'I'll just see if he has time.' There was a pause while she spoke in Afrikaans on the internal phone. Then she looked up at me, smiling again: 'I'm sorry, the park warden's in a meeting. He's too busy to see anyone today.'

'Ah, how about tomorrow?'

'I'll just check, hold on please.' Another brief chat on the internal phone. 'No, I'm sorry, the park warden is busy all this week. If you make an appointment after next week he may be able to fit you in.'

Cait had warned me that I might have trouble. I became very polite. 'I'm terribly sorry to keep bothering you, but you see I'm making a radio programme for the BBC about the Xhomani land claim and I'd hate for the park not to be able to give their side of the story. Is there anyone else I could talk to – anyone in the park who officially deals with the Bushmen?'

'That would be the Social Ecology Department,' said the brunette. 'Mrs Engelbrecht, the park warden's wife, is in charge there. I'll see if she has any space in her schedule.' After a third consultation in Afrikaans, the girl, obviously relieved to be rid of me, said, 'Mrs Engelbrecht says she'll see you now – her office is just down the hall there, last door on the right.'

'Thanks, that's great, thanks very much.' Rubber soles squeaking on the polished linoleum, I went down the hall and knocked at the door the girl had indicated. A female voice answered: 'Come in!'

Sitting behind a large wooden desk, her back to a window, was another slim attractive woman, with long blonde hair neatly tied back. She had pale, rather watery blue eyes. Standing by the desk, and looking as if he had just been in conversation with her, was a young coloured man, about my own age, with a wispy moustache and soulful brown eyes, dressed in khaki shorts and shirt with epaulettes showing the parks board insignia of a stylised kudu's head. Mrs Engelbrecht, also in uniform, introduced herself, and then the young man: 'This is Steven Smith, my assistant social ecologist.' We shook hands. 'Pleased to meet you,' said the young man in heavily accented English.

I recalled that 'Smith' was the name of the Mier leader Cait had told me about, the one who had said the land claim would only happen over his dead body. As I sat down I asked the young man if he was any relation.

'I'm Piet Smith's son, yes,' he replied, looking me right in the eye.

Then the woman spoke, half wary, half apologetic: 'Unfortunately I didn't know you're coming' – she used the mixed-up grammar of an Afrikaner unused to speaking English. 'You should have made some reservation, or something. Because then I'll, sort of, have enough . . . time to talk to you about it. I have to work through head office by handling journalists. I have to tell them that I'm handling people, and on what.' She paused: 'Did you come with Cait?'

'I came through with Cait Andrews, yes,' I admitted, trying to make it sound like a good thing.

She looked at her hands, then at me again: 'Well, on what exactly do you want to know?'

'Just some very straightforward questions. The first one is . . . er . . . does the Parks Board, the Kalahari Gemsbok National Park administration, support the Bushman land claim?'

The blonde woman took a deep breath and leaned forward over the desk. 'You see, on the land claim itself . . .' I switched on the tape machine. 'Don't record me!' she cried, suddenly alarmed. I made no move to switch the machine off. She shot me a panicked look, but did not insist. Instead she pursed her lips and said, 'Actually, we are not allowed to talk anything about the land claim, because it's not only us that's affected by the land claim – us as national parks. The *Mier* are the other part, and *we* are the other part and the *San* are the other part, so there's three partners in this whole thing. And they – not us – the *other* partners, decided on the negotiating table, that they'll *never* talk on the claim if it's not settled.'

Confused by this odd answer, I tried a prompt, 'So . . .'

'So I cannot say anything, I *may* not.' The woman glanced over at Piet Smith's son, as if for encouragement. But his expression was non-committal. He leaned against the wall, watching.

I tried a different tack. If she couldn't talk officially, then how did she feel personally about the Bushmen. Did she feel it would be a nice thing to have them back in the park?

She went off like a bomb: 'I don't know what Cait told you, because she's not actually . . . she doesn't know at *all* what's going on in the negotiations because she's not sitting in! Because the claim isn't just about land, they're claiming different kinds of things like access, or hunting, or a village, or what-what.' She paused, then went on in a more placatory tone: 'We are actually working *closely* with the communities. My post is Social Ecology. I'm based here to work with communities, not only on environmental issues . . .' She sounded as if she was reading from some kind of garbled script.

I tried to steer her back to the matter in hand. Did she feel that it would damage the park's ecology if the Xhomani had access to hunt a little, gather a little, collect firewood and thatching grass and so on?

'You see,' she switched to a patronising tone, 'You've got to understand the desert better . . . The people that's living now next to the park isn't the people that lived here forty years ago.'

'But some of them were born and brought up in the park . . .'

'Yes, but only a few. They do remember some tiny parts, but they're not really *living* as Bushmen any more . . . You can't just live like it was forty years back again, you see . . .'

'But they didn't choose to live the way they live now: they left because they had to!'

'No, they did not,' she whispered conspiratorially. 'That's the stories, that's not really the truth. The *real* truth never comes out.'

'What is the real truth?' I asked

'When the park was proclaimed there were no Bushmen in the park. They were never sent out.'

'But I was talking to *Ou* Anna just this morning,' I protested, 'who I guess is eighty or more. She and Dawid say that they were all born and raised in the park . . .'

But the woman was adamant. 'Not when the park was proclaimed. They came in from Namibia in the 1940s. The park was proclaimed in 1930. So they migrated, like the animals, they used this *whole area*, and the Mier area, and the park area. And I've got the inscriptions of the diary where they came here and where they left again. The parks board actually bought them rations because the animals migrated from this area . . . and they were hunting with dogs, and their dogs was killing the game, and you know the Bushmen in the past did *never* hunt with dogs, so they could not stay in the park. . . .'

Was she, I asked, saying that the present-day Xhomani were no longer real Bushmen?

'No, I'm not saying that at all. I only say that they don't *live* like Bushmen any more.'

'What if they were given the chance to?'

'Listen, they've got really social problems with alcohol. A lot.'

'But won't that only get worse if they go on living in the conditions they're in? They say that what they want is to hunt and gather, work with the tourists . . .'

'Yes, but one wouldn't like to use them as circus animals . . . There's a lot of people putting romantic ideas in their mind. They have to really decide themselves.'

'But they've told me that that is exactly what they want; to follow their traditions and also to work with the tourists and show them the veld . . .'

The woman faltered. 'They're very much influenced by a lot of people from overseas and all over that want to make them *do* things. But that's not what they *really* want.'

'So it would be OK to have them in the park?'

'In a cultural village, yes. It's not really safe for them, there are predators.'

'But they're Bushmen, don't they know how to avoid predators? Haven't they done so for tens of thousands of years?'

'The Bushmen of 1940 didn't ever have so much alcohol that the people of Welkom have now. And if they only have a lot of alcohol one night, the lions would just come in and kill them all.'

The woman smiled, as if she had just won a point. But, I asked, did she really think the Bushmen were so incapable? After all, most of the tourists in the park got drunk every night, and the rangers probably did too. If they were clever enough to do it in a safe place where lions couldn't come, why would Bushmen do any different?

Didn't they know the dangers of the bush better than anyone?

Mrs Engelbrecht ignored this, answering instead: 'But I wouldn't go out there, and I know the veld also.'

'Not like a Bushman does.'

'I don't say that, they know it very well. So that's why I use some of their trackers for nature conservation projects . . .'

'So,' I said, getting heated, 'if those Bushmen, living at Welkom, the same ones who drink – if they can go out and walk in the veld as trackers for park projects and not get killed by lions, then why can't they do it on their own time?'

'Not if they're drunk.'

'But they're not drunk twenty-four hours a day! And clearly they don't get drunk when they track in the veld or you wouldn't use them. Why don't you trust them to take care of themselves? Are they really going to walk around drunk when they're out hunting?' I stole a glance at Steven, still leaning against the wall. He was attentive, but impassive as before.

Meanwhile, the woman changed tone yet again: 'I'm saying it's dangerous there for *anybody*. For tourists too. Tourists aren't allowed out of their cars.'

'But tourists aren't Bushmen.'

'You changing my words! It's not what I'm saying! I've got to go now. You know you took half an hour of my time and I'm really late for my other . . . appointment. I really would have liked to help you, but you're pressuring me all in a certain direction! I'm saying it's dangerous there for anybody! That's all.'

There came the sound of a heavy step through the door behind us. I turned in my seat: a tall, handsome, powerfully built man stood there, his big face tanned and lined by years of South African sun, brown hair cropped short and bleached blond in places.

'This is our park warden, Dries Engelbrecht,' said the woman, sounding half relieved, half apprehensive at her husband's appearance. The man leaned down and offered a hand. I introduced myself, looking into his pale blue gaze.

'But I just said we cannot comment at *all* on the claim,' Mrs Engelbrecht went on hurriedly. 'And he was just asking me some . . .'

The man continued to look at me. A hard anger seemed to be swimming close beneath the calm surface of his gaze. I explained that I was interested in finding out the exact position of the park regarding the Bushmen and their land claim. The young man, Steven, stood stiffly, almost at attention.

'*Ja!*', the man said, suddenly affable. 'One thing that I know that my wife doesn't know about, is there's a media release coming out, prepared by a guy who has been appointed a mediator in the claim – and that thing must be out by now, or will shortly be out. He would be the best guy . . . he would be the only guy that may talk to the press.'

Trying to sound as diplomatic as possible, I said, 'So no one here is actually permitted to talk . . .'

'No, we're busy negotiating. That's it.'

The woman looked up anxiously. 'Now, you really must excuse me . . .'

'Of course.' We all shook hands, the interview over.

Back at the tents, the others were having their siesta and snoring deeply. Feeling the need to talk to someone, I remembered Belinda, the coloured manager I'd met when we arrived, and walked back up the dirt road, past the administration building and through the gate into the mini-suburb where the park managers' houses were. It was pleasant here, the houses shaded by tall camel-thorn trees, with the dunes forming an orange-red backdrop. A small mongoose shot across the road, busily active despite the heat. I walked up to the house Belinda had described and, finding the door open, knocked and went in. She was sitting on a low couch, in fact just a mattress on the floor with a cloth and some cushions on it, and offered me tea.

I recounted the weird interview with Mrs Engelbrecht (which drew a grin, but no comment from Belinda), then moved quickly on to what seemed to me the key problem – this official doubting of the Xhomani's identity as Bushmen. If even the park's social ecology department, whose job was supposedly to look after their concerns, regarded the Xhomani as 'not real Bushmen', then what hope was there? I admitted to doubts myself having seen them act for the camera. Had they, despite their *xais* and skin aprons, their clicking language, their small, slight bodies and golden skin, ceased to be Bushmen, and merged into the drab generality of Africa's rural poor?

'So,' said Belinda, her big, brown steenbok's eyes amused, 'Here you are. On a mission, hey? But to do what, find out what exactly!'

'You know, I'm not sure. I thought it was to come out and report on the political situation – but you know it's more personal than that. Maybe just to understand what this Bushman thing actually is. To chronicle the events as they happen.' Feeling restless, I got up and let my gaze wander around the room. There were many photographs stuck to her walls. Pictures of Belinda with long hair, in a city suit, in the uniform of a hostess for South Africa's Trans-Lux bus line, on the arm of a big, good-looking man with a moustache, in the snow in a place that looked as if it could be England.

'I feel that I've barely scratched the surface here. But I won't be back until next year sometime. For the rest of this trip I've got to go up to some of the other Bushman places, to Botswana and Namibia again to try and get a fuller picture of what's happening with the Bushman groups up there. I know I can't get to them all, but I think that to really understand I've got to see as many as possible. I feel as if, with this land claim, the Bushmen can reverse the whole history of wrong-doing in southern Africa, or at least start the process of reversing it.'

As I left Belinda's house, I stopped, seized by a sudden idea. 'Listen, next time, when I come back, would you interpret for me?'

'*Ja*, well,' she answered, seeing me to the door, 'That's a few months off. Barring accidents or acts of God I should still be here. You know where to find me.'

5

A Human Zoo

From Welkom our next stop was to be Kagga Kama, the private reserve where the rest of the Xhomani were living as show Bushmen for the tourists. But first we went to the Red House to say farewell. Most of the people, including Sanna, *Ou* Anna, Antas, Leana, Vetkat and Oulet, lined up rather formally to take leave of us. But Rikki and Jakob held back, seeming almost hostile. Everyone there smelled of stale alcohol – there had obviously been a big drink-up the night before. However, Jakob agreed readily enough when Dawid asked him to come with us down to the road: before we left, explained the leader, he wanted us to see the Xhomani's little craft stall, set up to try and tempt into stopping the few tourists that drove by each day, to and from the park.

The stall was no more than a dead branch planted upright in the sand with a tattered, hand-written sign that read: '*Boesman Verkoop* – Bushmen for Sale'. It had few wares – a handful of tortoise shells filled with a grass powder that was used partly as perfume, and also, as Cait explained, to bring healers out of trance. Next to these, a few necklaces strung alternately with reddish wood beads, neat white discs of ostrich shell and shiny black acacia seeds. There were also some small bows of gemsbok horn. Nowadays, said Dawid, the horn and eggs were no longer foraged from the veld, but had to be bought from local farmers, which made it hard to make any real money from selling them. The crafts were exquisite in themselves, but taken as a whole, the scene was unimpressive and even a little pathetic. As we stood there, several cars roared by, smothering us in their dust-clouds.

One stopped, however, disgorging a youngish couple, dark-haired, well-fed Italians. They wandered over and began to finger the crafts. Jakob took one of the small bows and held it forward encouragingly. 'No, no,' said the tourist, waving his hands, 'Am pacifist . . .' The man smiled apologetically and walked back to the car, and they drove off into the heat. Dawid looked at us. 'Hopeless,' he said, his expression at once frustrated, sad and amused.

We boarded a plane at Upington, where the Kalahari meets the wide Orange River, and flew south to Cape Town for a night. Next morning we drove back north in Cait's Toyota through the high, rainy passes of the flat-topped ranges that separate the lush Cape from the dry Karoo. In a vast, dry bowl between two spurs of the Cederberg mountains, the road changed from tar to dirt. It looked treacherous and, sure enough, Cait pointed out a place where, five years before, a vehicle taking a group of Xhomani down to Kagga Kama had overturned. Dawid had been badly injured, she said, and three people killed – his daughter-in-law, a child of Jakob's and a young man who had recently revived the ancient tradition of Bushman rock painting. Dawid had spent weeks in a Cape Town hospital and was now full of metal pins and rods – which explained his hobbling gait. 'So drive slowly,' warned Cait as I took the wheel and guided the truck up the long mountain track to Kagga Kama's gate. We arrived at the main lodge, a big, single-storey stone building surrounded by smaller stone cottages, and from there took a narrower, rougher track uphill to a small, mist-shrouded collection of stone, corrugated-iron and timber shacks.

We got out into cloud – cold, damp and clinging. A harsh, consumptive coughing sounded from somewhere among the shacks, and out of the darkness materialised a thin man, with unusually fragile, almost skeletal, features: a small hooked nose, deep sunken cheeks and eyes and a delicate jawline. He could have been anywhere between twenty-five and fifty, and was tall for a Bushman, with an air of palpable melancholy behind his gap-toothed smile of welcome. 'This is Izak Kruiper,' said Cait, 'Leader of the Kagga Kama Xhomani.'

Izak led us out of the cold, light drizzle that had now begun to fall, into his house, which comprised one small room with a brushed dirt floor. A low fire of glowing embers warmed the middle of the room, sending up thin grey plumes that hung below the corrugated iron ceiling and snaked their way out through the gaps between the roof and wall. Around the fire squatted several Bushmen, who smiled as we came in. Lys, Izak's wife and Rikki's sister, greeted us from where she sat huddled in a blanket, a *doek* wrapped around her head. She had exaggeratedly wide cheekbones and buck teeth, but a certain grace and beauty nonetheless. Next to her sat two smaller young men. One had a vacant, watchful stare: John, whispered Cait, was Dawid's second son, and the one who had been declared the next leader of the Xhomani when Dawid died. Beside him sat his elder brother Toppies, whose handsome face was scarred and troubled-looking. Tienas, his almost impossibly thin young wife, nestled close to him, wrapped in a blanket as Lys was. Next to them sat a couple who were obviously seriously stoned: a pretty, small, birdlike woman called Elsie, who was giggling and singing to herself, and her tall, thin husband Sillikat, whose face betrayed obvious traces of white ancestry. He had a moustache and curly, woolly hair. He looked like Phil Lynott, the half-caste leader of the Irish rock group Thin Lizzy. Wide-eyed children, their faces upturned in the firelight, filled the gaps between the adults, completing the circle.

We squatted down and shared a welcoming joint, but everyone was tired and we soon bid our respective goodnights. However, on our way out of the shack, before walking down to the stone guesthouse that Cait had booked for us, I took in the firelit circle of faces one last time and felt a glimmer of recognition. The scene before me could have been straight out of a painting by one of the early eighteenth-century adventurers that I had so often seen in the books of African history that filled my mother's bookshelves. The picture would be entitled something like 'Hottentot robbers in the Langeberg', Khoi and Bushman sheep raiders, *skelms* (rascals), who ought to be brought to justice, or better still hanged or shot down on the mountainside.

Lying in bed later that night, my mind drifted back over that long, sad history which I had read so much about. In the eighteenth century these mountains – the Cederberg – and all the other ranges between the Cape and the dry Karoo had witnessed a particularly deliberate Bushman genocide. It was 1774, and the Dutch Cape colony was expanding faster than its administrators could cope with. Several official attempts had been made to draw a definite boundary, but renegade settlers kept pushing north, dragging their unwilling government into an inevitable struggle with the natives. A war of sorts developed, with Bushmen and dispossessed Khoi herders running off with livestock, or occasionally filling a shepherd or farmer with poison arrows. Eventually, after repeated appeals from the colonists, the Cape government reluctantly financed three commandos, or posses, each comprising several hundred Dutch burghers and their Khoi servants, in a three-pronged assault across a front of five hundred miles into the mountains that separated the Cape from the Karoo. The Swartruggens and Cederberg, the two ranges which touched roughly at Kagga Kama, marked the western front of the General Commando, as the expedition became known.

As usual, the KhoiSan bands retreated up into the rocky table lands where, hitherto, they had always been safe – the ground was too broken to gallop on and the landscape honeycombed with convenient caves to hide in. But this time the enemy was too numerous, and too systematic in its pursuit. Beyond the mountain ranges stretched the flat, waterless Karoo, where a horse could run a man down in minutes. Unable to go either forward or back, the Bushmen did a most un-Bushmanlike thing. They fought, making a stand on the summits, using caves, cliffs, ledges and boulders as fortresses. After the first few engagements the Dutch, who knew something about sieges, simply sat and waited out of arrow range until they judged that the defenders' water had run out. Then they sent in their Khoi servants to do the dirty work.

One Bushman leader from this bloody episode left his name in history: Koerikei, whose clan lived in the Sneeuberg Mountains, at the eastern end of the General Commando's offensive. As the Boers rode up the tortuous path, their horses slipping and stumbling on the sharp shale, their muskets primed and ready, Koerikei, at his wits' end, jumped suddenly out from his hiding place and shrieked at them: 'What are you doing on my land? You have taken everything, all the places where the eland and the other game live. Why did you not stay where you first came from, where the sun sets? Why do you not leave us in peace?' A short time later Koerikei and all his band were dead.

Next morning, the cloud had lifted revealing a view of breath-taking beauty, a seemingly endless vista of yellow rocks and dark moors into which, from the north, tumbled a jagged rampart of peaks and mesas: a distant army of stone whose helmets and spear-points stood dark against the sun. The air, dried by the morning wind, had dispelled the previous night's rheumy damp. Overhead, two Cape crows, their bodies grey-white and their heads hooded black, came tumbling, cawing loudly. Somewhere out among the rocks a male baboon challenged a rival – the sound something between a human shout and a dog's bark.

We walked the short distance to the lodge. A row of vehicles was parked on the sandy space in front of the big, low-built stone building, and from inside came the happy sound of people breakfasting – tinkling cutlery and glasses, low buzz of conversation and the smell of fresh coffee. Kagga Kama obviously did not lack for clientele. A small foyer containing a reception desk and little shop selling crafts made by the Xhomani, gave onto a dining room where, at a dozen or so round tables, sat parties of mostly middle-aged tourists dressed in bright holiday clothes. Flitting among them were Kagga Kama's white staff in the usual game-reserve uniform of khaki shorts and semi-military-looking shirts with epaulettes.

'Cait! Cait Andrews!' came an Afrikaans voice. A large white man, not in uniform, sat among a group of staff at the centre table.

'That's Hennie de Waal,' said Cait in a low aside to Chris and I. 'Son of the owner. He's managing the place now. Come, I'll introduce you.'

Young De Waal welcomed us heartily but with ill-concealed unease. As soon as the hellos were done, Cait shot us a meaningful look and Chris and I slipped tactfully away, leaving her and De Waal to talk. We found an unoccupied table, ordered coffee and sat taking in the scene. Surprisingly, the majority of the tourists were not white, but coloured – middle-class Cape Town descendants of the Cape's conquered first peoples. Did they feel any sense of KhoiSan solidarity, or did they regard themselves as separate from the show-Bushmen they had come to see as any white tourist would? I guessed we would find out. Halfway through coffee one of the khaki-clad girls at De Waal's table stood up and announced that before going to meet the Bushmen, there would be a short talk in the next room, detailing some aspects of their culture and explaining how they had come to be at Kagga Kama. Chris and I got up and shuffled in with the crowd, finding seats at the back. When everyone was seated, the girl came to the front and delivered what was obviously a well-rehearsed lecture, learned by rote.

The first part of her story was accurate enough, recounting how the Xhomani had been 'kicked out' (her words) of the Kalahari Gemsbok National Park in the early 1970s. She then talked of their subsequent social breakdown: 'There was alcoholism, even prostitution, many, many problems. But in 1990, the SABC's 50/50 television series made a documentary about it. So our management went up and invited them to come and live here . . .' She continued briskly. Here at Kagga Kama the Bushmen were encouraged to keep up their traditions, to hunt antelope and gather the reserve's plants. 'We don't pressurise them to meet with the tourists, they come of their own free will. They make a very good income here, up to a thousand rand in a week sometimes . . .'

She introduced the question of the land claim. The management, she said, were confident that the Bushmen would stay on even if the claim were successful, as life at Kagga Kama was so good. 'They even have a TV, powered by a solar panel. While we're talking now the kids up there are probably watching *Black Beauty* . . .' I thought back to the previous night: the rough, smoky shacks, the tubercular coughing, the figures huddled in their blankets against the damp.

Then, the talk over, it was time to go and meet the Bushmen. Cait intercepted us outside the door, as the tourists moved away to the vehicles that would drive them the short distance up the mountain to the 'viewing area' where tourists and Xhomani would meet. We took our own vehicle, which had Chris's camera in it, intending to film the interaction. As we drove up the rough track Cait told us what De Waal had said.

'You know, I thought he'd quiz me about you two but no, he made me an offer. He said that together we could corner the Bushman craft market. Apparently the Xhomani crafts sell really well here. He said I should get more from up north, buy them cheap, bring them down here and split the profits with him. When I told him I didn't think so he said: "Well, you must be making money . . ." It's as if he can't see how anyone would bother getting involved with the Bushmen unless it was to make bucks! Anyway, here we are.'

The Xhomani were waiting for the tourists inside a neat semi-circle of traditional grass shelters. Izak, Lys, Sillikat, Elsie and Toppies were there, as well as a couple of younger men – John and a short, more muscular companion called Hendrik, whom we had not yet met. There was also one very old, fragile-looking woman. All had exchanged their ragged Western clothes for springbok and steenbok skins, which displayed their lean, golden curves and angles to full advantage.

The Xhomani sat, heads bent, each one busy with some craft or other. Izak and Sillikat were painting small gemsboks and hunters onto smooth slabs of stone, mixing the pigment made from a powdered red rock mixed with water and fat in an empty, upturned tortoise shell. The women made ostrich-eggshell beads, filing smooth the small circular fragments of hard shell and drilling holes in them for the string. To do this, they used ingenious little hand-drills that resembled miniature bows. By drawing the bowstring backwards and forwards, while holding onto the wooden piece in one hand and keeping the sharp metal bit steady with their toes, they bored perfect holes in the brittle beads. A few infants, clad in junior-size *xais*, lest their nakedness offend the tourists, played in the dust or wandered aimlessly from adult to adult. The older children, no doubt harder to control, had been left back at the shacks.

The tourists arrived, disembarking from the open-sided safari vehicles under the watchful eyes of two male guides. Some carried video-cameras and squatted down immediately among the Bushmen, shoving their lenses in close, or saying 'Hey, look up, smile.' Because the majority of the tourists were from Cape Town and spoke Afrikaans, there was more direct interaction than a foreign group might have had. The Bushmen handled it all like pros. As we walked among them, filming and taking notes, I overheard Sillikat telling one middle-aged couple how to stalk game and how to read tracks in the sand. 'He's bullshitting,' whispered Cait. 'That one was born in a town – Rietfontein up near the Namibian border, in the Mier country. He's probably never been hunting in his life.' One male tourist squatted down next to the shy, old woman – who ignored him, and went on grinding *saun*, the herb that, when crushed, produces the aphrodisiac, perfumed powder that brings healers out of trance. Squinting up through his sunglasses, the big man put his arm around the elderly woman's frail, bare shoulders, and asked his wife to take his picture with 'my new girlfriend. Hey, how many wives do these people have?'

Once again I was seeing history come to life. The tradition of displaying Bushmen and Khoi for the amusement of Westerners goes back to the earliest days of the Cape. The most famous case was that of Saartje Baartman, aka 'The Hottentot Venus', a Khoi woman (though people at the time referred to her as a 'Bushwoman') who had found work as a domestic servant in Cape Town around the year 1810. Like many Khoi women, she had two characteristics that differentiated her from European females: steatopygia (an excess of fatty tissue around the buttocks) and extended labia, known as the 'Bushman apron'. Saartje Baartman, it seems, possessed these two features in a particularly exaggerated way. One day a Scottish ship's doctor, William Dunlop, looked up Saartje's skirt and, amazed at what he saw, hit on the idea of taking her home to Europe. Promising to make her a wealthy woman, Dunlop persuaded Saartje to accompany him to London. There he exhibited her in a cage on Piccadilly, making her dance when he held up a stick.★ Though crowds of people thronged to gawk at Saartje's bum and vagina, not everyone in Regency London was amused. Saartje and Dunlop were taken to

★Carmel Schrire, 'Native Views of Western Eyes', published in *Miscast*, UCT Press, 1996 and 'Bring Back the Hottentot Venus', *Weekly Mail & Guardian*, 15 June 1995.

court by an anti-slavery organisation. She admitted that she was in Europe of her own free will and that she was getting half the money from the exhibitions. Dunlop took her to Paris where, in 1815, she caught influenza and died. The French anatomist Cuvier then removed her genitalia and preserved them in a jar of formaldehyde, in Paris's Musée de l'Homme.★

Another Bushman exhibit, on show in London in the 1850s, attracted the attention of Charles Dickens, who expressed the following sentiments, no doubt common at the time:

> Think of the Bushmen. Think of the two men and two women who have been exhibited about England for some years. Are the majority of persons – who remember the horrid little leader of that party in his festering bundle of hides, with his filth and his antipathy to water, and his straddled legs, and his odious eyes shaded by a brutal hand, and his cry of 'Qu-u-u-u-naa' (Bosjeman for something desperately insulting I have no doubt) – conscious of an affectionate yearning towards that noble savage, or is it idiosyncratic in me to abhor, detest, abominate and abjure him?
>
> I think it would have been justifiable homicide to slay him. I have never seen that group smoking, sleeping and expectorating around their brazier, but I have sincerely wished that something might happen to the charcoal smouldering therein, which would cause the suffocation of the whole of these noble strangers.†

Not all Bushmen were lucky enough to be displayed alive. The killing of Bushmen for sport and in reprisal for livestock raids became so commonplace by the nineteenth century as to hardly warrant mention in the regional archives. The museums of South Africa, modern-day Namibia, and even some in Europe,‡ are littered with

★Ibid.
†Quote from Dickens is taken from the leading article in *Household Words*, 11 June 1853, subsequently reprinted in *Miscast*, UCT Press, 1996.
‡There are, to my knowledge, three trophy heads in England – two in the British Museum and one in Cambridge (see Alan Morris's essay 'Trophy Skulls, Museums and the San', in *Miscast*, UCT Press, 1996). Flayed skins, skulls and other trophies are also stored in museums in Germany, France and probably Holland.

the physical remains of these killings: trophy Bushman heads, skulls, flayed skins, hands and scalps, all mouldering in shameful obscurity in the storage vaults.

The tourists at Kagga Kama might not have been asking the Bushmen women to lift up their hide skirts, nor were they reviling them as Dickens did. But the way in which they wandered among the Xhomani, pushing their camera lenses into faces, at working hands, at bare breasts, showed clearly that they had little concern for the feelings of the people they had come to see. Eventually, having exhausted their rolls of film, the tourists began filing back to the vehicles; it would soon be lunchtime.

As the last of the tourists boarded the waiting vehicle, one of the two uniformed guides, a tall, slender young man of about twenty-five came over to us. 'My name's Stephan,' he said, his voice low and urgent. 'Look, I think we should speak. There's really terrible things going on here. The owner's making up spurious debts, I've seen the books. And there's intimidation too. I've been waiting for someone to talk to. Can you come down to the bar later tonight?'

'We can,' said Cait, and the young man turned and walked briskly back to his waiting vehicle.

We walked up the rocky hillside, now very warm in the midday sun, towards the Bushman shacks. 'A good Afrikaner, that,' I said.

Cait grinned. 'You shouldn't be so surprised. There are lots of good Afrikaners. Perhaps on your travels you'll come across another one: Michael Duiver. He used to work here too, and he took me aside just like this one did and told me I had to find a human rights lawyer for the Bushmen, even before I had spoken to Dawid. Michael left, couldn't stand it here. He's working with Bushmen up in Namibia now . . .'

Back up at the shacks Izak had changed out of his show skins and back into jeans and T-shirt, his thin body and scrawny neck somehow made smaller by the cloth. He sat outside his little cottage, better built than the others, with stone walls and a couple of annex rooms tacked on the back that we hadn't noticed on the night of our arrival. He was smiling, enjoying the still gentle morning sun, but in daylight the place looked even rougher, more tumbledown. Rubbish lay everywhere: rusted loops of wire, broken plastic toys, bits of wood, old pieces of metal, smashed glass, sheets of roofing tin lying about, all in stark contrast with the surrounding rocky beauty.

We sat down and asked if we could interview him. 'Yes,' he replied amiably. 'You can ask me anything. That is why you are here.'

Izak smiled ruefully at the first question though. 'Why do we live here? Well, here we live well,' and he gestured around him. Indeed, despite the mess and the dilapidation of the shacks, they were larger and more solid than those I had seen at Welkom. 'But', he said, turning his eyes to the north, 'It's not home. It's not the Kalahari. Not the red sand. You feel so free there. If I had even just a tiny bit of ground there I'd be happy.'

'But at least you can move around here freely, can't you?' I asked. 'I mean, you can hunt here, gather . . .'

Izak turned his eyes to me again. There was laughter in them. 'You know, we can't hunt here. Years ago we tried a little, when we first moved down, but the *baas*, you know, he didn't like it. And here it's rocky country, you have to creep and stalk. It's not what we're used to. We grew up hunting with dogs across the open dunes. Here you can't see the spoor – too many stones. You can't run over these sharp stones. A dog, you know, that is my rifle, but they won't let us keep hunting dogs here. As for the plants, we hardly know them. Most of what is here is different.'

'But couldn't you learn the new plants, learn how to hunt over this ground, use traps and so on? I mean, Bushmen lived here in the past, didn't they? They must have hunted and gathered here?'

Izak looked north again: 'It's not home.'

'Then why do you stay?'

Izak considered awhile before answering, his eyes still on the northern mountains. 'We have to stay here until we clean our souls. You know, it's true, there were Bushmen here before, we feel their spirits. We see the messages they left us, the paintings, in the caves here. Something terrible happened to them. A killing; but it was they who called us here from the Kalahari and we must stay here until they tell us we can go, perhaps to take their spirits up to the red sands with us.'

I scribbled frantically. This was just the kind of spiritual talk I wanted to hear.

'But you know,' Izak went on. 'We also feel a sense of debt. To Mr De Waal, I mean. We have an income here. We send money home to Welkom. Whatever we feel about the place, De Waal came at a time when we needed money very badly. He saved us, you could say. But also we don't want to push it with him. Sometimes, if he's angry, the water doesn't arrive for three days or more. No, for the moment we're staying.'

'Even if you win the land claim?'

'Ah, the land claim. You know, the real reason we need the land is to bring back the rain. Since the Bushmen lost their land the rains have been bad, it has been dry. It's like old Regopstaan said; only we can bring the rain back, we the little people. But we can only bring back the rain by dancing. And we can only dance if we have land to dance on.'

Before we took our leave, Izak said to us, 'One thing. Keep your eyes open today. If you see anything strange going on with any animals you see in the veld, I want to know.'

That afternoon, while Cait and Chris took siestas, I went running, away down the rocky track westward towards the superb view of the knuckle-fisted Cederberg. The afternoon was mountain-warm rather than Kalahari-hot, but still the animals seemed to be sleeping. My eye eventually fell on three wildebeest perhaps a half-mile off but clearly visible in the clean mountain air, staring at me as I approached with something in their stance that suggested a mixture of belligerence and bovine complacency. It seemed unwise to test which was uppermost in their minds, so when I was perhaps two hundred yards off, I turned and began my loop back. As I panted uphill towards the lodge, a movement on the ground caught my eye. Two baboon spiders, tarantula-like arachnids about half-a-hand across, had jumped out of my way and now crouched on a rock beside the trail.

Should I report these sightings to Izak? According to Cait, Izak alone of all the Xhomani men, had given up both drinking and *dagga* which, if taken without alcohol, the Xhomani call *N/um*, meaning 'strength' or 'that which begets wisdom'. Izak was subject to visions, she said, visions which were often apt to come true. Yet apparently he reckoned his own powers as nothing compared to Dawid's. It was his hope that one day Dawid would be able to assume the full mantle of a Bushman leader, to get back the healing powers that he had lost through the years of dispossession, alcohol and survival in the non-Bushman world.

Back at the cottage I put my head into Chris's room. He lay on the bed asleep. There was a scuttling noise from the floor, and a mouse, bold as brass, sat looking straight at me. I took a step towards it. It didn't move, but faced me down. Then, from the room behind, came a tapping noise. I turned to see a small brown bird flying up and down the window pane, tapping its beak on the glass. And directly after that, came Cait's voice, 'Come and see!' In her room, on the curtain next to her bed, sat a large green mantis.

Much later, sitting around the fire in the red sunset with Izak and the little clan, we shared *braai vleis* cooked over open flames. One of the men, Hendrik, stepped into the fire-circle. He was stripped to the waist and wore, instead of the usual rumpled, torn trousers and shirt, a *xai* with a wildebeest's tail attached to the back. Around his ankles were strings of grey caterpillar chrysalises, emptied of their larvae and filled with small stones and chippings of ostrich egg. They made a swishing sound as he walked, not unlike maracas. Izak clapped his hands, applauding.

Hendrik began a dance in which every stamping foot, every dip and twist of the torso, every movement of the arms, expressed a pure and utter joy. Unlike the dances at Makuri, which had invoked particular animals, this seemed a dance of the spirit. Sweat ran down Hendrik's face as he moved, puffing his own rhythm to himself deep in his throat – the same deep-booming sound that male ostriches make – keeping hypnotic time with the ankle rattles, eyes closed. The watchers around the fire gradually began to clap, finding his rhythm. His was a dance, somehow, of hope, of faith. Then, with a final stamp, Hendrik left the circle of the fire and disappeared back into the gloom.

As if on cue, the Xhomani opened their mouths and, faintly at first, began to sing a hymn in Dutch, to a tune that was unmistakably Baroque. Some eighteenth-century missionary, travelling through the vastness of South Africa's great interior, must have brought the song from Europe and taught it to the Khoi and Bushman bands he met. And these people, finding beauty in its measured cadence and its words, which were words of God, had taken it for their own and taught it to their children.

Yet also reverberating through this hymn was the whole heritage of death, disaster and despair. The Xhomani sent their voices soaring out over the mountains that had seen the annihilation of their forefathers and it tore the heart to hear them, so tenderly did they sing.

When the song was done, it seemed right to tell Izak about the mouse, the mantis and the bird. Cait translated my words into the harsh, guttural consonants and strangely flattened vowels of Afrikaans, which, like the hymn, the Xhomani had made into their own *Boesmantaal* (Bushman tongue). Izak considered his answer for some while. Darkness was falling quickly and we heard the faint, high, regular call of a night bird.

'That bird,' said Izak. 'You hear it?'

'We hear it.'

'Now look at the moon, you see how tonight it lies at an angle, cupped? Both those things mean rain is coming; good rain. That bird – the rain bird – you hear only when the rains are coming, and the moon is lying like a cup, waiting to be filled with the water. The mouse, that's him' – and he pointed at Chris, 'It is a good sign – strength. The mouse goes about its business, working away quietly. Nobody knows it is there, until its work is done. Only then do the people notice that all along the mouse was busy, working away all the time, creating, building. And the mantis, that's her,' Izak pointed at Cait, 'She's one of us. And the bird, that's you. You are the one who carries the message.'

When we went to say goodbye next morning, Izak and the other Xhomani had already gathered at the little show Bushman village, waiting in their skins for the tourists to arrive. As before, Izak sat painting a gemsbok and a bow-and-arrow-wielding hunter onto a small, flat slab of rock, dipping his porcupine-quill brush into the little upturned tortoise shell that held the red paint made from small blood-coloured stones crushed to powder and mixed with animal fat. More than by the painting, my interest was piqued by these stones. I asked if I could buy some from him to give to my artist mother back in London. Looking up, Izak replied that he would rather give me the stones. If I wanted to buy something, why not buy a painting?

'Fair enough', I replied. 'What about that one you're doing now?'

Izak looked thoughtful. 'It isn't finished. But there is another, which I painted yesterday, in the little shop at reception. You could buy that one.'

I agreed and, pocketing the small red rocks he gave me, said goodbye. Izak, Sillikat, Elsie, Willem and all the Xhomani with whom we had had direct dealings, all said the same thing: 'We will see you again.'

Down at reception, Izak's bargain still fresh in my mind, I asked the receptionist if the shop had a rock painting done yesterday by Izak? '*Ja,*' she replied, 'He brought it down in the afternoon.' It was a particularly fine one, she added, walking the few steps into the little shop, and taking the rock down from its shelf to show us.

Even cynical Chris had to concede his wonder. On the rock's main surface were painted three figures, a woman and two men, dancing under a crescent moon, which lay on its side like a cup, two wave-like designs representing water sitting inside it. The woman figure had an insect-like, mantis-like head. The male dancer on the right had the head of a mouse. The one on the left had the tapered head and short beak of a small bird.

6

Old Magic, New Beliefs

Taking Izak's words to heart, I resolved to be that bird – to travel out into the Kalahari to 'bring the message' and learn what I could. First, that meant travelling down to Cape Town to interview Roger Chennels, the human rights lawyer representing the Xhomani's land claim. A lean, muscular man, he had a strong handshake and high – if cautious – hopes. The claim would go through sometime, that was without question. But the Mier farmers and park management, he admitted, were serious in their opposition. 'Technically we don't have to negotiate at all. The land minister, Derek Hanekom, has actually approved the claim. But the ministry doesn't want to just go in like that – it's not sound politics and it would make for bad neighbours for the Bushmen in the long run.' So they had to try to do their best to persuade both Mier and the park to accept the legality of the claim, though it might be years before the Xhomani saw any land.

Somewhat disheartened, Chris and I had left the lawyer's office and then parted company ourselves, he to go and hawk his video tapes around producers' offices in the USA and UK, while I headed north, to Gaberone, Botswana – and cousin Frank. A day after arriving at the headquarters of his now thriving organisation, Veld Products Research (his old dream of harnessing the wild foods and medicines of the Kalahari having finally been realised), I was heading north at the wheel of one of his Toyota trucks, an interpreter by my side, provisions and camping gear in the back, making for a village in south-central Botswana called Khekhenye. Here, VPR was working with a group of !Xoo Bushmen whose local hunting rights had been taken away, and whose territory had been appropriated for grazing by the local BaKgalagadi tribe.

It was a long drive, through flat grasslands stretching out on either side of the straight, black ribbon of tar. I had hitched this same road eighteen months before with Kristin, en route to pick up the Land-Rover that had taken us into Makuri that first time. It had been tarred since then, and now the miles flew by faster. I was also following the footsteps of Allen Loxton, my mother's alcoholic, journalist father, who had travelled this very road back in the late 1950s, when it was no more than a narrow sandy track. The purpose of his trip had been to write a series of articles on the Kalahari for the *Sunday Times*. I had resurrected these pieces and brought them with me. 'You can only get the "feel" of the Kalahari,' he had written, 'even in the freedom of fast flight over its vast tracklessness, if you can picture it as a tawny, hazy immensity in which nothing ever seems to reach anywhere . . .'

By now it was dark and owls swooped across the headlight beam. We turned off onto a rough track. Lydia, the interpreter, woke up, disoriented. Squinting at the white moths fluttering beyond the windscreen, she smiled: 'This is my place – old Kalahari.'

An hour later we were inside a wooden stockade, waking up Khekhenye's head man Sekelere to ask him to show us the hut that had been designated for our use. But when morning broke next day, and Lydia led me outside to explore the village, I saw that this was not quite the 'old Kalahari' she had spoken of. The place looked more black African than KhoiSan, composed of large, thatched rondavels, each standing within its own timber stockade, rather than the more traditional little grass shelters or beehive huts I had seen before. Even the people who hailed us and waved as we walked by their stockades looked much more black African than Bushman – or *Basarwa*, as they call Bushmen in Botswana. So much interbreeding had obviously occurred between them and the local BaKgalagadi and BaTswana tribes – whose larger settlements lay a day's walk off through the bush, and whose goats and sheep grazed the environs of the village – that the golden-skinned, slender Bushman look seemed to have disappeared altogether. Moreover, Lydia told me that the clicking language we were overhearing as we walked was not !Xoo but BaKgalagadi, the language of their more powerful neighbours, which gave an indication of how far down the social hierarchy Bushmen were in Botswana, as even the BaKgalagadi were regarded as second-class citizens by the dominant BaTswana tribe. Few people wore anything approaching traditional dress, but rather cheap cottons and shiny polyester. To the casual observer, there was nothing 'Bushman' about Khekhenye at all.

It quickly became obvious that here was a culture in the throes of change. After a more involved meeting with Sekelere, we followed the noise of a heated conversation coming from behind one of the huts and came upon several people clustered around and listening to a pair of arguing men. We sat down quietly at the edge of the group and, after a few moments, Lydia whispered, 'It's a religious debate.' The adversaries were one Sefitlao, a lean, old pagan, and a young man called Opi, who was – apparently – the village's foremost Christian. Just as we sat down, the young, charismatic-looking Opi was replying to something the pagan had said, his tone heavy with reproach: 'But all healing comes through Christ.'

The pagan Sefitlao snorted, as if he would not deign to answer, and there was a general pause. Taking advantage of the silence, I asked – through Lydia – whether Khekhenye's traditional religion was based around healing. The people, who seemed to accept both our arrival and my butting in without demur, murmured assent, and in response, two young men, who introduced themselves as Cera and Meme, grabbed a passing toddler and performed a quick ritual, dancing around him and taking turns to kneel and make sucking, blowing motions at his belly. Then, as abruptly as they had begun, they sat down again and the infant pottered off undisturbed as if such things happened every day. Which they probably did.

'That was a healing dance for a child who is depressed because its parents are arguing,' translated Lydia, as the young men explained what they had done. This sounded more like middle-class New York than the deep bush but I made no comment.

Just then, an old, almost bald woman sitting at the edge of the group spoke up: 'All this is just talk. The *badimo* [gods], all of them, are in the hands of God. God is all gods and all things.' And with that, the meeting broke up.

I was still musing on this strange episode, when Lydia asked me if I'd like to see the people who were working with Frank's organisation, VPR. As we bumped slowly out over the ruts and anthills of the surrounding plain to meet them, she explained how the system worked. Cousin Frank's organisation bought thatching grass and other veld products from the villagers for cash, then sold them on at local markets to recoup as much of the expense as possible. Some products, for instance Kalahari truffles, were even resold abroad to restaurants in South Africa and Germany. The seeds of a ground-growing vine called Devil's Claw were exported to pharmacies in Europe and the USA where they were much in demand as a homoeopathic cure for arthritis. Certain grasses and dried flowers were even sold as exotic 'fillers' to florists in London. On top of this, the VPR workers encouraged the villagers to plant wild fruit trees in their compounds – I had seen a few saplings that morning – for their own subsistence eating.

We came upon the villagers reaping the long grass with hand-sickles, working in a long line like harvesters in some old Dutch painting. Lydia made the introductions and they showed us what they had found while reaping: edible tubers called *thokwe*, to be taken home and cooked; another called *tshoba* with water-bearing flesh similar to the root that the hunter Fanzi had dug up when Tom and I had gone hunting from Makuri the year before. There were also a number of medicinal plants. One of the men, a lean, bearded elder called Dotar, caused much laughter and clapping among the women by digging up some roots called *ledang*, which were said to ease menstrual cramps and ensure a healthy womb.

Looking down at the hole he had dug, I noticed some small, jewel-like arachnids crawling there which I recognised as velvet spider mites. 'God!' said one of the women, following my gaze. Then, in rapid-fire imperatives, she called to the reapers to load their grass bundles into the back of our truck as fast as possible.

'What's happening?' I asked Lydia.

'She says the god is telling her big rain is on the way and we must get the grass under cover.'

Looking up, I saw only a few wispy clouds in an otherwise

unbroken blue. But I helped stack the grass bundles into the back of the Toyota nonetheless, and drove the lot back to the village. Twenty minutes later, the sky had turned the colour of gun metal – the clouds seemed simply to have materialised from nowhere. There was just time to get the precious grasses under cover before the rain broke in what the Bushmen call a 'male' rain – a storm so violent that it kept us in the huts for eight hours.

That evening, as the rain hammered on the tin roof several of Khekhenye's young people, all friends of Lydia's, gathered in our hut to laugh, joke and swap stories. Mostly they talked sex, and delighted in asking me how whites did it. What about this homosexuality thing they had heard about, for instance? Red-faced, I found myself being coerced into giving a hysteria-inducing (and ill-informed) description of gay culture, even down to the specifics of anal sex. As the hours passed, however, the conversation turned more serious. It was indeed a changing time for them, they said, and not just in attitudes towards religion. Everything was changing, and they did not know whether it was good or bad. The young men, in particular, felt bereft now that they had lost their traditional role as hunters. Cera, the smiling youth who had shown me the healing dance with the infant, and Opi, the young Christian, offered to take me out next morning to an area where there was still game.

It took us some hours to drive out to this place, far enough from any settlement for the game to thrive undisturbed – a vast meadow of waist-high, sun-dried grasses at whose centre stretched a wide pan of rock-hard, grey mud. We got out into absolute silence. When our car doors slammed shut, the sounds were like rifle shots in the still air. Though the day was cloudy and dark, I made out some moving shapes on the far side of the pan – a herd of springbok, perhaps a hundred strong.

Cera and Opi, in their ragged trousers and cotton shirts, set off at a fast trot through the swishing grasses and onto the pan. As they hit the dried mud surface, they veered to the left and picked up speed. As one, the springbok herd began to move too, running parallel with us at a leggy trot; a shimmer of brown and white bodies, lyre-shaped horns and delicate, fast-moving legs. I ran just behind my two guides, pleased at being able to keep up with the young Bushmen and the springbok they were chasing. Then, as the herd launched into a gallop and Cera and Opi changed gear with them, leaving me behind, I tripped on a ridge of dried mud and fell sprawling. I was up and running again immediately, but by then Cera and Opi had become small dots at the far edge of the pan.

They stopped, and waited for me, grinning. As I panted up to them, they drew back the strings of two imaginary bows. A large male springbok stood perhaps thirty yards off, looking right at us, flanks heaving, the rest of the herd having disappeared into the tall grasses. An old animal, no longer able to gallop more than a short distance, he had been marked out and run down. Opi and Cera bent forward from the hips as I had seen Benjamin and Bo do when shooting, and let fly their make-believe arrows. A split second later, the old antelope had recovered its breath and bounded off after its fellows.

We walked on, perhaps for forty minutes, from thicket to clearing to meadow, following a narrow, winding trail, until Cera suddenly stopped and looked down. Lying on the trail was a single, fresh gemsbok dropping, shiny and black like an olive. He knelt down and, with his finger, made a depression in one of the hoofprints, placed the dropping in it, then covered it over with sand. Having brushed the sand smooth again, he stood up and put his hands on my shoulders, turning me so that I was looking back the way we had come. Opi was already standing so, his eyes shut. From behind, Cera's fingers reached for my eyelids and pushed them closed too. We stood like that for maybe ten breaths, facing back down the trail, eyes screwed shut, until Cera whispered, 'OK, OK' and gently turned me around.

There on the trail, a bowshot away, stood a big gemsbok bull, heavily, magnificently muscled beneath his beige and light brown coat. Black stripes ran along his muzzle from eyes to nose. Long, straight black horns extended upward, his deep liquid eyes regarded us evenly, without fear. He swished his tail, knocking away the incessant Kalahari flies, standing broadside on, offering his shoulder for the arrow. As he had done before, Cera bent forward from the hips and mimed his shot, and as before, the big creature waited for the imaginary arrow to make its descent before whirling round and thundering off down his well-trodden path.

'Ah Rroo,' said Cera, using the nickname he had given me: 'This was our way.'

But not a word more would Cera say over his magic with the gemsbok, neither when we drove home or later, when the young folk gathered at our hut once again. The following evening, however, he and Lydia took me to the hut of Dotar, Khekhenye's principal healer.

Lying on a soft kaross of jackal skins, half-hidden in the smoky gloom, the bearded man unearthed a collection of little, hide-wrapped bundles from their hiding places in the rafters and the thatch. 'Of course,' said Dotar, as he assembled the bundles before him, 'these medicines need a dance to work, you don't just take them like medicines from the clinic.' He unwrapped a piece of thick root and rolled it towards me: '*Moikero meetsa* – good for the kidneys and bad periods in women. I charge two hundred pula for this one.'

'People have to pay?'

'Of course,' Dotar sounded surprised. 'Healing needs an exchange to work. Now, Cera here –' and he pointed at the grinning, lithe young man, stretched out upon the skins, 'He still owes me fifty pula from when I cured his diarrhoea . . .'

Cera groaned, clutching his hands over his abdomen and screwing up his face as if in pain: 'Ah, but I still have the cramps, you haven't cured me yet, you old fraud. You should be giving me money.'

Dotar laughed, and went back to his bundles. '*Tshaosa* bark, good for the shits.' He held forward a little section for me to taste. It was bitter and dried the mouth as you sucked it. '*Ledang*: you know what this is for. And if you shred it and mix it with some of the *moikero meetsa* it'll cure a barren woman. That's an expensive one – a thousand pula,' he paused, 'or a cow.'

'You take livestock?'

Again Dotar laughed, surprised: 'Of course.'

'But what do you do with it?'

'What do you do with a cow? Eat it!'

He picked up a small tortoise shell, filled with a black paste. 'I smear this one, *nxole*, on my hands during the healing and it helps me to see what is wrong with someone, or an animal . . .' Next came a cross-section of another big root: 'From the *mokalane* tree – it keeps animals, the cows and the goats, fertile and healthy. You chop it up and put it into their water and the livestock drink it. Also expensive, this one. The BaKgalagadi like it.'

Later, as we walked back to the hut, I marvelled at what I had witnessed: Antas and her quiet healing on Cait, Izak and the animals and the painting, now Cera and Dotar. There seemed to be magic at every turn.

But early next morning, I was returned to earth with a bump. The truck refused to start. We had been intending to leave next day. Now, said Lydia, we would have to wait three days for help – when a group of missionaries were expected to arrive – and longer if they couldn't fix it. On her advice I elected to walk with a backpack into Motokwe, the nearest BaKgalagadi village, with one of the young men as a guide, to buy enough supplies to last us until the missionaries arrived. As we walked the morning grew ever hotter and the bush became more barren, more over-grazed, more full of goats and thin, listless cattle. When at last we arrived at Motokwe's ramshackle store, a sumo-sized BaKgalagadi woman demanded to know what I was doing there.

I explained that I was a journalist, whereupon she became suddenly enraged.

'A journalist! You're not that journalist who was trying to take the picture of the Princess Diana when she was dying, poor woman, in the car!' She advanced on me, eyes blazing.

'No!' I assured her, caught between fear and astonishment. 'I'm not that kind of journalist.'

Princess Diana had died only a matter of weeks before, yet the news had penetrated even here. Amazed at the reaction, I filled my backpack with tins, paid the lean, expressionless man behind the counter and set out on the long walk back.

Three days later the missionaries arrived. They came at evening.

To greet them, the whole village came alive with song: the sound of hand-claps and stamping echoed out among the thorn trees and grasses. The following morning, there was a service under a tree to which a simple wooden cross had been nailed. Opi (in clean, respectable shirt and trousers) and the one black missionary led the villagers through a set of Victorian-sounding hymns. The five young white South African missionaries sat, red and sunburnt, to one side of the ragged congregation. Everyone was there, including Lydia, Cera, Dotar the healer and even the old pagan Sefitlao.

The whites stood up to sing, producing a guitar from behind their bench, on which one of the girls strummed some rather loose chords while the others launched into 'He's Got the Whole World In His Hands'. After the first verse, the congregation began to shuffle and cough. A baby started crying and its young mother thrust her breast into the yelling mouth to silence it. The older children, less patient, began to fidget. Then it was sermon time. The tall BaTswana pastor got up and cleared his throat: 'Jesus asks not one thebe★ from you,' he began. 'All he wants is your heart.' Almost immediately he nodded to Opi who went into the crowd with a collection bag that, miraculously, produced a few coins and even a stained note or two. Then, focusing his stern, spectacled gaze on the restless children in the front of the congregation, the pastor described in gruesome detail the torments of hell. No longer distracted, the children listened with wide, fearful eyes.

Finally, the service over, I introduced myself to the missionaries, explaining the situation. Two of the men, Nico and Len, accompanied me back to the Toyota, quickly diagnosed the problem as an air bubble in the diesel fuel line and showed me how to fix it.

Cera came to our hut that night, brimming with enthusiasm. The missionaries had brought good things – food, medicine, clothes – some of which had been given to him. But it went beyond that. 'They are offering a better way for me. You know, I sometimes go to Motokwe. I drink, and then I fight. Always getting into fights, and losing my money. These people will show me a better way . . .'

★Small Botswana coin: 100 thebe = 1 pula.

I left the men of Khekhenye hard at work laying the foundations for the new church: Dotar unloading sacks of concrete from the missionaries' truck; Opi and Sefitlao wielding picks, singing in the morning sunshine.

I had two days to rest back at Frank's place before the next leg of my journey took me north again to see Frank's son, my cousin Michael, whom I had last met as a twelve-year-old boy illegally smoking my cigarettes on top of the red ironstone ridge behind Frank's old house. Michael was now doing field research for his Ph.D in anthropology, and had chosen for his study group the Khwe, or River Bushmen, of northern Botswana. I arranged to join him where he was now living with his wife Katrin, in the main Khwe village of Kwaayi, deep in the swampy heart of Botswana's Okavango Delta.

This vast wetland is one of Africa's great natural wonders – a river that flows not into the sea but into the desert. Aeons ago, the broad Okavango river, which rises far to the north in the distant highlands of Angola, was blocked from its course to the sea by an uplift at the south-eastern end of Africa's Rift Valley, and diverted southward into the Kalahari. As it spilled into this great, flat plateau, the river widened into a vast, jewel-like delta of lagoons and marshes, some two hundred kilometres across, before draining into the insatiably thirsty Kalahari. Every year this miraculous wetland renews itself with a great flood fully six months after the annual rains up in the Angolan highlands have swollen the river sufficiently for its waters to cover the entire Delta. For the rest of the year the region is a mixture of ponds, marshes, isolated lagoons, forests and spreading, lawn-like natural pastures; a watery Eden, teeming with life, in the midst of unrelenting dryness.

I had been here before, while researching my second guidebook and had explored the game-rich meadows and waterways on horse-back, on foot and in *mokoros* (dugout canoes) poled punt-like by the local Bayei fishermen. I had stayed, like any other white tourist, in well-appointed safari camps and lodges. No one had told me that there were Bushmen living here. I had discovered their existence only recently, while reading my grandfather Allen Loxton's Kalahari articles.

Sitting in the little bush-plane that was flying me into the Delta, I re-read one of his pieces, entitled 'Crying Sands and Odd Tales of Web-Footed Kalahari Bushmen'. He wrote: '. . . it is true that these primitive people, whose knowledge of the swamps is invaluable to the White crocodile hunters who employ them, are as aquatic as any humans can be. There is something almost uncanny in the ability of the primitive swamp people, on even the darkest nights, to guide the crocodile hunters back to their camps down miles of hippo runs, up twisting, doubling watercourses and lagoons . . .' Even so, as I had found with his article about the Khekhenye area, Allen did little more than mention these River Bushmen as local colour before turning to the main story about the region's whites, in this case crocodile hunters.

Although the rainy season had begun, little moisture appeared to have fallen on the Delta, and our plane cast a shadow like a moving crucifix on grasses shining yellow in the sun. Here and there were small ponds, and an occasional larger lagoon, fringed with palms, their straight, slender trunks reflected along with the deep blue of the sky. Animals were in plentiful supply. Elephants, like grey, slow-moving ships, passed below us frequently. A group of topi, close cousins of the hartebeest, cantered across a dry meadow, kicking up puffs of dust as they went. Across a wide, winding stream, fat-rumped, boldly striped zebras and smaller brown flecks – either impala, or red lechwe (stocky, marsh-dwelling antelope that take refuge in the deeper pools whenever danger threatens) – grazed together.

In this part of the Kalahari, it seemed, the Khwe Bushmen had more traditional resources at their disposal than any group I had yet visited – more even than the Ju'/Hoansi. What was more, according to Frank, they had recently been granted a land claim – the first Bushman group in the whole sub-continent to achieve this, despite the fact that the Botswana government was still evicting Bushmen from other wild areas. The worst region for this was just two hundred kilometres south of the Delta in the Central Kalahari Game Reserve.

Here, reported the newspapers, whole villages had been forced to move, and their people resettled in appalling conditions in camps just outside the reserve.

I was collected from the rough airstrip by a young Khwe Bushman called Brown, whose English was perfect – acquired, I learned, by working at the local safari camps. Many of the young men at Kwaayi, where we were heading, had experience in the camps which would stand them in good stead now that they had become landowners. The Khwe, he informed me, intended to run their own hunting and tourism operation and to break away from working for the white camp-owners.

Kwaayi turned out to be a large, straggling place along the north bank of a narrow river on the far side of which rose the dense forest of Moremi Game Reserve, a wilderness full of big, dangerous game. There were no large stockades here, but like the huts of Khekhenye, Kwaayi's were built in the conically thatched BaTswana, rather than Bushman, style. Some I noticed, were constructed from tin cans held together with mud.

In the middle of the settlement stood a lone, concrete-built shack – cousin Michael's house. Brown dropped me here, saying he had to get back to work at the safari camp that employed him. I pushed open the door of the little building and looked inside. So this was the anthropologist's life: one ill-ventilated room containing a desk and chair, cardboard boxes of food stacked in rows against the wall. Rolled up in one corner were two backpacks and two sleeping bags. In another, a pile of firewood. I unpacked the food I had brought and put it into the boxes. Then, having nothing else to do, and not wanting to explore the village until Michael returned, I lay down outside in the shade of the eaves, shut my eyes, and fell asleep.

I lay there for perhaps an hour, when a shadow fell across my face and I woke up, to see a man standing over me. Rubbing my eyes, I saw it was another young man of about Brown's age. And like Brown, the young man spoke perfect English, though his voice was softer. 'I'm Merafe', he said politely, shaking my hand. 'You must be Thuso's cousin.'

'Thuso?'

'Yes, we call him that. It means "helper" in our language.'

Over the next hour, the young man filled me in on the background to the land grant. It was a similar tale to the Xhomani's, only more successful. Back in the 1960s the Khwe's ancestral land had been declared a reserve – the Moremi Wildlife Reserve, now across the river – and the Khwe had been moved out. For a few years they were shunted between one temporary site and another until finally, in the late 1960s, they had been settled here at Kwaayi. It had been a betrayal, said Merafe, without emotion: their head man, one Kweke Sirere, had helped cut the trails and build the camp sites for the reserve, believing the officials' promises that his people, even when moved, would benefit from the coming tourism. Yet all that had come was the loss of their land and a few low-paying jobs in the local safari camps and lodges.

In 1992, the government had decided to move them again, and this time the Khwe had refused. Head man Sirere, now elderly, had sent a ten-man delegation to Botswana's capital, Gaberone, demanding an audience with the then Minister of Local Government, Lands and Housing. They had been amazed, admitted Merafe, when the minister had called them into his office and listened. With his encouragement, the Khwe had set up a community trust, and the government had given them not only the land on which Kwaayi village lay but that on which the local safari lodges had their concessions. Now they were landlords themselves and could charge the lodges rent and also set up their own hunting and eco-tourism operations. Various NGOs, including the Kellogg Foundation, had donated funds to help them do this. But recently things had got bogged down; old Sirere had died and the village, governed by a committee until a new leader could be decided upon, was trying to find the best way forward.

But why had Kwaayi been singled out for help, I asked, when almost everywhere else in Botswana Bushmen were still being dispossessed? Merafe thought a moment: 'We are lucky here. There are a lot of white tourists. The government makes a lot of money from tourism here . . .' Maybe, he admitted, the government did not want tourists coming into contact with unhappy Bushmen who could express their grievances.

At this point my cousin Michael and his wife Katrin walked into the hut and, excusing himself, Merafe slipped out, leaving us alone. Katrin made tea, and Michael picked up the story where Merafe had left off. This was a difficult time, he confided. The land grant had come suddenly and there was a lot of dissension among the now leaderless Khwe as to what to do with it. All favoured some kind of combination of hunting and eco-safaris, but they had no lodge, no vehicles, and no experience in setting up or running such a venture, despite the fact that many of them had spent years working in the local camps and lodges. The village committee had divided into factions; young men like Brown and Merafe who were literate, spoke English and worked in the safari camps, were the most powerful of these, but it went against tradition for young men to wield such power. The villagers wanted an elder as leader, but no one could decide who it should be.

On top of this, there was a division between 'old Kwaayi' and what Michael called 'Kwaayi Two', a straggle of newer huts at the west end of the village where Khwe Bushmen from the swamps and marshes that lay north over the Namibian border had recently come and settled. Many of them had been conscripts in the South African army (which ruled Namibia until its independence in 1990) and had fought against the guerrillas of SWAPO – now the ruling party of that country. Fearing reprisals from the local black tribes who had supported SWAPO, these ex-army Khwe Bushmen had come south to Kwaayi. The villagers of 'old Kwaayi' resented these newcomers, especially as resources were in short supply.

It was indeed ironic that for all the surrounding wealth of game and wild land, Kwaayi's people were still going hungry. The problem lay in legal technicalities rather than in actual physical resources. Before the land grant the Khwe had been allowed to do a limited amount of subsistence hunting. Now they owned the land, but as landowners they could practise eco-tourism and controlled sport hunting: legally, they could no longer hunt for the pot. There were no stores nearby and people came only irregularly into the village to sell supplies. Some families had begun chasing leopards and lions from their kills in order to get a meal. And, as this was as illegal as hunting, if caught they could go to jail. My journalist's instincts were stirred. Would that, I asked, be something one could see? Michael thought it quite probable, if we talked to one of the more influential elders, a village matron who made her living selling *khadi*, a liquor made from *moretlwa* berries, to the local Ba Yei fishermen. She would know if anyone was going out to a kill.

In the cool, smoke-scented, morning, Michael and I went to consult with the *khadi* woman, picking our way between the waking compounds, and keeping a weather eye on the large bull elephant which was tearing the branches from a tree at the northern edge of the village, a hundred yards or so away. When we reached a slightly larger compound than the others, Michael shouted a greeting in Setswana, and we walked into a sort of courtyard between the huts. The woman we had come to see, yellow-skinned, fat and cheerful-looking, sat on a makeshift stool at the far end. She returned our greeting, before motioning for us to sit down on the ground next to her daughter, a tall, skinny girl called Kanjiye. The daughter had mischievous eyes and short dreads sticking out in all directions, and was busy ladling liquid – presumably *khadi* – from a large plastic bucket into a smaller one. Next to her sat a man, bigger-built and darker-skinned than the other young men I'd seen so far in Kwaayi. He seemed shy, smiling and looking down as we came in, his diffidence belying his Herculean physique. Michael explained that I was his cousin, that I was writing a book about the current state of the Bushmen in the Kalahari. He told them what we had discussed the night before. The women seemed unimpressed.

'Go out to where the leopards killed?' laughed the lanky girl. 'You'll get us in trouble! No,' she said, 'Let's talk about more interesting things.' She was looking for a new boyfriend. It was time she took a new one, maybe a white man, maybe your cousin, she said, pointing at me, before pealing off into another torrent of laughter as Michael translated. Her boyfriend didn't seem to mind, but smiled on at the dusty ground. Half an hour later, however, she had summoned two youths to take us out. They led us away into the bush, chatting cheerfully all the while, keeping to the open country between the forest and the river. We walked for an hour or so, the day growing hotter, until the two lads called a halt by the river, so that they could cast for catfish and bream with the lengths of fishing line that they carried in their pockets. When each had caught a fish (they were patient, expert anglers, and there was a hypnotic pleasure in watching them make their slow overhand casts), they turned and led us onto another trail, which seemed to wind back in the direction of Kwaayi.

To pass the time until we reached the kill, I asked them questions. Did the people here still hunt at all? Yes, of course they did, answered the boys, but it was done quietly, using dogs and spears for warthog. Some of the older men still went after small buck – duiker and impala – with the poison arrows, but this was dying out. You went to jail if you got caught. Were there still healers in the village, I asked? This produced a laugh. Medicine was still strong, they giggled, pointing at a big tree growing at the edge of the forest, whose gnarled branches were hung with long, cylindrically shaped fruits. That tree had great *muti*, for instance: if you pissed against it, your penis would grow and keep growing until you went back and pissed on the exact same spot. Then, having had their joke, the youths grew serious. No, they admitted, there were no more powerful healers in Kwaayi. Healers from the outside sometimes came to Kwaayi, but that was all.

After some time, we rounded a corner and came upon a small group of young women and girls, all stripped to the waist, sitting on a shaded patch of grass working with knives upon what looked like a great pile of pink squid. In the centre of the group sat Kanjiye, who hailed us, her long breasts waving as her arm did.

We sat down on the grass, grateful for a rest in the shade. The kill site might be miles off yet. For a minute or two, we watched the women work away at the pile of what turned out to be water-lily roots. Using sharp knives, Kanjiye and the other girls lopped off the superstructure and stuffed the main bodies of the roots into little cloth bags. Kanjiye sliced two sections of root and offered them to us. The taste was of radish, with the same spicy kick, and the flesh released a cool, fresh burst of liquid into the mouth as soon as you bit into it. When we looked up, we saw that the boys had walked on without us. We just caught a glimpse of their backs turning a corner in the trail, back towards Kwaayi.

'So,' said Michael, in a joking tone, 'I thought we were going to a kill.'

Kanjiye laughed, then retorted: 'You think I would show you those kinds of secrets? Ha! I'll wait till you're gone, then we'll go and find where the meat is.' And she went back to her work.

We waited, accepting defeat, until she and the other girls had trimmed all the roots, packed them into bags, and eventually led us slowly back to Kwaayi. Coming into the village, we passed a pack of running, yelling children, among them a couple who were obviously half-white. Michael explained that several of the local safari operators had fathered kids in Kwaayi, as had the local Bayei, BaTswana, BaKgalagadi. If I looked around, he said, I would be hard put to find any kids with Bushman fathers at all.

The local safari operators may have been happy to father children in Kwaayi, but they seemed far less content to think of the Bushmen as potential business competitors. That afternoon, Michael, Katrin and I crossed the rickety log bridge across the river, and drove through the forest of Moremi to visit three lodges whose managers Michael wanted to interview as part of his research. Merafe asked to come with us and I sat with him in the flatbed.

At the first lodge – a cluster of reed-built chalets on a green, tended lawn overlooking a wide lagoon – the young, bearded white man in charge treated us and Michael's questions with suspicion. When asked how many people from Kwaayi he employed, he replied, guardedly, 'only four'. The rest of the staff, thirty-six in all, were mostly BaTswanas hired from Maun, a town to the south of the Delta. Did he buy crafts or any other products from Kwaayi? Yes, he responded, the camp bought the odd bundle of thatching grass to put on the walls for decoration. He also bought baskets but thought the quality poor: in his opinion the people at Kwaayi didn't understand dyes and colour and their designs were limited and simplistic. Then, as if aware that he wasn't coming across too well, he asserted that at least he paid his workers more than Botswana's required minimum wage of one pula, fifty-nine thebe per hour. So how much did the camp pay, asked Michael? The manager coughed and looked sheepish: 'One pula, sixty.'

Did many of the tourists who came ask questions about the Bushmen; were they aware that Bushmen existed in the area? '*Ja*, man, I tell them the Bushmen are there' – he waved a vague hand out at the lagoon and the forest lining its further shore. But it seemed it was not part of the general information given out at the camp. Tourists came to the Okavango to see game, not people.

At a neighbouring camp, the middle-aged manageress (also a white South African) admitted that, of a staff of twenty-four, only three came from Kwaayi. As for tourists asking about the Bushmen: 'Some have heard of the River Bushmen and want to see them,' she admitted, 'But they're expecting your pedigree Bushman and, let's face it, you don't see him here.' The manager of the third camp – a young BaTswana – said that he had never even heard of the local Bushmen himself.

On my fifth day in Kwaayi, Michael took me down to what he called 'Kwaayi Two', where the Namibian Khwe, those that had fought in the war and feared reprisals there, had settled in smaller, more traditional-looking huts at the far western end of the village. There I met Mathias, a small, depressed-looking man in his forties, and heard his story. He had been born in the Okavango, but during his teens his family had moved up into Namibia to get away from the local BaKgalagadi who, he said, used to come to the Khwe villages wielding giraffe-hide whips, whenever they needed manpower. They would round up the men and take them away to work, and they would do bad things to the women. So his people had gone across the border to Namibia. Here, as a young man in the early 1970s, Mathias had joined the police, then been conscripted into the army. In 1978, his unit was sent up into Angola, where South Africa was helping UNITA commander Jonas Savimbi in his bid to oust the Soviet-sympathetic MPLA government. Mathias and his battalion were thrust into the front line.

'Yes', said Mathias, with dull emotion, 'I killed. I did not feel good inside. But it had to be done. We fought because we were hungry. We needed food, needed pay. I sit here hungry now,' he added, with some defiance in his voice. 'If the army came here needing recruits I'd take the job again.'

'Did you know the reason for the war?'

'They never told us.'

He was bitter at the reception he had been given in Kwaayi, and said that he and others like him were being treated as second-class citizens by their own people. When questioned about the land grant and plans to develop tourism, Mathias shook his head. 'I don't know what they're planning here. They don't include us from this end of the village. They say we are not even proper *Basarwa*. Ask the fat woman. It's her project.'

I asked Mathias if he would take us out to the bush next morning but he declined. It would cause jealousy and dissent in the village (Michael agreed with this). But somehow I eventually talked both him and Michael round and that evening, my cousin cleared it with the village factions.

At dawn the three of us set off, but whatever I was trying to prove, the foray with Mathias turned out to be no more than another token walk in the bush. He led us into the forest, a spear over his shoulder, and brought us up close on a herd of impala, showing us where and how he would hunt them if it were back in the old days, before walking us back to Kwaayi. We gave him fifty pula for it and Mathias was overjoyed. When will you come again, he asked? I looked at the eagerness in his eyes and felt distaste for my own power.

The following day we had to drive back to Maun, as Michael and Katrin had business to sort out there. Time was running out for me too, though I felt that my work in Kwaayi was somehow unfinished. Apart from Merafe I had not interviewed any of the young men of the village; my understanding of the place still seemed shallow. On the drive out we met Brown again – I had not seen him since he picked me up that first day. I asked if I could interview him, explaining that I felt I would not have any real grasp on the place until I had. Brown's response was surly: 'We are getting so sick of people like you coming here and asking questions . . .' And with that he turned on his heel and walked away.

Michael, Katrin and I were stunned at this. As we drove on up the track, Michael said he'd never seen Brown so hostile. Perhaps our foray with Mathias had caused dissent after all. Perhaps it was simply a show of independence. Despite the fact that they now had title to their land, and stood to make serious money, the people here seemed in some ways worse off than Dawid Kruiper's destitute band, or the hunters at Nyae Nyae, or the villagers of Khekhenye. These others somehow seemed to retain a lightness of heart, a more obvious social cohesion, a certain strength and happiness that seemed lacking here, for all the wealth in game, natural beauty and donor money. I remembered too what the two youths had told me about there being no healers left in Kwaayi. At no point had I heard or seen the people dance.

7

Trance Dance at Buitsevango

We said our goodbyes at Maun. Michael and Katrin had to head down to Gaberone to tie up loose ends there, while I was due to meet Kristin in Zimbabwe, two days' travel away. But before leaving Maun, I had some new friends to drop in on – the Hardbattles.

The Hardbattle family was a Kalahari legend. Van der Post wrote about them. My cousin Frank had told me stories about them. A half-Bushman, half-English dynasty founded by a Yorkshire-born, cattle-ranching pioneer back in the 1940s, they came from Ghanzi, the little frontier town that sits at the gateway to the emptiness of western Botswana. I had met them by chance while en route to Kwaayi, when I had stopped in Maun for a couple of days to arrange the light aircraft that took me into the Delta.

Old Tom Hardbattle, an ex-policeman, had come to South Africa around 1900. Like my great-grandfather Harry Schapiro, he had been initially sidetracked by the Anglo-Boer War, before heading up into the interior to make his fortune in cattle. Around that time the mining magnate Cecil Rhodes (whose company, De Beers, still dominates the world diamond trade) had dreamed his dream of flying the Union Jack right across Africa from the Cape to Cairo. Part of this plan was to open up the Kalahari for white ranchers loyal to the flag, who could keep a watchful eye on the black tribes to the north and the German colonists to the west. Vast ranches were carved out in the Ghanzi district and offered cheap to anyone tough and adventurous enough to take them on. Tom Hardbattle was such a man.

The area was virgin bush, but well populated with Nharo and BaKoko Bushmen, who the pioneer farmers tried to press-gang into working as ranch hands. The Nharo adjusted to the coming of the ranchers with stoicism, while the BaKoko stayed aloof, hunting and gathering as ever in the free lands north of the ranches and watching as their Nharo cousins were gradually reduced from hunters to serfs. Some ranchers treated their 'Bushies' well, others tyrannised them. Tom Hardbattle did something altogether original: he married the daughter of one of his Nharo farmworkers and sired four children on her.

Several decades later, John, the eldest child of Tom Hardbattle and his Bushman wife, formed the first Bushman political group: First People of the Kalahari. In the early 1990s, John began campaigning for Bushman political representation in Botswana and, more specifically, an end to the forced removals of Bushmen from Botswana's Central Kalahari Game Reserve. Sadly John Hardbattle's sudden death from stomach cancer in 1996 led to the collapse of the campaign.

On the drowsy afternoon before I flew into Kwaayi, a friend in Maun had taken me for a cold beer at the Duck Inn, the town's main watering hole. There, by chance, he had introduced me to Andrea and Tom, John Hardbattle's older sister and younger brother, and I had explained to them, briefly, about my book. There was nothing, at first glance, to suggest that either of these people had any Bushman blood. Andrea was tall, blonde and handsome in a northern European way, and spoke with an Afrikaans accent. Her brother Tom, by contrast, was pure Yorkshire, from his crew-cut grey hair and beer belly to his broad accent. Even so, if you looked twice, there was a hint of mixed blood, something delicate in the make-up of their faces, something in their high colour, that had a whisper of KhoiSan.

Although they were still grieving over the death of their brother, they gave me an interview that same night. Sitting with them under the electric light on the veranda of Andrea's long, low bungalow, I didn't know where to begin. Did they know what was going to become of First People of the Kalahari? Were Tom and Andrea going to take up the political standard? Did they still have much of a Bushman family left? While I talked, and Andrea's two Staffordshire bull terriers licked my bare legs, I did not notice the effect my questions were having. Only when I happened to catch Andrea's eye, and saw that it was glistening with tears, did I realise my insensitivity. Embarrassed, I began to apologise.

'No, it's all right,' said Andrea, sniffing. 'You can ask. It's just that it's very hard, you know. We were so close. Growing up here, like we did, and then being sent away to England, and then not seeing each other for years, and now to lose John so suddenly. This year I thought I would never smile again.'

Their earliest years had been spent with their Bushman mother (who was in fact only half-Bushman, her father having been an Afrikaner ranch foreman who had impregnated a Nharo woman and left her to bring up the baby), running wild with the other Nharo kids on their father's ranches. But old man Hardbattle was more practical than sensitive: once the children were old enough he had sent them away to England, to live with working-class relatives in the North. The four children – John, Andrea, Tom and a second girl called Polly – were not to see their mother again for more than twenty years. Instead they found themselves isolated in a cold land whose people had never heard of Botswana, let alone Bushmen or the Nharo, and they quickly learned to hide their exoticness. They would speak Nharo together, but only in secret. Then, for reasons that both Tom and Andrea seemed unclear about, John had been sent away to live with another relative in Yorkshire, while they stayed in Lancashire. The years passed, and the children learned to become English, finishing their schooling and learning trades as their father had intended. But John and Andrea (and, latterly, Tom) still missed the hot wild land of their birth. Only in the 1970s, when a letter came from the family lawyer to say that old man Hardbattle had suddenly died, did the two elder children, John and Andrea, go back to claim their inheritance.

They found things greatly changed. During their childhood, the Ghanzi ranches had been open-range, the game mingling freely with the cattle. Now, hundreds of miles of fences had been put up, and the wild animals were gone, having died of thirst in their hundreds of thousands along the wire that now blocked the old migration routes. Moreover, the ranches had fallen into decay and since the old man's demise much of the livestock had been rustled off or had strayed. Andrea and John also found that most of their father's money had been embezzled by crooked lawyers and accountants, leaving them with land but no capital. To top it off, their mother (who still lived in a traditional grass hut, eschewing the big house), hardly seemed to know them. She had had several other men since their father had grown old, and had borne various half siblings of Herero, Nama and Nharo Bushman paternity.

Nevertheless, John had tried to make the ranches work again, while at the same time – with the help of a charismatic Ganakwe Bushman friend called Roy Sesarna – becoming more and more vocal about the abuses suffered by Botswana's Basarwa. This eventually led him to found First People of the Kalahari in the early 1990s. Andrea, meanwhile, had pursued a more ordinary existence, working as a hairdresser in various towns and cities in South Africa and Botswana, returning to the ranches only occasionally.

When John died suddenly in 1996, Andrea had been at a loss for what to do. She contacted her remaining siblings to discuss the future, but Polly, the youngest, was too rooted in England to come back to a bush-life that she had left almost thirty years before. Tom, however, recently divorced and between jobs as a refrigeration specialist, heeded the call and flew out. Neither he nor Andrea had any background in ranching. Nor did they intend to take up the political torch – that, they felt, was up to John's friend Roy Sesarna. So they hit on the idea of tourism, of setting up some kind of eco-, or ethno-travel idea similar to Benjamin's idea in Namibia. The Nharo family had agreed and now, having given up their respective jobs, Tom and Andrea were trying to drum up interest among the tour operators in Maun, the headquarters of Botswana's small but lucrative safari industry.

'What about your mother?' I asked. 'How does she feel about it all?'

Tom cracked open a new beer. 'When we were little,' he said, taking a sip, 'she used to sing to us all the time. A special song for each of us kids that she always sang when we were with her. When we went away she stopped singing, didn't sing for years, decades.

Nor did she sing them to Andrea and John when they came back. But just a few weeks ago, last time we were at the ranches, she began singing them again; Andrea's song and mine.'

Next morning I had departed for Kwaayi, but with an invitation to come back and see them when I came through Maun again. They were planning to take some safari operators into the Hardbattle ranches to stay with their Bushman family – once again a kind of prototype trip to see if such a thing would be viable. The Nharo family had told them to bring the visitors to a trance dance, a healing dance, that they would be holding in the December full moon.

After a month's belated holiday in Zimbabwe with Kristin, she took off once more for the States and I headed west, back into Botswana, stopping at Victoria Falls to pick up a photographer friend, Mondi. It took three full days to drive to the Hardbattle ranches.

About three hundred kilometres from Ghanzi we picked up a young woman hitch-hiker; a coloured, Afrikaans-speaking, good-looking girl on her way to visit some relatives. What were we doing in the Kalahari, she asked? We told her that we were going to stay with the Hardbattles. Did she know of them? Of course, replied the girl, everyone knew about the *Engelsman* who had married a Nharo woman.

But we should be careful among the Ghanzi Bushmen, she warned us. Some of them, she said, killed outsiders if they ventured into their territory.

'Really?' I asked, incredulous. 'That doesn't sound like any Bushmen I've ever met.'

The young woman was adamant. We didn't know these Ghanzi Bushmen. Some of their doctors even changed themselves into lions, or leopards, at night and went out hunting, stealing livestock or even murdering people.

Mondi and I looked at each other. 'We're going to stay with some of these Ghanzi Bushmen now,' I said. 'Do you think they're going to murder us?'

'No,' said the girl thoughtfully. 'You're going to the Nharo, who work on the farms. They are good – though they are getting too "*high*", wanting too much money. But the BaKoko, north of here: *Aai*! They're naughty.'

'And have you ever met one of these shape-changing Bushmen?'

'Yes! Of course. There's an old man north of here, a BaKoko. Everyone knows about him! Ask anyone in Ghanzi.'

'But have you seen him do it?'

I never got to find out because at that moment the temperature gauge went berserk and we had to pull off and stop the car and the girl hitched another lift. After giving the vehicle half an hour to cool we drove on, making the Hardbattle ranches in the last of the daylight.

It was lonely country, criss-crossed with deep, sandy tracks leading through a sea of waving grasses, following tumbledown barbed-wire fences that stretched beyond the horizon. Although the land was enclosed, these Hardbattle ranches were vast – perhaps the size of a small English county – and all but uninhabited, with no more than a handful of homesteads and Bushman encampments scattered through the whole territory. We passed Jakkalspits, a white-washed, colonial-style house that had been the home of both old Tom Hard-battle and his late son John. From here the track led straight, due south, for what seemed an age. Once or twice a small steenbok crossed in front of us, silhouetted in the red sunset, but for the most part we were alone.

The track brought us at last to a deep, dry riverbed shaded by a natural parkland of tall, widely spaced camel-thorn trees, on the far side of which was the little, shady copse of thorn and seringa where Andrea and Tom had pitched the camp. We crossed the riverbed and pulled in, to find that there were some other guests from the safari companies already there: a young freelance guide called Paul and his girlfriend Michelle, who worked for Okavango Tours and Safaris, one of the more established companies in Maun; and, to my surprise, Cait Andrews, my guide from the Xhomani, with her two children. It turned out that Cait was a friend of Andrea's and had heard about the trance dance while passing through Maun on her way north to vacation in Zambia.

The Bushmen were particularly excited about the coming dance, said Andrea, because a well-known healer was coming down from the north to lead it. The same healer from the north who could change shapes, I wondered silently? There was excitement, too, said Tom, because elephant tracks had been found on the farm for the first time in many years, and a leopard had been prowling around the camp the past two nights: both good omens, according to the Nharo. We ate and drank, and chatted until it grew late. Were the Nharo going to come in later, I asked Andrea. No, she told me; they had their own camp a short distance away through the bush.

As if on cue, from the darkness there arose the sound of singing, the high-pitched, shrill singing of a dance beginning. Andrea and Tom, far from appearing pleased, looked at each other and rolled their eyes. Andrea got up, went to the edge of the camp and shouted in Nharo for the singers to stop.

'Why?' I asked, 'Why shouldn't they sing?'

'No,' said Andrea, 'They'll keep us up all night with it.' I saw the whole thing through her eyes, that if the family was going to make the tourism idea work, then the white clients must be allowed to sleep undisturbed. Yet surely that singing would be just what her future clients would be coming here to experience.

We rose at dawn. Wondering how to pass the long hours before the coming dance, I asked Andrea if it would be possible to go into the bush with some of the Nharo, if any of them were going hunting that day. Andrea took Mondi and I over to the Bushman camp to ask the clan's best hunter, an old man called Xashe, if he would mind taking us out. The man was sleeping when we arrived, and Andrea had to wake him up to ask him. Understandably, he gave us a grumpy reception. He couldn't go hunting now, he said, because he had strung his bow with wire, intending to play it as an instrument for us later. If we wanted to hunt we would have to wait until he could get back to his other place in the bush and fetch a sinew string.

By the time Xashe reappeared the sun was high and the day growing warm. Whatever game might still be afoot would surely be starting to lie up now. Still, the small man led us out into the hot, sun-bleached grasses, weaving expertly between the island-clumps of low-growing shrubs to avoid their skin-piercing thorns.

We walked for hours, seeing nothing, until at last Xashe stopped in the shade of a low thorn tree and sat down to smoke. Only when a minute or so had passed did we realise that the old hunter had in fact brought us right up on the prey. Mere yards away, upwind, so it neither heard us nor smelled Xashe's smoke, a small russet-coloured steenbok was grazing. We had been hunting the whole time. Suddenly excited we readied our cameras and pointed them at Xashe. But the old man did not pick up his bow. Nor did he even rise from where he sat, smoking at his leisure until, at last, he coughed and the little antelope looked up, saw us and was gone.

Chastened, we arrived back at camp in the full, blistering, glaring heat of midday. Everyone was stretched out in the shade of the big central tree, dozing. They gave us a lacklustre welcome as we walked in and headed straight for the ice-box. We shared a drink of cold water with the old hunter, then flopped down in the shade. The whole bush seemed to be drowsing, doves cooing soporifically on the hot wind. I closed my eyes and fell quickly to dreaming. In the dream there was music, soft notes weaving among the dove-song, the rustling leaves and insect-singing grasses. I opened my eyes and saw Xashe, the end of his bow in his mouth, tapping gently at its steel string. He had restrung it with wire, turned it back into an instrument. I closed my eyes again.

When we awoke, in the early evening cool, Xashe had gone. The doves had also stopped. Instead we heard sharp, chattering voices and a small procession of bright-eyed young boys entered the camp, led by a tall, lean adolescent naked to the waist. All carried long, thin sticks of *moretlwa* wood, white and newly stripped of bark.

'Aha,' said Tom, getting to his feet. 'The stick game. I haven't played this since I was a kid. Come on.'

Down on the dry riverbed, on a flat, open bit of ground, the tall boy made a long, low mound of earth, gently slanted at one end. Onto this little slope he piled dry grass, patting it down to lie smooth. The boys arranged themselves single-file in a line some twenty yards from the mound, and began, one by one, to trot forward. Each did the same, starting slow and accelerating rapidly until, one yard out from the mound, he raised his right arm and threw the stick down hard on the slanted edge so that, landing flat, the stick took off, and – seemingly of its own accord – flew straight forward. Most flew several yards, but the two smallest and wiriest boys sent their sticks some fifty yards or more. Anyone standing in the way would have been skewered.

They offered us a go. Tom went first, confident that he'd remember the technique from his boyhood. He got up a good run, raised a powerful arm, threw his stick down flat just as the boys had done, but, fish-like, it just flopped once and lay still. Mondi impaled his stick into the mound. Mine bounced dangerously backward, causing me to jump back with a yelp, much to the boys' merriment. Paul, after several tries, got his to fly a few feet. But the boys were beautiful to watch – all grace and perfectly timed, economical, effective movement. They played until the light began to fail, their sticks flying further and further with each try.

As dusk fell, we re-entered the camp, to see under the big central tree a huge hulk of a woman, her head wrapped in a scarf. She sat on the ground, deep in conversation with Andrea. 'That's Mother,' whispered Tom, as we went to the cooler for a beer. The woman neither looked up nor acknowledged us as we passed. There was authority in the way she spoke, the way she sat, in the steady immobility of her features, in the way Andrea bowed her head as she listened. She was far larger than any Bushman I had yet seen. The face was fine-boned, though, for all the jowls and wattles that hung below her jaw. Clearly she had once been a beauty.

Still speaking to her daughter, the old woman pulled up her much-patched skirt, revealing great legs swollen with large, angry red blotches. 'The healing tonight is for her,' explained Andrea later. 'For the pains in her legs.'

We ate under the stars. It was a warm night, the breeze soft. As we sat, I remembered the question I had meant to ask before, about the shape-shifting healers from the north. Tom and Andrea had heard about them but the healer tonight was Nharo, from the north but not as far north as the BaKoko lived. It was the BaKoko who had that reputation.

Andrea then told a story about one of their neighbouring ranchers, a big, red-headed man of Irish descent called Edward Flattery. One night, his Nharo ranch-hands had woken him to tell him that lions, were in the cattle corral. The rancher and his men rushed out, banging pots and pans and firing into the air, and the lions fled into the night. But when they checked the spoor, the ranch-hands saw blood next to the footprints. One of the lions had been gored. Knowing the danger of having a wounded lion around, the rancher took his best trackers, filled his pockets with shells, and set off on the spoor. They walked northward as the sun rose. By mid-morning they had come to the edge of the ranch, beyond which stretched wild land, BaKoko territory. At that point, said Andrea, the spoor changed from a lion's to a man's.

The Nharo ranch-hands refused point-blank to go on. Flattery, intrigued, said that he would continue, even if it meant going alone and eventually a few of the Nharo reluctantly agreed to go too. They tracked the blood and the spoor until at last they came upon a cluster of grass shelters, where a clan of BaKoko Bushmen sat resting in the shade. Flattery and his men entered the circle and told the people that they had tracked a lion to the edge of his farm, and that the spoor had brought them here. He received only blank looks and shrugs in reply. They knew nothing of any lions, said the BaKoko. Then the rancher looked over at one of the furthest huts and saw a man lying down, nursing a wound such as a cow might leave if it had gored you in the side. He and the Nharo Bushmen turned right around and did not stop walking until they were home.

According to Andrea, these BaKoko were not merely known as shape-shifters and mischief-makers. Their 'doctors' were said to be the most powerful of all, able to sniff out evil-doers and make them atone for their actions, as well as to heal the sick. A few years before, for example, three very young Nharo girls had been raped by a trio of white farmers. Such cases were by no means rare but somehow this one had got to court. Predictably the girls, none of them older than twelve or thirteen, were intimidated (as were their parents) into saying that they had told the men that they were of legal age and had been willing partners in the affair. The farmers were acquitted.

Three years on, two of the farmers had died in strange circumstances – one in an accident and one from a kind of wasting disease, and the third, it seemed, was ill. Word in Ghanzi was that a BaKoko healer had gone into trance and challenged the farmers' spirits to take responsibility for what they had done.

The moon rose, and the Nharo men, women and children began to come into camp, gathering around the fire. The happy cacophony of talk and laughter died away for a moment when the great bulk of 'Mother' (whose name was Xwa) came swaying in out of the dark and sat down outside the circle. She carried a little girl in her arms, lolling against her vast bosom, completely at ease. The talk and joking began again, punctuated as always by hoots of laughter and deep, phlegmy smoker's coughs. The expectation, anticipation, was palpable. After perhaps an hour – it was hard to tell, for no one was keeping track of time – a few of the women began, gently, to sing and clap, only to fall silent again and resume their chatter, as if limbering up for the coming work. Little by little, these short snatches of song and rhythm became longer. It was impossible to say exactly when the chorus began, but at some point the conversation fell away and there was only song, swelling, loud, fast yet steady, tied to a rhythm of many palms coming together in complicated sequence. The men had somehow managed to extricate themselves from the inner circle, and now sat in their own group on the far side of the fire, leaving only women in the chorus. A short distance from the fire, on our side of it, the old matriarch sat unmoving, her face still as stone. Music and moonlight washed over her as she sat, like the bulky figurehead of a boat anchored in a gentle sea.

A lower, deeper voice began to weave and boom in strange harmony with the women's. A small man wearing a battered felt hat and an old, threadbare jacket, emerged from the dark behind the old woman, who did not look up at him as he passed and walked towards the singing circle, but continued to stare straight ahead, as if he were not there. Then a second figure appeared, a long, lean shape, shirtless, showing ribs and lean stomach muscles. As he walked his legs rattled, for around them were tied rows of stone-filled cocoons that hissed in rhythm with the singing. The flames lit up his face – it was the same tall youth who had led the stick game. He and the smaller, older man – who had shed most of his clothes at the firelight's edge and was now also bare from the waist up – stepped through the circle of women and into the circle between them and the fire. There, slowly, they began to dance.

The two men danced and danced, their bass voices and the hissing leg-rattles adding depth and resonance to the women's song, which slowly grew in volume and intensity until the old man staggered, lurched, then stopped, tilting back his head and screaming as if in pain, the veins standing out clear on his neck and forehead. At once the younger man caught and steadied him from behind and then reached into the fire, drew out a handful of burning embers and rubbed them onto the older man's bare back.

Neither man was burnt. Instead, the older one seemed to return to himself and, shaking his head in little, twitching shakes, continued to dance around the fire.

Andrea leaned over to me and whispered: 'It's the helper's job to make sure he doesn't go into trance too quickly, that he enters it at the height of his power. So he brings him out of the trance the first few times by using the coals.'

'But why aren't they burnt?' I asked. Andrea did not answer.

Three or four times, the healer staggered and screamed – once half-falling into the fire itself – his helper repeating, each time, the business with the burning embers. Then, at last, the healer gave a loud scream, a shriek in fact, as if someone had run him through. He leapt out from the fire, over the heads of the singing women. Once in the darkness he staggered a moment, disoriented, then jumped upwards, grabbing a branch of the camp's central thorn tree, and swung there howling, while the women sang on and the helper danced alone. With maniacal strength, the healer gave a great forward swing that landed him hard on his knees in the sand some fifteen feet from Xwa, the old mother. Still screaming, but now sobbing too, he rushed forward on his knees, reached out and grabbed the old woman's legs, running his hands down them, pulling at them, still sobbing while the chorus sang and the old woman, impassive as a statue, looked resolutely over the healer's head, into the darkness, letting him handle her as he would.

Then, without warning, he was back to his feet and leaping back over the singing, clapping circle of women to re-enter the dance once more, dancing with a sweating intensity that made it almost painful to watch. His voice and movement conjured agony, guilt, spiritual anguish, illness, nausea, fear, hate, envy, anger, plucking them from the night like dark spirits to flow through him and back out into the surrounding night like poison. One wanted to shut out the sight of him. Again and again he would stop, shriek – as if the pain was just too much – and go leaping over the heads of the chorus to kneel before the old woman and pull away at her legs as if trying to rip them from their sockets. Through it all the old woman sat, immobile, seeming hardly to notice the drama around her.

I looked at the others. Mondi was glued to his camera, snapping away. The safari people sat stock still in the flickering light, fully absorbed. The same went for Tom, Andrea and Cait's two teenage children. Cait herself had crept nearer the circle and was holding out a small microphone, recording the music, the shrieks and the wails. Paul was video-taping it. It seemed the right thing to do, to try and document this extraordinary happening (extraordinary, at least, if you were not a Bushman). I ducked away to my shelter, where my own tape-recorder lay inside my pack, rummaging a few minutes to find it. When I came out, a different voice was shrieking and yelping. The healer had stopped at one of the women in the circle and laid his hands on her head. He and she were sobbing together, her hands reaching up into the air. When he released her, uttering a great yell as he did so, her whole body bucked violently and she fell sideways, moaning. The healer pulled her upright, caressed her almost lovingly, and the woman quietened. He moved on, the helper behind him, going one by one around the circle. In between the women, the children watched, eyes and mouths wide open in unselfconscious awe.

I sidled up to Andrea: 'What's he doing now?'

'He's going around all the people, healing everybody. It doesn't have to be a specific ailment like Mother's, it can be psychological or spiritual. He draws the bad energy out, into himself and then spits it out for the wind to take away. That's why he screams – it's the pain of taking their pain into himself, and then releasing it. This is a very hard healing.'

As she spoke, the man leapt once again over the heads of the singers and went back to the old woman, pulling at her legs as if his life depended on it. 'You see,' whispered Andrea, 'It's unusual for him to go back to one person so often; it's usually done much more quickly than that. He must be finding it difficult.'

'And the men sitting outside the circle, will they be healed too?'

'No, you only get the individual healing if you sit in the circle. It's sad, but the men here aren't too comfortable with it any more. It's a bit of a source of conflict in the clan actually. Some of them want to identify more with Western, or at least BaTswana ways. A lot of them just don't want to put in the work of being part of the circle. But they still want to be close to it. They know it's powerful. So like us they get some benefit just by being here even if they don't really take part.'

Still the dance went on. One by one, though, the people outside the chorus circle began to slip away. First the men, stealing off on noiseless feet, then the children. A little later the old woman rose and silently, slowly walked into the night. The healer and his assistant danced on oblivious. Yet something in the atmosphere, some tension, seemed to have lifted. Now when the healer laid hands on the women, he no longer screamed and sobbed, but sang a softer, dreaming song whose melody fell gradually down a minor scale, ending almost on a sigh. The women no longer bucked spasmodically and cried when he touched them, but sang with him, in softer, lower voices.

Of the whites, only Mondi and Andrea were left. Then, a little later, they too had gone. I sat on alone, watching as the moon dipped lower and lower, the singing grew sleepier in sound and the rhythm slowed. Soon the healer was no longer laying on hands, merely dancing slowly around the fire, singing softly to himself. It seemed that his trance had broken, for his eyes were focused now and he smiled at me as he passed. It was then that I did what I had been longing to do all night. I got up from my seat at the camp table, went over to the circle and sat down. The women, smiling, made space for me. I picked up the rhythm and sat, clapping with them, basking in the deep, almost slumberous peace that the dance now seemed to have created.

I slept the longest of anyone, only waking when the day was already baking hot. Blearily, I joined the others under the tree to sit and drink coffee. Most of the guests had to get back to Maun – Cait and her kids, Andrea and her daughter, and everyone connected with the safari trade except for Paul, who was coming on to the Central Kalahari with Mondi and me. Tom suggested that we ask one of the Nharo men to come with us to interpret: Karnells, a young man who spoke English and acted as unofficial ranch foreman. He knew the area well, said Tom, and was also a great bush mechanic, and had all the hunting and gathering skills.

Everybody clearly felt touched in some way by the dance, but unsure exactly how, needing time to let the experience settle. No one wanted to be the first to speak about it. Just at that point the camp was suddenly astir with young women and girls, singing and clapping. They wore their best dresses of bright floral prints, skin cloaks and headbands patterned with coloured beads, long white necklaces of ostrich eggshell which wrapped around the body front and back like slender bandoliers.

There was no announcement, no explanation of what the dances were to be, nor of what they meant. In the first dance, the women and girls stood in a bobbing, clapping line, the first holding a *tsamma* melon – the water-bearing fruit that matures in the dry season, and sustains life through the rainless months – a symbol of plenty. The woman holding this large, round, natural ball sprang out from the line, executed a few steps in time to the song then tossed the melon behind her, so that the next woman had to leap forward to catch it while the first jogged back to the end of the line, rejoining the song. So it continued, with each woman and girl performing her own short solo before tossing the melon back to the next dancer. Anyone who failed to make the catch was treated to raucous laughter.

When the melon dance was over, two of the older women produced a long rope of plaited grass fibres and began a skipping song, chanting as the rope made complicated loops and waves which the young girls leapt over like gymnasts. Then the two youngest girls locked their left legs together and, while the grown-ups clapped, hopped around and around in a dizzying circle until one had to break free and fell down hard on her bum, much to everyone's delight. Hardly had this finished than the three oldest women, great-grandmothers of seventy or more, shuffled into the shade under the big tree carrying between them a long bow, some seven feet in length, strung with wire. Laying it down, they took an upturned bowl from the camp table and put it under one end of the bow to make a sounding box. Then, sitting, they began to tap along the length of the wire, producing a slow, dreamy tune like the one Xashe had conjured with his mouth-bow, only richer, deeper.

The eldest began to sing, at the same time making coquettish gestures with her arms, hands and head. Andrea whispered: 'Three young hunters are out in the bush, thinking about girls. She's becoming what they're thinking about, if you follow me . . .' I looked again. Despite her wrinkles and gnarled, knotted joints, this old lady *was* now a flirtatious teenage girl, one who knew she was pretty, and wanted to be looked at but not touched. As the song drew to a close she chuckled softly, as if at old times fondly remembered, and became her aged self once more.

It was time to go. Down came the tents, the tables were collapsed, the cooking pots and utensils packed into boxes, all of which were carried to the vehicles, loaded onto the roofs and tied down. When the goodbyes were over I went back to my vehicle to fetch my camera, wanting to take a 'team photo'. As I trotted back to the copse, where the others still were, I passed a rough shelter of branches, standing slightly away from the camp site. The flap was up and my glance fell on the figures inside. It was Xwa, her huge, heavy-breasted body standing unclothed while one of the other women rubbed some oil or ointment into her skin. In that brief moment I glimpsed the old woman's legs. The red swellings that had been there the previous night were gone.

8

Into the Central Kalahari

The road into the Central Kalahari Game Reserve (CKGR) seemed endless; a shallow canal of thick, slippery rutted sand through which the Land-Rover rolled and pitched like a boat in choppy water. On either side, miles and miles of empty bush. No sign of livestock even, no stray donkeys or goats hanging out in this hot, shimmering, silent wilderness. Predictably the temperature gauge started to fluctuate again. I ignored it the first couple of times, hoping the problem would go away. It didn't.

We got out and opened the bonnet. The engine was hot, but it was hard to tell if it was really over-heating, for the day itself was a proper Kalahari scorcher. Karnells advised driving on, but a few miles further the needle flew up again. 'We haven't tried swearing at it,' I said. 'What's the worst swear word we know?' Everyone agreed it had to be 'Cunt'. We stopped the car, got out and, on a count of three, all yelled 'CUNT!' at the top of our lungs, except for Karnells, who yelled *Nwi*!, which means the same thing in Nharo.

Miraculously, the temperature gauge gave us no further problems. We drove on into the mirage-laden heat, pushing, coaxing the vehicle hour after hour through the sand. Suddenly the engine gave a roar as a wheel caught in a loose rut then flipped out, the bump causing my foot to accidentally depress the accelerator. The vehicle began to spin, then rocked once, twice onto two wheels, righted itself and came to a halt, broadside to the road, the four of us inside releasing a simultaneous sigh of relief. A good moment to take a break: in another half-hour or so, Karnells told us, we would be at New Xade, where the dispossessed Bushmen of the Central Kalahari had been relocated.

Pulling the vehicle off the road, we strolled along the verge, looking for wild vegetables to eat that night and filling a cardboard box with spiky wild cucumbers (what the Bushmen call gemsbok cucumbers), *tsamma* melons and sour plums. We checked over our journalistic equipment – making sure that video camera, tape-recorder and other cameras were all working. Once at New Xade we would have a very short time to make contact with someone, interview them, and move on. The word in both Maun and Ghanzi was that, owing to all the bad press, the Botswana government had now placed a moratorium on journalists going into the CKGR, or even talking to the Bushmen who had been moved out.

New Xade materialised quite suddenly; a vast, cleared sandy space dotted with big army tents, a few thatched rondavels and some more traditional grass shelters. Groups of Bushmen sat or squatted in the shade of these, fugitives from the fierce glare reflecting off the dry, sun-blasted earth. They watched us with dull, uncurious eyes as we drove past. In a place where several huts came together, and where a casual glance would not spot us, we stopped and got out. Karnells greeted the people, who slowly got up and shuffled over to see what we wanted. As he explained that we were journalists a man in his late thirties, thin and anxious-looking, stepped forward and said we should be careful – if anyone in authority saw us we'd all be in trouble. We would have to ask our questions quickly.

Offering my microphone to the man, I asked him: 'Why are you here?'

The reply came at speed in the Ganakwe Bushman language: this man clearly had much ire to vent. Karnells, frowning with the effort, summarised: 'He says the government is just putting them there. They don't like it here – they are hunting here, but they can't find animals. There's no water. They just want to go back.'

'Do they know why they've been brought here?'

'They don't know why. The government has just put them here.'

'Do they know if they're going to be here permanently?'

'There's nothing here. The government people said they would help them, but there's no help. No borehole.'

I tried a different tack: 'Why does he think he's been brought here?'

'We ask,' replied the man through Karnells. 'We wait for an answer.' The small, ragged crowd around us had grown larger. He went on, speaking with more passion: 'The government is just throwing us away . . . If we could just get some help . . . First People have been here, journalists have been here. But we are just sitting, just waiting . . .'

In the middle distance, a vehicle painted government-issue blue was moving slowly among the huts – coming closer. We would have to wrap up quickly. 'Has the government made them any promises, offered any compensation for the move?'

'Yes,' answered the man. They had been promised a lot of things – money, and cattle, boreholes, seed and ploughs, tools, donkeys, bricks for houses (none of which had arrived) – all compensation for a move which, he said, they hadn't wanted to make in the first place. They had been sitting here since July. It was now December, and all they had seen were handouts of food because they could no longer hunt, and a few donkeys that the lions had eaten.

'Did they see these promises in writing?'

'Yes,' said the man, they had seen paper. But now – nothing.

I thanked him, shut down the tape machine and then joined the others in unloading some of the supplies we had bought before leaving Ghanzi – sacks of maize-meal, tinned meat, bags of rice – which were received with appreciative shouts. The man I had interviewed said, through Karnells: 'Listen my friend, we need money, very, very badly. I have some crafts to sell, my bow . . .' and he sprinted off to a hut or tent somewhere on the other side of the road. The blue government vehicle, meanwhile, had stopped about fifty yards off. We saw people getting out, going to another hut, looking over their shoulders at us. Paul gestured towards our vehicle and Karnells was biting his lip. We all got in, and I fired up the engine. But as I was edging out through the little crowd, the man came running back. He held out a hollow ostrich egg, decorated with a neat, geometric pattern of small dots burnt into the hard white shell. I had seen such things in use at Nyae Nyae as water-carriers, either as canteens or stashed in secret places, under logs or in holes, to be used when hunting in the dry-season bush. He thrust it through the window into my lap. The work was exquisite, probably weeks in the making. 'Fifteen pula!' he said in English, his voice so urgent that I automatically reached into my shorts pocket and produced the notes. He took them and burst into tears, grabbed my hands through the window and kissed them, then broke away, running back to the huts. In the rear-view, I glimpsed the government vehicle moving, coming our way. I slipped the clutch and two minutes later we were out on the empty bush road, heading east.

Much later, with the light growing gentler and the worst of the heat gone, we arrived in Xade, now emptied of its people. Unlike New Xade, which was scorched and barren, this place was well vegetated, shaded and sheltered by wild fruit trees. But the huts – which were of woven grasses stretched over wicker frames – lay in ruins, their tops bashed in as if by a giant fist. We got out and took photographs. In my pocket, I had one of the reserve's official information leaflets. It made interesting reading.

> Larger than Belgium or Switzerland, the 52,800 square kilometre Central Kalahari Game Reserve, which was set up in 1961, is the largest game reserve in the world . . . The people commonly known throughout the world as the Bushmen, but more properly referred to as Basarwa, have been resident in and around the area for probably thousands of years. Originally nomadic hunters and gatherers, the lifestyle of the Basarwa has gradually changed with the times and they now live in settlements, some of which are situated within the southern half of the Central Kalahari Game Reserve. Government is now encouraging these people to move to areas outside the reserve in order that they may be provided with modern facilities, schools, clinics etc. and integrate them into modern society.

I read the last bit aloud to Karnells. 'They are lying,' he said simply.

The two Wildlife Department officials at the reserve's entry post, a kilometre or two up the track from the ruined village, eyed Karnells suspiciously. What was our purpose for visiting the reserve? Tourism, just tourism, we replied, and drove on.

In fact, our destination was Molapo, the home village of Roy Sesarna – the head of First People of the Kalahari since John Hardbattle had died. The people here, so we had heard, had announced that they would resist any attempt to move them. We had no chance of reaching Molapo that evening, so we found a clearing with a lone tree to camp under, cooked up the gemsbok cucumbers we had gathered earlier, and listened to a pack of wild dogs hunting some small antelope past the southern end of the wide clearing. The sound – high and babbling – was somehow demonic.

On impulse I asked Karnells if he knew the stories about Bushman healers turning themselves into lions or leopards.

'Yes, I know these stories.'

'Do you think they're true?'

'Yes,' he said, quieter now, 'They are true.'

'Do you know anyone, a healer, who can do this?'

'Yes, I know some of them.' Karnells mumbled uncomfortably.

'The healer the other night, at the dance, was he one of these?'

'No,' replied Karnells, after a moment's hesitation. I could tell from his tone that he was growing more and more uneasy, that any moment he'd clam up altogether. 'So is there another healer from the north, from north of Ghanzi?'

'Yes, there is a powerful one there. He was trying to heal John Hardbattle when he was ill, when he was overseas and ill. And at Molapo where we are going, there is another one. A woman.' As usual, that was as far as the conversation went.

We rose at dawn and set off again in the Land-Rover, sometimes picking up a little speed across the hard-baked surface of a pan, sometimes floundering through sand so deep that we seemed to be driving through turgid water. Mopane trees, their butterfly-wing leaves dappling the road with light and shadow, gave way to great, sunlit meadows. Game appeared and disappeared – kudu, gemsbok, the occasional secretary bird or kori bustard stalking through the long grass, and once a martial eagle, largest of the many Kalahari raptors, his crest raised in challenge as we chugged underneath his branch. At last, in the late afternoon, we crossed yet another pan, watched by a lone springbok ram, and saw a thin woman off to our left vigorously waving us in. A few seconds later, the scene was transformed by a yelling, jumping mass of kids, surging around the doors and windows while behind them came women, dressed for the most part in skins, and men, some in *xais*, some in torn cotton and polyester, some in both. We had arrived.

The old woman who had waved us in came forward, took my hands, led me to a clear space, and sat me down opposite herself on sand that was white and full of quartzite sparkles. At this, the rest of the people – some fifty-odd – sat down too. Karnells, in his role of interpreter, settled between us, sideways on so that we could both see his face.

Where else in southern Africa would one find a female leader but among Bushmen? Seen from close to, her face had a startling, angular beauty, a delicate pattern of small, vertical tattoos decorating her temples and accenting her cheekbones. Through Karnells, I introduced myself and the others, explained that we were journalists and would like to talk about the political situation in the CKGR, but that we would also like to see how life was here, maybe go hunting and gathering. If it was all right, we would like to stay a couple of days.

As Karnells translated my requests, I let my gaze wander over the village. It was big, almost as big as Kwaayi: there must be at least two hundred people living here, I thought. The huts were large, and of a style I had not seen before, resembling large haystacks with low doorways. A few goats, donkeys and horses drifted about the place. There were stronger-looking stockaded corrals dotted here and there between the great, shaggy huts, presumably for these animals to be locked away from predators at night. It appeared these people kept domestic animals, although I had been told that the Ganakwe Bushmen of the Central Kalahari Game Reserve lived traditionally.

Yes, answered the old woman, these things we wanted to do, to know, were good. There were three hunters right here who could take us out this very evening if we wished. As for the political talk, that could come later. At a word from her, three lean young men got up from the small crowd of seated onlookers and went off to their huts to fetch what they needed for the hunt.

Just as I was getting to my feet, brushing the sand off my shorts, Paul leaned forward from behind me and whispered: 'Aren't you going to ask her, you know, about the shape-changing?' Perhaps because my head was still fuzzy from the drive, I did – against my better judgement. Were there healers in the village, I asked? The woman smiled and inclined her head. Was she a healer, I asked? The handsome old lady inclined her head again. I pressed on: Did she, or any of the other healers here know about this thing of shape-changing from man to lion or man to leopard? Had she heard of this?

Karnells was obviously embarrassed but he made the translation. The old woman looked down at the ground a moment before turning up a face that no longer smiled, and answered, with finality, that no, she could not do this thing, nor could any other healer here.

The three young hunters returned, dressed in shorts, skin capes, battered old running shoes and baseball caps presumably traded from whatever tourists passed through this remote place from time to time. They carried digging sticks and spears, but no bows. So this could be only a small-game hunt as spears were good for something near that could not move fast. Two of the hunters obviously had Bantu fathers, while the third, who was smaller and thinner, looked to be a full-blooded Bushman.

Accompanying the hunters was a fourth young man, in a white shirt and grey nylon trousers that reminded me of my old school uniform. He spoke English. As we walked out of the village to the south, he introduced himself as 'Mohubu', which immediately caused Karnells to giggle. I raised an eyebrow; 'It means belly button', whispered Karnells and went into such a paroxysm of silent laughter that he bent double for a moment as he walked. The young man didn't appear offended, indeed he seemed to share in the amusement, smiling broadly, then introducing the hunters – Moipollai, Moseise and Setilo – which set Karnells off again. Respectively, the names meant 'Don't Kill Yourself', 'Sun is Hot' and 'No Horns'. Was this a joke?

We crossed the pan and entered a patch of grassland where *moretlwa* bushes grew. Several times the hunters stopped and dug up an edible root or tuber, showing it to us and explaining its use. One root, which Karnells called wild spinach, was hollowed out with a knife. The hunter called 'Don't Kill Yourself' knelt, laying a stick horizontally above a wad of dried grass and, while 'No Horns' held it down, he rubbed another stick, a harder one, into the softer, making fire. Immediately, 'Sun is Hot' produced some tobacco from his shorts pocket and stuffed it into the hollowed-out root. He grinned, like someone doing their party trick, lit the pipe and had a smoke, looking up at us as if to say 'Howzabout that then?' When the tobacco was done, they turned for home. That, apparently, was that. We had been out less than half an hour.

This was no hunt, but a show for the tourists – an easy buck, in other words. I wondered if I would ever learn. How could we expect to waltz in, flash some money around, say 'Take us hunting, show us shape-changing' and expect to be treated as anything but the fools we were? Nevertheless, the young men seemed aware that we had been short-changed. Tomorrow they said, as they left us back at the village, they would come again and take us out properly. Meanwhile we should go and make camp, which we did, a discreet half mile north of the village under a great Marula tree. It was still light long after we had stopped gathering wood and had built our cooking fire. Springbok came drifting in across the big meadow that surrounded us – there was certainly no lack of game around. That night we all got drunk on wine, Karnells too. Sometime after the fourth or fifth glass, he startled us by leaping to his feet, snatching up a pair of pliers from the vehicle's nearby toolbox, bending down into the darkness and coming up with one of the largest scorpions I have ever seen. The highly venomous thing writhed and twisted in the metal grip, its huge sting stabbing impotently at the air just an inch from Karnells' hand, while he laughed and laughed.

The hunters were as good as their word, coming for us just after dawn and looking far more business-like this time, carrying bows as well as spears, and a long flexible pole of *moretlwa* wood, with a hook at one end. They led us at a brisk pace, without dawdle, chat or laughter, and locked straight onto a steenbok spoor. At a point where the trail narrowed to just a few inches across they knelt down and set a snare, manufacturing a rope on the spot from tough grass stems twisted together with a little open noose at one end and the other fastened to a bent-over sapling and secured with a little twig.

We walked on a mile or two, until we came upon a set of wide holes in the ground – a warren of spring hares, shy, nocturnal Kalahari rodents that hop on their back legs like small kangaroos. As we stood watching, the young men fed the pole of *moretlwa* wood carefully into the largest hole, expertly manoeuvring around the corners of the tunnel, hoping thereby to hook one of the rodents as it slept. During these hot summer months, explained 'Belly Button', they hunted small game only. The kudu, gemsbok and wildebeest hunts – highly organised affairs using horses and dogs – took place only in the dry winter, when a man and a horse could run without getting heat stroke and the meat didn't spoil.

But, he added, this kind of hunt was happening less and less often. Until recently each hunter (or rather each hunter's household), had known what they could take each year: one kudu, two gemsbok, four springbok and thirty steenbok. Now the wildlife officers were saying the rules had changed; no one was sure these days whether or not he was poaching. And they could no longer hunt eland at all, which was a problem, because at least once a year the heart of an eland should be burnt and the smoke sent into the sky to bring rain. Not long before, wildlife officials had accused one of Molapo's hunters of killing an eland and had taken the man in for questioning. He had later been found, beaten to death. Others had also been taken for questioning and had had the tight rubber rings that farmers and ranchers use to castrate lambs and goat-kids fastened around their testicles. Yes, he shrugged, now that the government wanted them out of the reserve, this was how life was going.

At that moment 'No Horns' let out a triumphant cry: he had hooked something! He called urgently to his companions, one of whom grabbed him around the middle from behind, helping him pull back, maintaining the tension, while the others pressed their heads to the ground, listening for the squealing of the caught animal below. As soon as they had located the sound they began to dig down through the hard-packed, dry earth with sticks and hands.

Until I watched these three Bushmen dig out the spring hare I had not fully appreciated how desperately hard traditional life in the veld could be, the life that I and so many like me happily mythologised. Even a long hunt, such as I had seen with Tom, with the task of butchering and carrying heavy meat over long distances in the heat, does not compare with this digging down with bare hands through hard earth six feet or more to where the quarry, a small meal, but a meal nonetheless, lies snagged on the hook. It's extremely tough digging that kind of depth through hard earth with a spade, let alone bare hands. The three young men took turns at it, curtly refusing our offers of help as if they knew that we would only be a hindrance. While one dug, his body white with dust, another would rest and the third would keep up the tension on the pole. I looked at their hands as they came up from their turns in the hole, and saw that their fingernails were neither torn nor bleeding, as ours would have been, and I marvelled at their strength.

While we looked on, taking notes and pictures, running the video camera, Karnells stripped off his shirt and took a turn at the ever-deepening hole, to accelerate the work. 'No Horns', squatting down out of sight in the hole, gave a sudden shout. We rushed over to look. He had the strange creature – far larger than a European hare – by its long tail. He had detached the hook from its side: we could see the red wound, the large, nocturnal eyes blinking confusedly in the sun. As soon as its two long back legs touched the ground the spring hare tried to hop away, but in vain, so firm was the grip on its tail. It looked desperately sad, exposed and curiously resigned. The hunters shouted for joy, exuberant with their success, but they did not prolong its suffering. Karnells, picking up a nearby fallen branch, killed it with one sharp, well-aimed blow to the head.

Gutted and skinned, the spring hare was cooked immediately in a hollow scooped from the earth, covered over with the hot charcoal of a quickly-made fire. The hunters shared the meat with us, though we felt too guilty to take more than a bite or two. It tasted sweet, like rabbit. The meal done, they dismantled the nearby steenbok snare, which had caught nothing, and led us back to the village, content both at having full bellies and knowing that they were to be paid for the pleasure.

On our return, the old woman was sitting waiting for us, a group of villagers behind her. 'So, now,' she said, 'you had some questions about our life here.' I badly wanted a drink of water and a lie-down in the shade but, shamed by the hunters who were still energetic even after their labour, I rallied and tried to think of questions. I was still embarrassed by my *faux-pas* of the previous day. At first we talked of general things, how much we had enjoyed going out with the hunters, how impressed we were with their skill, then, feeling more confident, I asked if the things that 'Belly Button' had told us were true – about harassment from the wildlife officials, even to the point of beating Bushmen to death.

The old woman inclined her head: it was so, she answered. Now, whenever a government truck came into the village, people ran into their huts, not knowing what trouble might be coming. For some years they had been dependent on a supply of water (for the livestock rather than for the people) which was brought by truck to a large container in the centre of the village. But the trucks were coming less and less often, sometimes not for days at a time. Little by little the animals were dying. Yet a few years ago, the government people had been telling them to become farmers, and had even given them goats. Now it seemed they were trying to kill the animals and even, sometimes, the people.

'But why?' I asked.

'It is to make life here too bad,' came a young woman's voice in English from somewhere in the back of the group. 'So that we will start to think that life here cannot go on, and so we will climb onto the trucks and leave, like those from Xade.'

Startled, I looked around, trying to locate the voice. My gaze followed the other villagers' to light upon a young, slightly built, very pretty woman with dark skin and a neat, clean dress, who sat a few rows behind the old woman leader. 'But we are resisting,' she went on, speaking confidently into the silence that had been left her. 'This is our place. Our life is here, has always been here. The government tells us that it wants to develop this place for tourism, and cannot have people living where the game animals are. They say that we are killing too many animals and keeping too many goats, but they are not telling us how to conserve, or working with us, they are just saying we must go.'

'Who are you?' I asked.

'I am Bulanda Claudia Gwanxlae Thamae, the wife of Roy Sesarna, head of the First People of the Kalahari,' replied this striking woman, in the same measured tone.

As the crowd dispersed back to the village, the young woman agreed to record a proper interview with us. She could be no more than twenty-five, I guessed, yet her self-possession as well as her obvious language skills (the best I had encountered since meeting Benjamin), were striking. Here is a leader of the future, I thought, as I found my recording equipment and returned to where she sat, in the shade of our tree. She took control immediately, demanding to know, before we began the interview, what we had agreed to pay the hunters and how much we were going to give the village for the camping. We told her and she approved the figure, saying that the safari operators who came through from time to time with clients often paid next-to-nothing, or promised to pay and then reneged.

She was a mine of surprising information. The Bushmen of the CKGR were not only going to resist being moved, she told us, but had actually filed a land claim, under the guidance of First People of the Kalahari, with Roger Chennels' company. Also, she said she had met prospectors from the de Beers diamond mining company in the bush not far from Molapo. They had told her that this land was now theirs to do with what they would. I had read, a week or two before, that a de Beers spokesman had admitted to a British journalist from the *Telegraph*, that the company had found diamonds in the CKGR, although he had given an assurance that as far as they were concerned, the Bushmen could stay.

Later, at Bulanda's invitation, I went to her hut to record something she had prepared in writing. Reading aloud, she launched into a long and complicated set of demands, enunciated clearly, as if she was speaking at a conference, rather than sitting in the dust with a crying infant on her lap. Her people had been in the Central Kalahari for 30,000 or 40,000 years, she said. They did not want to move. They wanted development, but they wanted it here, in their own place. If the government was worried that this development would damage the wildlife and the environment, as they claimed, then it was up to them to teach the Ganakwe how to avoid this, not to move them. The British had set this place aside for the Bushmen before independence: she cited the chapter (14.C) in the Botswana constitution that stated that Bushmen had been given rights to their land. She demanded that government funds be made available to train Basarwa doctors, nurses, teachers, so that people could be treated and taught in their native languages. She pointed out that no Bushmen, no Basarwa, currently sat in the country's House of Chiefs, nor in the Parliament and accused Botswana of practising apartheid.

When, at last, she had fallen silent, I asked, 'Do you think Molapo will still be here in a year's time?'

'Yes. We will refuse and stay.'

'But if the government stops bringing you water here, how will you survive?'

'Sometimes we put the fat of the eland in the fire and the smoke will go up to the sky, then the rain will come. We can survive, because all of our life is here . . .'

I finished recording and asked Bulanda why she was not in Ghanzi, giving her skills to First People of the Kalahari. Because she needed a healing, she replied. She had come back to Molapo because she, like all the others at First People, had been made a target of bad *muti* (medicine) from the BaTswana people, angry at their challenge to government policy. John Hardbattle, she said, had been a victim of this same *muti* – it had been that which had brought on the sudden cancer that had killed him the year before.

But how could Bushmen be a target for bad *muti*, when they had such powerful healers of their own, ones who could even turn themselves into lions, I asked? Bulanda smiled. Yes, First People had even thought of asking some of the BaKoko healers to take on lion shape to go and kill those people in the government who were hurting them. 'But,' she said, sighing, 'Bushmen do not make this kind of medicine. It is forbidden. So it will be a long, and slow fight, everything political.'

I seized my chance and asked her if she knew one of these shape-changing healers. Oh yes, came the reply. The most powerful BaKoko healer lived far to the north and west of Ghanzi. She hadn't seen him for some time, but she knew him quite well. If I liked, the next time I came back she could help me find him. His name, she said, was Besa.

PART THREE

THE GOOD LITTLE DONKEYS

9

Revelations at the Red House

It is always a shock to travel from the southern hemisphere back to the north – especially in December. I swapped the desert's summer swelter for a wind-battered family Christmas at my sister's house, perched high on a Welsh mountainside, but the Kalahari followed me there, as luck would have it, with the arrival of Andrea and her daughter Alexandra from Ghanzi. She had come over, partly to look into marketing her Bushman tourism idea, and partly to see family.

I was preoccupied with the healer Besa, and asked Andrea if she had heard of him. He was quite famous around Ghanzi, she said, though she hadn't heard of him for some years. I made up my mind to get back out there as soon as possible. However, it took me a few months of freelancing to raise the necessary funds to go in search of Besa, especially as the trip would also have to be long enough for me to follow up the Xhomani story and get to some other parts of the Kalahari I hadn't yet seen.

But in April 1998, I was on a plane back to the Kalahari.

I began the journey at the Red House, among the Xhomani where Belinda, the young coloured manager from the Kalahari Gemsbok National Park, had agreed to interpret for me. April is a strange transitional season between the end of the rains and the beginning of the long dry. You can't predict the weather. On one day the temperature and humidity will rise steadily through an afternoon of pounding white sunshine, only to pass off suddenly, ushering in a night so chill and dry it chaps the lips and makes you shiver in your sleeping bag. Then again, the night might turn soft and gently warm like a tropical sea, seducing you into bedding down on the dunes, only for a late rainstorm to come charging out of nowhere.

It was just such a night. Dawid, naked to the waist, crouched by the fireside, the red light illuminating his lined face and small, lean body. Even in his sixty-third year, the old man retained a certain youthfulness, not so much in his face, a labyrinth of lines and creases radiating out from a nose that had been flattened and skewed from some fight or accident long in the past, but more in his body, supple from a lifetime of desert living, and in his eyes, which smiled out at the darkness as if to say 'I'm still here'.

Next to him Sanna, his wife, hummed gently to herself and clapped quietly, perhaps remembering a dance. A *doek*, or scarf, was wound around her head. Her long breasts were bare. Unlike her husband, Sanna seemed old, her face bore the marks of years of childbirth and loss, and the memory of the land she had seen taken away.

'*Ja, Mama!*' Dawid exclaimed in Afrikaans, as if to break the silence, and reached into a little leather pouch lying by his side. He drew out a small package of *dagga*, marijuana, unrolled the paper, emptied out the contents and began to sort the seeds and stalks from the leaf in the palm of his hand. '*Ja Mama,*' he repeated, stuffing the *dagga* into a pipe made from a hollowed-out section of shin bone. 'Let's smoke.'

The night before, my second since arriving back in the Kalahari, Dawid had invited us to take part in a dance. So we had come, feeling excited, expectant, honoured, ready to stay up all night for the trance, wondering if the whole community would be there. Yet when we had arrived, only Dawid and Sanna had come out of the cavernous Red House to greet us. Everyone else had stayed inside their huts. So we sat and smoked, and waited for the evening to unfold.

A small, bedraggled, loose-gaited silhouette emerged out of the darkness. Bukse, Dawid's younger brother, sat down. Everything about him twinkled, suggested mischief. Grinning from his ragged old clothes, he reached for the bone pipe and took a deep drag. Sanna's song grew louder. Then, with a quick, unexpected grace,

Bukse jumped up and began a slow, stamping circle around the fire. Dawid put down the pipe and started clapping in time with his wife, nodding for us to do the same. The song was different from the usual run of Bushman music: there were no complicated, interwoven beats, no high, wailing song. This one had a structure recognisable to a Western ear. A definite three-time, like a slow waltz, and instead of the usual improvised devotional phrases, a clear round of lyrics. Bukse sang as he danced:

> *Ou Mackai te Kiraha*
> *Ou Mackai te Kiraha*
> *Na ke !au Kwena Hocha*
> *Na ke !au Kwena Hocha*

Bukse turned and stretched out his hands to me. As I stood, Bukse grabbed me, put me in front of him and, still singing, began to dance me around the fire, his knees pressing into the backs of mine so that – like puppet and puppet-master – we made the same stamping steps together. Then, out from the darkness beyond the firelight came Antas, the ancient woman who had healed Cait Andrews, her wrinkled breasts hanging flat against her bony chest. She stood in front of Belinda, took her by the hand, pulled her upright with surprising strength and did with her as Bukse was doing with me.

Round and round we went, Dawid clapping the rhythm, we stomping it and trying to follow the words that Sanna, Bukse and Antas sang. Then, as abruptly as it had begun, the dance ended. Bukse released me from his tight embrace. 'See,' he said, pointing to the circle of footprints. 'Now we have danced together.'

I asked Belinda: 'Do you know what the song means?'

'Yes,' she laughed, 'I've heard it a lot over these past months. But let Dawid explain.'

Old Mackai, said Dawid, had been the leader of the Xhomani before Regopstaan. During his time, great changes had come to the red dune country – the Mier farmers had pushed north and the National Park had been declared. Fences had gone up everywhere, ending the old life when the Xhomani had wandered up and down the Aub and Nossob rivers at will, although for a time life had been good, or at least not so bad. The Leriche family, who had farmed at Twee Rivieren before it became the park headquarters, were its first wardens. They had let the Bushmen stay on. 'Sometimes they were good to us, would let us hunt, and walk around. Sometimes they beat us, or made us work, or said we couldn't hunt.' Shortly before Mackai's death, the old leader had given his people a prophecy in the form of a song: *Ou Mackai te Kiraha, Na ke !au Kwena Hocha* (Old Mackai is growing old, and the strangers are coming). Dawid coughed, clearing his throat, and said simply: 'That is the song.'

Belinda and I stared at him rapt, intent, wanting more. Looking at us, he burst out laughing, opening his eyes wide in imitation. 'Like two baboons catching their reflections in a pan!' he roared, then burst into a hacking fit of coughing. '*Ja Mama*', he said, shaking his head once he had recovered, 'First Mackai growing old and the strangers coming. Then Regopstaan's prophecy, which you know. I know Cait told you: *when the strangers come there will be big rains, and then the little people will dance. And when the little people of the Kalahari dance, the whole world dances.* You know this one, I think.' Dawid fixed me with a mischievous eye.

We sat in silence, waiting to hear more, but in that half minute, as if from nowhere, a cold wind sprang up. Suddenly the air smelled of rain, the wind began to race, blowing sand. To the north, a great bolt of lightning cracked white across the night, then real African thunder, loud as an exploding bomb. Dawid shook his head: 'Where did this come from? A wind like this brings scorpions, they run in front of it. We should not sit here now. There's a big rain coming, we must go inside and sleep.' Belinda and I sprinted for the car, parked in the sand nearby, as the first fat raindrops fell.

The following night we found the whole clan gathered inside the Red House. Dawid welcomed us in, sat us down at the fire and began to talk, as if picking up a previous conversation. 'Blood, it's all the same. No matter what you are – full blood, half blood, quarter –' he fixed Belinda with a glittering eye. 'Black, white,' he turned to me, stretching across the low fire and squeezing my arm, 'in the end, blood will find blood. The same, all of us, all from the same stem . . .'

At that moment Bukse staggered in, drunk. His shirt and trousers, always ragged, hung in soiled shreds. On top of this he wore a *xai*, the Bushman's skin loincloth. Dangling loosely over his groin, it looked absurd, like an outsize, furry scrotum. Dawid fell silent, frowned and looked up at his younger brother. With a loud cough, Bukse pulled a half-bottle of brandy from his pocket and insisted that Belinda and I share a drink with him. The rest of the clan looked on, waiting to see what would happen.

Dawid said quietly: 'Bukse, sit down, I'm talking now. Sit down and be quiet.'

Bukse raised his fists: 'Who are you to tell me what to do? You aren't the leader! The only leader I respect is Mackai!'

Immediately Dawid was on his feet, shouting back: '*Ja*! Mackai gave the leadership to me! Left me to lead a pack of drunk, useless . . .' he could not go on. Spitting with rage he reached out a sinewy arm, tore the *xai* from Bukse's groin and threw it into a corner. 'How dare you wear the traditional clothes when you're drunk! How dare you insult the ancestors!' There was a moment's silence. Then Dawid pointed out into the night: 'Go then! Go if you don't want me as leader! Go join Jakob and Sillikat and the rest of the whiners by the side of the road. Go back to your hut in the bush!'

Bukse swayed, then collapsed into a little heap of shredded clothing, sobbing to himself. Dawid looked down at him, 'You, you're a *fok-gat* [fuck-arse].' Then to the silent faces of the clan: 'How can I lead such a pack of fools?' On the fire before us, the pot began to boil. Dawid regarded it for a long moment, then said, almost to himself: 'I should take that boiling water and throw it over them all.' Then he sighed, looked up at us and shrugged his knotted old shoulders, 'But then I'd be a bad leader, wouldn't I?'

Belinda got up, throwing a long shadow on the Red House wall. '*Oompie* Dawid, I can see this is a bad time. Perhaps we'd better go.'

Dawid nodded, still staring into the fire. 'Perhaps you had better go. Come back in the morning when things are quiet. There is still a lot I need to tell you.'

Ever since I'd been there last, the Xhomani had been like this, said Belinda as we drove back to the Red House again the following morning: a perpetual emotional roller coaster.

In the three short months that I had been away, much had happened at Welkom, not only in terms of the land claim, which had moved on several stages, but also for Belinda, whom the Xhomani had virtually adopted. Inevitably, she had been drawn into the politics of the Xhomani themselves, and to some extent, the land claim.

The organisation that was handling Bushman affairs in South Africa (SASI, the South African San Institute) and Roger Chennels, the human rights lawyer, had managed to get the Minister of Land Affairs, Derek Hanekom, to agree to a tentative date in April for the signing of the land claim. The Bushmen had been very excited all through the preceding months. But nothing had happened. There was silence from the SASI office in Cape Town, silence from the ministry in Pretoria, silence from the park. The Bushmen sat in the dunes, wondering, frustrated and angry. In their frustration, they had begun to turn on each other: there had been a lot of drinking and violence. Rikki, Jakob, even old Dawid, were beating up their wives almost daily, and the children were asking Belinda a question she couldn't answer: 'Why do the grown-ups drink?'

Sillikat, who had come back from Kagga Kama for a while, had answered the question one night: 'You want to know why I drink? I drink because I feel like a caged animal. In the old days this clan, when we disagreed, would have split up, different families going off to live where they pleased, coming together again as they pleased, no problems, no fighting. But we can't move, can't go anywhere except the road. So we drink, and when we drink, the anger comes, and we fight.'

Some had moved – but only as far as the road. Jakob and Leana, Sillikat and Elsie, Bukse and his wife, had all established little grass shelters every few kilometres or so between Welkom and the park, and each had set up their own stall in competition with the others. Money earned from craft sales and occasional film crews (organised by Cait Andrews from Cape Town) was no longer filtering into the community as a whole, but staying with certain families. Some people were going hungry. Resentments routinely flared into confrontations. Sillikat had been stabbed in the neck by Elsie after beating her one night. Rikki had been set upon by the whole clan, and the subsequent battering had laid him up for a week. Kabuis, the Xhomani's best tracker, who was currently working deep inside the park with a team of biologists and earning good money, had been unable to protect his wife, Betty, from being beaten up by the other women in the clan, who were jealous of the money her husband brought home. The police had often been involved. Fines had been levied that the Bushmen could ill afford, and the threat of stiffer sentences now hung over Sillikat, Rikki, Jakob, and several others.

On the positive side, just before my arrival, Roger Chennels had organised a local workshop to discuss the land claim. Everyone of importance had been there: the National Parks Board, represented by Dries Engelbrecht, and also the regional director for the whole Northern Cape province, Dick Parris; Dawid and the Welkom Bushmen; the SASI representatives. They had met for two days and, despite much suspicion and frequently flaring tempers, all had agreed that, in principle, the claim should go forward, and that everyone's differences could be ironed out, given time. Belinda confessed that she now felt completely committed to the Bushmen's claim: 'I guess these past three months I haven't really realised it but now, sitting here telling it all as a story I can see. I'm going to be here until the Bushmen get their land. Until they're wandering in the park again like they used to. Until the story's done. Who knows how long it's going to take? But when it happens, I'll be here.'

We sat awhile, looking over the empty veld. To the south of us, a dust cloud appeared above the road. Soon a large white Toyota materialised out of the heat haze. 'That's a ranger's vehicle,' said Belinda sharply, putting out the joint she had just lit and returning it to the little leather pouch that Dawid had given her. But when it was a hundred and fifty or so yards away the vehicle stopped, and two men got out and began to walk on the bare sand of the riverbed. One I recognised as Malcolm, the rest camp manager. The other, smaller man, was Steven Smith, son of the Mier leader Piet Smith, whom I had met before in Henriette Engelbrecht's office and whom I knew to be the only non-white manager at Twee Rivieren apart from Belinda. 'I thought he was in the Social Ecology department,' I said, recalling his presence during that crazy interview. 'No,' replied

Belinda, her eyes on the two men, who seemed to be intent on something on the ground. 'He couldn't stand Henriette. Said she was too racist. He's transferred to work with the rangers.'

Off to the left some kind of animal had sat up in the yellow grasses that grew patchily along the edge of the sandstone cliff that marked the Botswana side of the wide riverbed. Then the silhouettes of three large cats emerged, sitting on their haunches and watching the two men, who were now pacing slowly along the riverbed, following whatever track they had come out to inspect. At this distance it was hard to tell what type of cats they could be. The three animals rose from their sitting positions and began to stalk forward towards the men. They seemed to be moving quite fast – perhaps intending to make a sudden rush.

Just as we were about to shout a warning, one of the cats stepped out into the space between two patches of grassland and displayed itself fully: it was a cheetah. Relieved, Belinda and I let out a long breath; cheetahs do not hunt people. But they are notoriously inquisitive, a trait which has led them to become an endangered species, for once their curiosity is piqued they will show themselves openly where more wily cats, such as leopards, lions or lynx, never will. The old adage of 'curiosity killed the cat' applies firmly to cheetahs. The three creatures sat down once again, simply watching the two men, who now appeared satisfied with whatever they had come to see and walked back to their vehicle. They climbed in and drove away. The show over, the three cats got up and slowly crossed the road to the South African side of the dry riverbed, climbing up into the dunes and disappearing into the dry wilderness beyond.

I was quietly pleased. They were the first cheetahs I had seen wild in the Kalahari. But Belinda was even more excited.

'No one's seen cheetahs at this end of the park for months. It means something's up. You remember how Izak told you to look out for anything unusual among the animals while you were down at Kagga Kama? [I had told Belinda about the incident with the mantis, the mouse and the bird.] Well, Dawid's been telling me the same thing all this past month. I'm sure this means something,

I've got a gut feeling. We'll go to Welkom tonight and ask him.'

We had two more strange encounters on the way back to Twee Rivieren. Though dusk was a good hour off and the sun still bright, we had to brake suddenly as a great horned owl swooped suddenly low across our windscreen, and landed on the branch of a camelthorn tree overhanging the road, glaring at us with great saucer eyes as if defying us. A mile or so further on, a large mouse ran out into the road, stopped and looked at us a long moment, then scurried off. Like owls, Kalahari mice are usually nocturnal. In the course of some years of driving African roads I had never seen one run out in daylight like that, much less stop and stare.

Walking into the Red House that night, Belinda and I received an enthusiastic welcome. Old Anna, who along with Antas was one of Regopstaan's two surviving siblings, grabbed me in her strong, lean old arms and started to kiss me roughly with lips that were dry on the outside and wet like peach-flesh on the inside. When Dawid came shambling in to separate us, amiably pulling his drunken aunt off me, she berated him and struck out.

'Ja Mama,' said Dawid, seating himself stiffly at the side of the low-burning fire and motioning for us to do the same. 'So what d'you say?'

Like excited children, Belinda and I told him what we'd seen in the park that afternoon.

In response Dawid said: 'You Rru, Rupi, Rupe-man,' he nodded at me, a teasing smile on his face. 'You're everywhere, yes? The bird, flying here, flying there. Well, Dawid Kruiper is everywhere too. What do you think I saw a couple of months ago down in Upington? You can't guess? On a computer, you people call it "internet", yes? They showed me: we looked up "Bushman" and "Dawid Kruiper", and guess what? I was everywhere! Me! Old Dawid, who can't even walk up the sand dunes any more!' He burst into one of his coughing laughs, the rest of the clan looking on. Belinda and I sat patiently waiting for him to come to the point.

'Ja!' he went on. 'And not just on the computers. I've flown around. To other countries even. A few years ago, Michael Daiber, that naughty man who used to be working with us down at Kagga

Kama, he and me, we went to Geneva, Switzerland, for the indigenous peoples' conference. Very important! Like Mandela, sitting up in the seats with the ladies coming round and giving us drinks.' Dawid's face puckered into a mass of happy wrinkles. 'I drank too much. And soon I need to find somewhere to let my water out. But I'm up in the sky, in this big sky bus – heads, heads, heads everywhere in front, behind, on either side. For sixteen hours I stayed in my seat, surrounded by that sea of little heads, dying to piss. I thought I would faint. You see, no one had told me there were toilets on the plane. I thought it was like a bus, but in the sky: sometime they would land and let everyone off for a piss, just like they do on the buses to Cape Town! Stupid Bushman!'

The old man paused, first to cough, then to reach out for the marijuana pouch. Clearly his story had just begun. So we, and the rest of the Xhomani, waited until he was ready to go on.

'Ah Belinda,' he said fondly, eyes twinkling, '*My wonderlekker meisie van die Kaap* [my wonder-lovely girly from the Cape]. The forefathers are watching, eh? Watching it all. *Ou Mackai te Kiraha, eh? Jasus!*' He lumbered to his feet, at once both awkward and limber and danced a step or two. Looking at me, he said, 'You have danced with the Bushmen now. Now you see the old man dance.' He pointed to his *xai*. 'Dancing in his nappy! *Eh-hey!*'

The laughter rattled in his chest. 'Yes, my friends. The park is a lion.' Dawid ran his hand over his greying hair and squinted up at the smoky rafters, as if looking there for inspiration. 'And who are we? We are the little people, the jackals that sit in the dunes and wait while the lions eat their kill. We wait and wait until finally the lions have had their fill and fall asleep. Only then can we creep in and eat our share. *Ja Mama*, we are the people that sit in the dunes and wait. But soon, soon, the jackal will ride on the lion's back.

'You know what Mackai meant when he said "the strangers will come"? He didn't just mean the people that are working for us, for the land – you Belinda, Rupe-man there, Roger, Cait, all the friends. No, he also meant all the broken people. The people in pain, the hungry ones, the ones without homes, without a place, the ones who need healing. The people like us, the little jackals. They will have a home with Dawid Kruiper, when he gets his land again. When he gets Dawid's land and the little people dance.'

Outside it began to rain, very gently. It was growing late and the old man clearly wasn't going to tell us what we wanted to know. Belinda got up, I followed suit, and we walked to the wide-open entrance. Dawid came with us, saying: 'Ah my friends, you see, you bring the rain. Just a little for now. It's good that you have your eyes open in the veld, that you're beginning to see the patterns there. This is just the beginning. Do you understand? The beginning. Keep on as you are, keep those eyes open. Come and see old Dawid again in a couple of nights' time and tell him what else you have seen.'

As we walked back through the light, misty drizzle to the car, we heard the people singing: '*Ou Mackai te Kiraha*' and laughing.

On the way home, we drove past the roadside huts. As we passed each lone fire, each solitary shelter of grass and branches, a figure would run out and wave us down; they knew Belinda's car. But when we got to the last shelter – Jakob and Leana's – no one came out. We slowed and heard shrieking, sobbing, so we stopped and got out, walked over to the dim fire just in time to see Leana lurch towards her husband, a sinewy arm raised, and strike him a heavy blow on the side of the head. He, sitting hunched and dejected, accepted the blow, then another, with an air of resignation.

'Ah Leana!' said Belinda softly, as we approached. 'Stop, stop now. What is it? What's wrong?'

'*Ay Belindy*!' yelled Leana, crying and weeping, and then, in a torrent of Afrikaans, spilled out her heart. Jakob had beaten her yet again, he always beat her, with sticks, with *assegais*. 'Sometimes I wake up and find his fingers round my throat! I'm not joking! Look at him there, quiet like he's never done anything wrong! Last night he choked me so that I almost died before he let me go. Then he laughed! He's sick! Sick!' As she spoke, Jakob just sat there, looking at the ground, saying nothing. Night after night it was like this, wailed Leana. She could not show her face and body in daylight for the cuts and the bruises. 'One day,' her voice sank to a low, danger-ous tone: 'One day I will kill him where he sleeps! If he does not kill me first.'

Both of them were drunk, but her words were sincere. Jakob would look neither at her nor at us. '*Belindy*,' said Leana, calming down, 'sing with me. Make my heart sing. Make my heart quiet.'

Jakob kept silent. But as they sang – a child's rhyme in the Nama language – the high hunch of his shoulders relaxed, and he reached under his blanket for his pipe. After a while, Leana sniffed, smiled a little embarrassedly, and went into her shelter to sleep.

I realised then that it was going to take a lot more than a land claim to heal the Xhomani.

10

The Same Blood

Time was slipping by. Each day, Belinda and I made forays into the park and saw the same animals, the cheetahs, the owl and the mouse. Yet each night, when we told Dawid he refused to speak directly about it. Meanwhile five days had passed and I had done nothing to arrange transportation and accommodation for the rest of the journey. So, while Belinda went about her morning duties down at the camp's reception, I monopolised her telephone, battling with the crackly, indistinct line, calling around the car hire companies in Upington and steeling myself to ring Gert and Cynthia Loxton. I felt slightly awkward about this, perhaps because I had been supposed to make contact with them way back in 1992 when I had been researching the South African guidebook, and wondered if they would be offended.

At last, having found the right vehicle, I took a deep breath and rang the Loxtons and found myself speaking to my cousin Gert. The conversation was difficult especially as Gert obviously found English something of a struggle. I was far too ashamed of my pidgin Afrikaans to try it on him. Still, we managed to arrange a day to meet at his farm, which lay on the tar road to Namibia and western Botswana, where I would be going when I left to head north.

I went down to the park shop to buy some groceries. At the cash register was a KhoiSan-looking young man, smart and in his regulation green military-style sweater. We chatted a little and I asked him where he came from originally.

'From right here,' he told me with a hint of pride, 'In the desert.'

'Ah, so do you speak Nama as well as Afrikaans then?'

The young man grinned, white and broad, 'I am Nama.'

'Ah, then do you know this song?' I asked, and sang the first line of the Nama song that Leana and Belinda had sung in the wet dunes the night before.

The young man's face clouded with anger. 'Why should I?' he snapped. 'I'm not a *blerrie* Bushman!'

When I told Belinda later she put her head back and roared: '*Ach ja*, I tell you, Ru, you don't know racism until you get among the coloureds. To them being associated with a Bushman is worse than being called a dog, common ancestry or no common ancestry. I know it's pathetic, we should all be *Hotnots* together. But you know, if you've got lighter skin, more European features then you've got a better chance. There's a whole hierarchy within the coloured world that you don't even know.'

Later, smoking a joint on the dune behind her little house Belinda began talking about Vetpiet, one of the Bushmen that worked in the park. 'He's one of the rangers. He's Dawid's age, maybe a little younger. They were brought up together. He and *Ou* Dawid used to work together in the park under the old head wardens – the Leriche family. Except that when the Bushmen were kicked out of the park, Dawid went, because he'd already been chosen as the next leader, and Vetpiet stayed. He still works here.'

'Dawid used to work as a ranger?'

'Yes, he and Vetpiet are cousins. Vetpiet's supposed to be the best tracker in the whole Kalahari. All the wildlife biologists that come here, they all ask for him first to help them in the field. If they can't get him they ask for Kabuis, that's Betty's husband, or Bukse – but Vetpiet's the one who still knows most about the veld. There are endless stories about him . . .'

I interrupted. 'I didn't know Bushmen worked in the park.'

'Yes', she said, impatient. 'Of course. Who else would the first wardens have got to do the job? There wasn't anyone else living around here who knew the Kalahari like the Bushmen did. No man, most of Regopstaan's sons and nephews worked as rangers at one time or another. Vetpiet's the last of that generation, but since Dries came to run the park, things have gone sour.'

Belinda then told me the story. Vetpiet, the son of a Xhomani woman and a local coloured man (who had not claimed the child) had been raised by Regopstaan. He and Dawid had therefore grown up together and worked together in the park as young men. After the Xhomani exodus, Vetpiet had become the right-hand man for the chief wardens, who had given him complete autonomy, his own rifle and vehicle, and relied on him to not only know everything that was going on with the animals, but also to track down and deal with poachers. However, when Dries Engelbrecht, the present chief warden, had taken over in the early 1990s, one of his first acts had been to demote Vetpiet and put a white man in authority over him. '*Ja*, he took away Vetpiet's gun and his vehicle and made him ride in the back of the white man's *bakkie* [pick-up] like a proper kaffir. One that knows his place. Vetpiet's very bitter.'

Vetpiet had complained to head office, but because Dries had not lessened his pay or his privileges, nothing had been done. Something of a quiet war was now going on between the two men. '*Ja*, you should hear Vetpiet sometime. Like now, he says poachers are coming in from the Botswana side, but that Dries won't let him go after them. He says the park's losing animals to these guys. And last year, when some lions got out through the fence on the Namibia side, Vetpiet said he was sure he could herd them back into the park alive. But he wasn't allowed to, and the farmer ended up killing them all. Vetpiet hates Dries, and I think Dries hates him for being a cheeky kaffir that won't do as he's told. And Vetpiet's worried, because if he oversteps the mark, he might lose his job and his pension, and he's close to retiring.' It seemed that the park's involvement with the Bushmen went way beyond a simple stand-off over territory.

We could not go to see Dawid that night, because Belinda had promised to attend a *braai* (barbecue) cooked by some of the student rangers in the park. It was a true gathering of the New South Africa with students garnered from every racial group. Their conversation was about the future of the National Parks, especially this one, which was soon to be declared the first of a series of 'peace parks', or trans-frontier parks in southern Africa, aimed at promoting open borders within the sub-continent.

Eleanor, a young coloured student, pointed out that the trans-frontier idea could hardly work, however, unless the park found a way to make money. The Kalahari Gemsbok Park was the second largest in South Africa, and one of the most visited. Yet it was nearly bankrupt, and the word from head office was that the current subsidy that kept it afloat would soon be slashed. Parks in the New South Africa were going to have to generate their own revenue. Cor – a young Afrikaner – explained: 'Under apartheid, everything was run by whites, or by blacks who would do what the whites told them. It didn't exactly make for an environment that fostered talent. So much money was wasted on bureaucracy, there was a lot of corruption. You got a lot of really incompetent, lazy people in positions of responsibility. That's the way the park is still run now. These guys, Dries and others, they don't care about the bush. Not really. They just want to push paper, draw a salary and be the big white *baas*. They've got no idea how to be entrepreneurs or make conservation work.'

'But surely that's where the Bushmen come in,' I said. 'If the park were to have them lead groups of tourists on hunting and gathering forays, tell stories, that kind of thing, wouldn't that generate a lot of cash? Wouldn't people flock in?'

This time Belinda answered: 'Of course it would, but that will take a leap of imagination that just isn't there at present. One of the other senior managers – a guy called Maarten Engelbrecht – same name as Dries but no relation, though he's Dries' right-hand man, told me the other day that every time I went to the Bushmen I was "dancing with Satan". That's the mentality you're dealing with.'

She went on, 'Most of these people are fine one-to-one. I'm sure if you needed anything, were short of money or whatever, Dries would help you out, look after you, see you right. He's a decent guy in that regard. It's just that this is South Africa. They think in terms of their own group. And the Afrikaners' group, the old-school *Broederbond*★

★The *Broederbond* (or brotherhood) was a secret society of Afrikaner businessmen, farmers and government workers who, while South Africa was still under British rule, used to meet and formulate plans for taking power. They are largely credited with engineering the landslide election victory that brought apartheid into being in 1948. Despite the arrival of the New South Africa, the *Broederbond* is reputedly still alive and well.

Afrikaners, are feeling threatened. Anyone who represents change is the enemy. It's the same with everyone, whites, black, coloureds. Your own group first, outsiders second.'

Much later that night, as we smoked a knock-out joint in the candle-light of Belinda's back porch, she poured out her own story. Born into an educated, politically active Cape coloured family, she had experienced her country's special brand of violence and negativity from day one. Her father, a church minister and local political lobbyist much respected by the community, had – behind closed doors – beaten her and her brother almost daily. Later, despite being the perfect daughter, she had broken the rules and married a white man, incurring all her family's wrath. 'You're supposed to marry the lightest skinned coloured you can. But a white man – that's betraying your race. God, the hypocrisy!' Her husband had then repeated the father's pattern, beating her whenever he felt himself not in control of his wife. 'Imagine how it was, Ru, having been the big rebel and married this white guy, and now realising it was a huge mistake. He used to say: "I can't control you, I wish I could control you . . ." How could I go back to the family and say – *ja* I made a mistake, this white man beats me. It would have been too humiliating, so I stuck with it, stuck with being the perfect wife, just like I'd been the perfect daughter, until one year we went travelling. Went to see his people in London. Travelled down through Africa together. And it was as if I suddenly woke up. So I left him, and the family couldn't understand it. Marrying a white man had been bad enough, but divorcing?'

A short time after leaving her husband, Belinda had gone to stay with an aunt in Johannesburg. One night, while unlocking the front gate of the house, she had felt a knife at her neck. 'Come with us', a voice had said, and she had gone, afraid to breathe lest the blade cut deeper in. The two men had taken her to a dark place not far away and stripped her. 'They were young black guys, Zulus I think, by the way they talked. Anyway, once I was lying there, before raping me, they hit me and kicked me for a while. And all the while I'm calm, I'm just praying; God, be with me. Be with me. And then they start talking, and I hear the one guy tell the other he feels he

163

must kill tonight, that he must have blood. And I knew I had to do something.' Incredibly, she had leapt to her feet, kicked the one with the knife hard in the crotch and run for it. They had given chase, but Belinda had made it through the gate, safely into her aunt's yard.

The aunt's reaction had been to tell her that it was her own fault, that such things would not happen to her if she went to church more often, if she led a more God-fearing life. After that Belinda had cut her long black hair (her father's and her husband's pride and joy) and applied to the National Parks Board, to take refuge in nature. 'So you see Ru, there's so much hatred, so much fear, so much mistrust, even among my own people. Even with you, there's a part of me that says, here's another white guy just wanting to use me for something. What does he want? To use me as a way of getting to the Bushmen? How's this one going to hurt me? It's probably the same for your cousins down in Upington – even if they have been to England. No man, here it's a different story. You can bet they're nervous about your coming; nervous of what their neighbours will say, nervous to have a white guy, even if he's a relative – especially if he's a relative – staying on their turf.'

Around us the night was thick, warm, close. 'So now you have my story – why I came to this Kalahari. To heal. Everyone comes here to heal, whether they know it or not. Even Dries. Even you. Whatever reason you think has brought you here, this interest in the Bushmen or whatever you say it is, the real reason is that you have something in you that needs to heal, you can be sure of that.'

Next morning, my last, I was down at reception, chatting with Themba, a student ranger from the Xhosa tribe, when one of the ladies working there said out of the blue: 'Hey, didn't Belinda say you were related to the Loxtons in Keimoes? Well, two people called Loxton have just checked in. Maybe they're cousins of yours?'

I wandered down to the sun-baked camp site and found a middle-aged man and his wife pitching tent. I introduced myself and, after a minute's talk, found that they were indeed cousins, albeit distant ones, from the town of Loxton in Australia, founded by cousins of the Loxton brothers who had come to South Africa. I asked them how long they were going to be in the area. Did they know they had Loxton cousins here in the Kalahari, in Upington? They didn't, so I filled them in on the story – Frederick William Loxton and the Baster *kaptein*'s daughter. They took Gert and Cynthia's phone number, and my address. They were moving on to the north of the park now, but they might try and look in on Gert and Cynthia when they went back south.

I wandered back up to reception, shaking my head at the coincidence, and thanked the receptionist for her tip-off. Her reply made me go dizzy. 'Here, wait a moment,' she said. 'Aren't the Smiths – Piet and Steven Smith, the Mier lot – aren't they related to the Loxtons as well?'

As luck would have it, I had brought a Loxton family tree that my mother had printed out for me. I raced back to Belinda's house to retrieve it. Sure enough, the connection was there – Piet Smith's father had been half-brother to Gert Loxton's father. It was tenuous, but the blood tie existed. Piet Smith, the head of the Mier, and the principal opponent of the Xhomani land claim, was my cousin.

'You're joking,' said Belinda, when I told her later that afternoon.

'No joke.' And I showed her the family tree.

The stories I'd heard about Piet Smith were not good – and not simply because he was opposed to the Bushman land claim. A local coloured man of the same generation had told me Piet had been one of apartheid's 'good boys', that he had been given farms in return for local co-operation with the white government – farms to which he had no legal title and therefore stood to lose, without compensation, should the Bushman land claim be successful, and a compulsory purchase of Mier land go through. What had this 'co-operation' involved, I had asked? The man had looked down a moment, then said: 'Anyone who was suspected of agitation, of anti-apartheid activities, anyone involved in the "struggle"; if Smith heard about it, he'd make the right phone call and say: Those guys, take them.'

But I asked, would there not be reprisals from within the community for a collaborator? 'No,' the man had told me. 'You don't keep a position like that without making people afraid. Piet Smith has power. Whatever he tells the Mier to do, they'll do.'

Rumour, often unsubstantiated, is the lifeblood of the Kalahari. I had also heard that Smith's uncompromising stance against the Bushmen stemmed from a simple if over-zealous desire to protect the interests of his own people. He resented – to the point of irrationality – anything he perceived as a threat to them. There were plenty of stories about him funding from his own pocket projects that he thought would help the Mier community.

Belinda's voice brought me back to the present. 'But you know Rru, this couldn't have come at a better time, because Steven's really been on the Bushmen's backs these past few months. Maybe he feels he has to because of his Dad or something, but he's really been up to shit at Welkom, and he's been stirring shit for me too.' Steven had, she said, visited Welkom on a few occasions, asking loaded questions about Belinda's dope-smoking. If she were caught doing this it could be a pretext for firing her. The Bushmen had successfully fielded his questioning but had been worried. When he came again, and yet again, they had become angry. Rikki, in particular, had been incensed – said Belinda. He had got drunk, climbed the fence into the park and threatened Steven at his own front door. The following day, sober, he and Bukse had given Belinda a piece of bitter bark. She pulled it out of her dope pouch and showed it to me – a small piece of grey bark about half the size of a fingernail. 'They told me to chew a little of this each day, and while I did it, to think of the bad shit about Steven. Then to swallow the juice and spit out the wood bits and not think about it any more. That way, they said, my relationship – and theirs – with Steven, would improve. I've only got a very little bit left, it's almost finished. And now look what's happened! Oh man, just wait until we tell *oompie* Dawid!'

Before going out to the Red House that evening, I took a deep breath and walked across to Steven's house, the sound of cheery voices and the scent of grilling meat wafting my way. There was no way to enter politely, no door to knock on, so I simply walked into the edge of the firelight and stood shyly while, as expected, the conversation stopped. Steven was standing, beer in hand, next to

Henna, his very pregnant wife. They and the guests, all coloured staff from the non-managerial compound over by the park's back fence, looked up with questioning eyes.

'Er, sorry to interrupt. It won't take long. Um, Steven, do you think I could have a quick word?'

'Sure,' he said, coming forward. We hadn't spoken, nor seen each other since that one afternoon in Henriette Engelbrecht's office. I told him, as succinctly as possible, what I had found out that afternoon. His deep brown eyes looked straight into mine, as if to make sure that I wasn't joking. For a moment he seemed almost hostile, then his shoulders relaxed, his eyes softened and he scratched his head, charmingly puzzled. 'So . . .' he said.

'So . . . cousin.' I grinned. He grinned too, and, after a moment of awkward shuffling, we both stepped forward to embrace. It was the only thing to do.

'Listen,' I said, 'I don't want to drag you away from your party. Are you around tomorrow?'

'Ja, I am, but I'm leaving pretty much straight after work to go home for the weekend.'

'OK, say I come by about four-thirty? I can show you the family tree my mum printed out for me, and we can make some kind of plan perhaps.'

'Ja, OK, do that . . . cousin.'

There were few people in the Red House that night. Only Antas and Anna hovered gently in the background, their humming and quiet singing mingling pleasantly with the deep, even breath of sleeping children and the tiny old man with the guitar who never spoke, but who always sat in the darkest of the corners, watching with small dark eyes like a mouse. Dawid grinned, bade us sit and, as usual, began to roll up a fat, conical newspaper joint while we told him about the repeated encounters with the same animals.

'Ja Julle [yes, you guys],' he said, as if to limber up his throat and his thoughts. 'These animals you've seen – each day the same ones – these are good signs. The mouse, that's strength, you know that. The quiet strength of one who works long, who works away, maybe without others knowing, but whose work eventually comes out

167

when the time is right. The cheetahs – now that is calm, gentleness. We call them "Bushman pets". They show that you can go after what you want, what you need, single-mindedly like a cat, but gently, not with anger like a lion. And the owls, now that is the ability to see further.'

He looked up to make sure we were listening. I could contain my news no longer, and told him what I had found out about Steven and Piet Smith. I had been expecting Dawid to fall over with shock. He didn't, but greeted the information with a single low, drawn-out whistle. '*Is dit*? [is that so?],' he said, almost matter-of factly. '*Is dit*? You, Steven and old Piet Smith cousins eh?

'It shows that Steven, even his dad, can't be bad as we thought, that they have good blood. You know what this makes me think? That we have been going about this all the wrong way. With hate, and fighting in our hearts – not the Bushman way. No, we have gone away from the love. Unless the land comes to us with love it'll be worthless, it won't sustain us. Unless the Mier and the park and all the others let us in with love we might as well keep on sitting here by the road. No, we are the ones who must show them how it must be done. If we don't have love in our hearts, how can we expect them not to hate us? And if the land comes, but not with love, then it will never be Bushman land. Not truly. We will never be secure in it if we claim it with fear and with hate.

'So Rru, look what you bring. And now, tomorrow off you go again – the bird once more – to see the other Bushmen, to spread the word, bring the word back. So you must go. When you come back we will talk again. But now it is time for you to go out,' and he waved his arm wide in a sweeping gesture that took in Welkom, the dunes, the wide sky, the park, the dry Nossob and Aub riverbeds that ran through them and all the vastness beyond.

I had said nothing as yet to Dawid about my mission to find Besa, although Belinda knew. Was it the right time to tell him? I turned the thought over in my head. No, somehow it seemed that to speak now might chase away the luck. I'd wait and see if I even found Besa. After that, maybe, I'd have something to say.

★   ★   ★

Before leaving the following morning, I went to see Steven. We kept it brief, being still shy of each other, and slightly incredulous at the turn events had taken. We swapped family addresses, looked again at the family tree. When I came back from the north, he said, he'd take me to see his father. But I mustn't expect the old man to be happy at the news.

11

Dream and Disillusion

At first sight, there was nothing to distinguish Gert Loxton's farm from any white Boer's: the white-washed, one-storey, tin-roofed Cape Dutch house, complete with curly gables; the three big, growly dogs – a Rottweiler, a shepherd and some kind of muscular hybrid of the two; the tamarind and eucalyptus trees shading a large, rectangular patch of irrigated lawn that shone dazzlingly green against the surrounding brown of the sun-baked landscape. Gert's wife Cynthia, a neat, good-looking matron with a fifties' hairdo and a floral-print dress coming down to mid-calf, gave me a controlled, cousinly welcome and led me into the living room. Once there I saw what marked this house out as different.

On one wall of the comfortably furnished room hung a big picture of Nelson Mandela. Few white farmers had any love for old Madiba. Nor indeed did many prosperous coloured households, most of whom now aligned themselves with the National Party, which had transformed itself since the apartheid days into a moderate party for Afrikaans speakers (most of whom, it should be remembered, were coloured, not white). Piet Smith was a Nationalist Party MP. The ANC was seen predominantly as the party for young, ambitious blacks, and mostly Xhosas at that. That cousin Gert – clearly a more prosperous coloured farmer than most – should be so openly ANC suggested something of an original turn of mind.

Tea and biscuits arrived and Cynthia asked me how I liked the Kalahari and enquired after my mother, entertaining me until Gert appeared. He was a man of middle height, with a thickset physique that made him seem taller than he really was; grey, once black hair, and the grumpy-looking, stoic face, khaki shorts, pants and socks pulled-up-to-middle-calf typical of the South African farmer. His face was still handsome, yet seemed set in a permanent frown. His voice, when he spoke, was soft. He enquired after my mother, Polly, my sister Hannah, my father. I realised, in a rush of relief, that behind this harsh exterior was someone very gentle. After a heavy lunch of macaroni cheese, Gert asked me if I would like to see the farm.

The land, which occupied several islands in the wide, sluggish Orange River, was an emerald surrounded by parched, rocky gold. Water from the river, fed into irrigation channels and judiciously applied to the rich, dark alluvial soil, gave life to serried ranks of Chardonnay and sultana vines, fields of alfalfa and tall rows of cotton. A small army of boiler-suited coloured and BaTswana farmworkers tended this green domain. We drove from field to field in Gert's silver *bakkie* (pick-up truck), surprising great herons that flapped unhurriedly into the air, and troops of startled vervet monkeys who, caught raiding the vines, went scurrying off into the riverside trees. Gert laughed: 'The monkeys and the baboons – that's a war we'll never win.'

But they had won the battle to keep the land during apartheid. 'Yes,' he acknowledged. 'It was a struggle holding onto this as coloureds. Not easy, not easy at all.'

As we drove around his paradise, Gert told the story. After apartheid had been ratified in 1948, the local Nationalist Party bosses had turned envious eyes on the Loxton land, as well as on the farms of the other prosperous coloureds in the district. By the early 1960s, when Gert and his brothers took over the farm, many coloured farmers had been forced to sell out, at a huge loss, to whites, because the Land Bank – the government's agricultural financial machine upon which farmers relied – cut off all coloured credit. Gert had managed to find private financing, but even he could not save all the family holdings. Some vineyards which lay technically within the city limits of Keimoes were confiscated under the Group Areas Act, which made it illegal for non-whites to live in, much less own, property in white areas. But the Loxtons held on to what they could. Realising they meant to resist for ever, the local race relations officials had then changed tack. They tried to persuade the family to re-register as white. The Loxtons stood firm: all but one sister, who did make the strange conversion (spending thousands of rand from her own pocket to fund a farce in which various Afrikaner clergy, witnesses and 'racial experts' were called into a courtroom to testify to her 'whiteness'). She was now a virtual stranger to the family, living far away in Johannesburg.

'Listen Rupert,' said Gert, his voice suddenly sharp as we bumped over a narrow bridge that spanned one of the many waterways that separated his bountiful fields. 'The problem in this country has always been racism – it's everywhere, in everyone. The farms around here – maybe 90 per cent of them are white-owned. They still won't deal with us. The people at the Land Bank, they *have* to deal with us now, but they don't like to. Racism's still the centre of everything. It breaks up families.' There was deep-seated anger in his voice.

On the way back to the homestead we passed a marble monument that the family had erected in 1994 to mark the centenary of the Loxton farms. '*Ja*,' smiled Gert as we got out and contemplated the small, hexagonal pillar whose polished surface reflected the blinding sun. 'When everyone else was celebrating the New South Africa in 1994, we were also celebrating our own century. It started with clearing wild land, now the farms have schools, computers, over five hundred people working on them in the high season. We've come a long way.'

'I guess the original Basters would be proud,' I said.

Gert looked at me: 'What is this word Baster? That's a historical word. We haven't used it for years. We're just Loxtons.'

And now, having broken the ice, it was his turn to ask questions. When we were back in the car he asked me what exactly was my purpose here? It was clear that this was no ordinary family visit. Taking a deep breath, I filled him in as best I could. When I had finished, he gave a soft whistle. 'Bushmen? A land claim? Well . . .' he chortled, both amused and bemused. 'Bushmen wanting land? I never knew that. What do they want land for?'

'Well,' I said, somewhat at a loss, 'They want the land back that they used to have, the land they were kicked out from . . .' I trailed off. 'Don't you think they should have land?'

'I don't take it serious,' Gert answered pragmatically. 'The Bushman likes to hunt. Them as farmers? No, I don't think so. Perhaps if someone gives them a piece of wild land, you know, with game . . . perhaps then tourists could come . . . take photos . . .'

I told him that this was what the Bushmen had in mind, more or less.

'Really?' Gert seemed genuinely surprised. 'People is interested in trying to make that happen?'

I assured him that many already were. Though, equally, many were trying to stop it, and I told him about the Mier, though not – as yet – about my discovery of the family connection there.

'Well,' said Gert thoughtfully. 'That's a difficult question. As a farmer I have to say I can see the Mier's concern. You know, we Loxtons too, we are also fighting a land claim to get back the property in Keimoes, the vineyards and other places that were taken away from us.' He paused, then laughed: 'So we're all Bushmen then.'

We drove on a short way before he spoke again. 'Tell me, are the Bushmen's ancestors buried on that land?'

Surprised at the question, I told him they were.

'Well, that's a very different matter. Still tricky but – I know a lot of those Mier farmers. They say that the Bushmen are just drinkers, lazy *skelms* what doesn't want to work.' He was silent a moment, then added, with a mischievous smile: 'Listen, when they see a Bushman, they don't see what you see – a man. They see a dog, a piece of rubbish by the side of the road that needs cleaning up.'

'So is their opposition just down to prejudice then?'

'Oh, you've really asked me a tricky question . . . yes, but also a lot of those Mier don't have titles to their farms, you know. They're probably worried that, if the government comes in and takes the land, they won't get proper compensation.'

I asked Gert if there had been any Bushmen on the Loxton farms when Gert was a child.

'Yes, quite a few,' he answered, reflecting. 'Not what you'd call "pure" Bushmen, not wearing skins and so on, but yes, they were there.'

'Did they sing, dance?'

'Oh yes, if you asked them to. If you'd come here ten years ago, you could have spoken to the last one – old Piet Nxumi. He was a real Bushman. I don't know where he came from, he was already an old man when he started working for me. Then there was old Sol, he also spoke the language, but he's gone. *Ja*, all these old folk on the farms used to gather *veldkos* [wild foods], go after the small game with dogs and spears and snares. My father knew all the wild plants from them and he taught us too when we were kids. He spoke their language too. I can't remember any of it though, it was all so long ago.'

Gert looked up into the blue sky beyond the dusty, insect-spattered windscreen. 'I had a Bushman nanny, *Ouma* Sanna. She would always heal us with plants if we got colic, or constipation. Sometimes she didn't even use anything, just rubbed our stomachs and sang a little and it would be gone. Many, many people around here believed that those people could cure cancer even. But now all that knowledge is gone. My father told us time and again about it. It took three plants to cure cancer, I remember he said. My father knew two of them, but they never showed him the third. They said that only Bushmen should be knowing that. I know they would make a solution of the three plants and then soak an animal skin and wrap it around the place that was affected . . . *ach* but I can't even remember. You'll have to ask your Dawid Kruiper. *Ja*, even when I was growing up, the Bushmen were almost gone.'

Back in the house, Gert showed me an old lithograph of Anna Booysens, the woman who had married my Loxton forebear. It was easy to see why my ancestor had fallen for her: a strong face, high cheekbones, a fine nose, dark eyebrows, sculpted lips and a determined look about her. In the same room hung a portrait of old Loxton, also good-looking, with a great, shaggy Victorian beard. The face behind the whiskers was familiar, he looked not unlike my cousin Bruno, the son of my mother's sister Lindsay.

We turned in early, and the following day I spent in Upington trying to arrange the vehicle that would take me back into the Kalahari. That second night Gert and Cynthia took me to dinner at a restaurant in town that overlooked the river. As we relaxed over the meal, Gert picked up the conversation of the previous day, with Cynthia listening and nodding. Race was something you just couldn't ignore, he said. It touched one's life at every level. For example, their son Trevor, who was my age and busy taking over the farms, had once fallen in love with the daughter of a staunch AWB family.* He had had to visit the girl at night, sneaking in through her bedroom window like an Afrikaner Romeo. Eventually, however, the affair had come out into the open and the two families, both outraged, had decided to meet. The girl's mother had stated her absolute opposition to the match. And, admitted Gert, neither he nor Cynthia could bear the thought of the farm going, however obliquely, to an AWB family – for that was how they pictured it if Trevor were to have a son by this girl. In the end, Gert had persuaded his son to give her up. And now, they chuckled, you should see the beauty that he had married.

Later, as Gert and I hit the whiskey, Cynthia having retired, he showed me a picture of his daughter-in-law. She was indeed a beauty, who would continue the family's tradition of good looks. A local girl too, and clever, a teacher in Keimoes. It was a shame I hadn't been able to come a week or two before so I could have met them – they were on holiday just now. With quiet pride, Gert refilled our glasses with J&B Rare. We went to bed drunk, laughing about we knew not what.

Next day, Gert saw me off at the farm gate. Maybe he would come up and see these crazy Bushmen next time, he said. Maybe he and old Dawid could compare notes about land claims. They were about the same age, after all, had both seen the changes come,

*The Afrikaner Weerstandbeweging, an extreme right-wing Afrikaner group dedicated to creating an Afrikaner state. Its bearded leader, Eugene Terr'blanche, pledged a race war if blacks took power. The AWB fizzled out of existence after Mandela's accession in 1994.

the old order begin to fall away. It might help erase the bad memory he had of the park: back in the 1970s, during the height of apartheid, he had taken the kids up there. They had pitched tent in Twee Rivieren's main campground, but when word had reached the park warden that non-whites were staying there, rangers had made them take down their tent and forced them to move to a barren area without water, without toilets, behind the staff quarters, before making them leave next day. The humiliation in front of his young children, who had thought that they or the family must have done something wrong, still twisted his gut to this day.

The road to Namibia was long, straight and seemingly endless. Small, dry conical hills, ancient spines of rock eroded by aeons of wind and frost into dinosaur skeletons; all flew by outside the window. I watched a pair of clapper larks – small brown birds – fighting in mid air, falling to earth together, then flying upward again, fighting on.

Little over a week had passed since I had returned to the Kalahari and already more had happened than I could possibly understand. What I could not yet see was any kind of whole picture, just a mass of stories woven and knotted together.

Late that night I pulled into the Chameleon, a backpackers' lodge in Windhoek run by an Australian friend, Jackie. As I had done with my friend Mondi the year before, I had arranged to meet up with an old buddy here, in order to share the driving and the costs. Greg and his girlfriend were already waiting for me, annoyed, for I was a couple of days late. And so, after a brief perusal of the Namibian newspaper headlines, 'Woman Gives Birth to Goat', at breakfast the following day, we hit the road north to Nyae Nyae and Makuri.

Two days of driving later, we arrived in Tsumkwe. Hoping to get a little information before making the final drive to Makuri, we went first to Nigel, the game-ranger's house, to find Vivaldi's *Four Seasons* wafting towards us through his open door. 'Come in, come in,' came the familiar, rough-edged voice, as we stood in the door-way, peering into the shady gloom. 'Long time no see. Sit down, sit down. I'll make you some tea. No, you make it, you know where everything is . . .' So, after making the introductions I went off to his spartan kitchen to boil a pan of water on the old gas stove. Stacked against the walls and windows were the same half-completed paintings of wildlife I had seen when I'd been there last. 'I've been experimenting with making paper,' I heard him telling Greg and Tracy. 'Look at this nice thick consistency. Know what I use? Elephant dung! *Ach*, but I never have time to finish anything.'

'So,' I said, coming back into the room with the teas, 'What's new?'

'You didn't hear?' said Nigel. 'They've won. The Ju'/Hoansi have won. Their land has been declared a game conservancy with them as custodians. The government ratified it. The Herero are out. More game's being introduced. It's a victory!'

'No, I hadn't heard,' I said, taking in the news. 'So what's the mood? I mean, the people must be celebrating, no?'

Nigel sipped his hot tea, beads of sweat appearing on his tanned, lined forehead. 'They haven't been letting off fireworks, if that's what you mean. But they know they've won. You have to pay a fee now, to go into the bush, you know.'

'What about Benjamin, have you seen him lately?'

'Benjamin? You'll have to ask around, man. I haven't seen him for a while.'

Makuri, when we reached it, lay in ruins, the mud walls of the little beehive huts tumbled to the ground, the thatched roofs fallen in. A short distance through the bush were a few new huts, but of a much smaller settlement. We walked in among them, passing the reddish hide of a recently killed hartebeest hung over a makeshift stand of poles to dry in the hot sun. In front of this, and surrounded by some young Bushmen I didn't recognise, sat old man /Kaece. He knew me immediately and jumped up, thrusting out his bearded chin, and began to shout in Ju'/Hoansi, rubbing his belly, rolling his eyes and holding out his hands to denote hunger.

Once /Kaece had run through his diatribe, he gave me a cursory embrace, like a curmudgeonly uncle forgiving an errant nephew, and sat down again, inviting me to do likewise. I asked the watching men if any spoke Afrikaans, and got a nod from one of them, a man of about thirty with a hunting bow slung over the shoulder of his tattered, soiled T-shirt. His name was Tomaas and he was a son of /Kaece's. He shrugged when I asked what had happened to the village. 'No tourists, no money, no one coming.' When I asked after Benjamin, he shrugged again. 'Maybe in Tsumkwe, maybe Baraka.' And Bo? 'Gone to Grootfontein to the army.' And Fanzi, Xau? Tomaas waved a hand out into the distance. 'Gone, gone.'

The old man began shouting again. 'We are hungry,' translated Tomaas. What about the game conservancy victory, I asked, in my terrible Afrikaans, surely that must have been good news? Tomaas did not answer himself, but translated the question to old man /Kaece, who merely snorted in reply, and repeated, angry now: 'We are hungry, give us food.' I took Tomaas back to our camp and he and I carried back the mealie meal, sacks of potatoes, and bags of tobacco and sugar that we had brought up from Windhoek. We laid them in a pile in front of /Kaece, who nodded, watching as the women of the village came forward, took the provisions, and carried them away to their huts. 'I will take you hunting tomorrow,' said Tomaas, 'And we will have singing and dancing . . .'

That night, /Kaece brought his people to dance for us where we had camped under the big tree. With so few adults and a mere handful of scampering children it was hard to make a circle, let alone create the full, throbbing chorus necessary for a good dance. 'Sing! Sing!' /Kaece yelled at the women, frustrated, unable to conjure the animals through his dance as he was used to. But the women sang desultorily, hardly bothering to keep their hand-claps in rhythm until, as if deliberately breaking things up, a group of hyenas began hooting and cackling right at the edge of the clearing. Everyone jumped to their feet at once, shouting to scare the night raiders away, and soon after that they too had gone, leaving us with the silence and the smoky, dying fire. Later, on the other side of the clearing we heard elephants feeding, tearing branches from the smaller trees. They were so close the deep sighs of their breathing were clearly audible. When we woke up next day there was fresh dung near our tents.

Tomaas showed up at dawn next day with old man /Kaece's younger son in tow, a lean, grinning youth. But the 'hunt' they took us on was a sham. Although the ground was criss-crossed with spoor, and we twice walked close to herds of kudu, after half an hour in the bush Tomaas turned for home and, smiling as if at a job well done, said, 'Now you must drive us to Baraka to buy soap and sugar from the store.'

In Baraka I tried to find Benjamin but the only information I could get was that he hadn't been seen for some time, was believed to be living on the eastern outskirts of Tsumkwe with an Ovambo girl, apparently his fiancée. I was told to try the *shebeens*.* So, having dropped Tomaas and his companion back at Makuri, I returned to town, stopping when I saw a collection of grass shelters surrounding a big plastic barrel. Some four or five people squatted around it, reeling slightly on their hams, cups in hand. Benjamin was not among them, but the Herero proprietor, the only man sober, told me to try another place, further up the track.

The second *shebeen* was larger than the first, with a ghetto-blaster pumping out African jive next to another big green barrel of home-brew. Around this, moving jerkily and erratically, a dozen or so Ju'/Hoansi men and women danced to beats more of their own than the music's making. As I drew up, they stopped dancing and came running over.

I got out, and was immediately mobbed. Hands grabbed at my arms, hair, voices demanded money, help, a ride, a talk, tobacco. I disengaged myself, or rather pulled the struggling, writhing human mass with me towards a tall, stern-faced Ovambo, obviously the proprietor. Behind him I saw another powerful-looking black man dragging a Bushman girl off into one of the huts. She was screaming and yelling, though whether in protest or delight it was impossible to tell. The proprietor knew nothing, so back I went to the vehicle, but could not prevent it from being boarded by the drunken, unarmed pirates. I made a futile defence, trying to simultaneously hold my door shut and beat off the intruders coming in behind. But to no avail. They swarmed, octopus-limbed, all over the back of the vehicle. Getting into the driver's seat I gave the engine a couple of loud revs to warn anyone in front to get out of the way and let slip

*Illegal bars.

the clutch. Triumphant at having won a joy-ride, my passengers roared and yelled as we chugged away.

A few minutes later, where the narrow track joined the main dirt road back to Makuri, I spotted Benjamin standing by a tree. I stopped, shouted his name. His face, which always called to mind a little hawk's, turned in my direction, but he had trouble focusing. He was colossally drunk. He stared at me a moment then, as recognition blossomed, he smiled, radiant: 'Rru!' I got out and he came over to me, swaying a little. We embraced, cheered by the people in the car. 'I was waiting for you,' he said, looking happily into my eyes and breathing fire into my face, 'You said you would come back and now you are here.'

'How are you?' I asked.

'I'm OK man, OK.'

'I hear you're getting married.'

'Who told you that?'

'The people over at Baraka.'

Benjamin laughed and punched me on the shoulder. '*Ach* those guys. They are telling many lies and bad things. I am so sick of them . . .' Benjamin lurched wildly in my arms, yet his lucidity seemed unimpaired. 'So are you getting married?' I asked again, if only to keep the conversation going, wondering what to do next. Benjamin laughed: 'Well . . . I'll organise it sometime. Where are you staying?'

'At Makuri. Things have changed there.'

Benjamin laughed again, and the laugh seemed not altogether kind. 'Well,' he said, 'I have not been to that place for a very long time. But let me come with you. I have many important things to say to you. About here, about the Nyae Nyae people, yes . . .' He trailed off, eyes losing their focus, and lurched a second time. 'Yes! I have had enough there. The foreigners there . . . those bastards . . . they want to make all the decisions. Not asking the . . . the . . .' He paused, as if searching for a word, 'Communities!' He beamed, triumphant.

'But Benjamin,' I asked my friend, 'Aren't you still working for them?'

'Yes,' he nodded, 'still senior field officer . . . translator. But maybe I will leave those people, maybe take a job in Windhoek as a teacher . . . in adult education.' He paused, 'What did you do at Makuri?'

'Some of the other guys took me out to the bush, but I missed Bo . . . and you . . .'

Benjamin eyed me. 'You went hunting? Who with?'

Tomaas, I told him. At this, Benjamin put back his head and gave a loud hoot. '*Heh-heyyy*! That man Tomaas! He was *cheating you*!' Benjamin punched me again. 'Ha ha! Let's go to Makuri . . . Yes', he nodded emphatically, 'and tomorrow, I will take you out, like before. But my friend Royal – you don't know him. He must come too. And our wives. All of us together!'

My joy-riders, who had spilled out during this conversation, tried to reboard as Benjamin and I went back to the vehicle, but at one angry snarl from him they scattered like hens. We drove for an hour from *shebeen* to *shebeen*, picking up his diminutive friend, Royal, then his fat wife, then finally a giggling, dark-skinned giantess well over six foot tall – Benjamin's girl. No sooner were they all in the car together than they decided they needed another drink. And some *dagga*. So back around the *shebeens* we went. By now the levels of drunkenness had risen a notch or two. At one place, a young woman lay on the ground, thrashing and tearing at herself as if in some kind of fit, clawing blood from her own flesh, spittle flying. Pointing at the flailing, writhing girl, Benjamin's friend Royal burped, giggled and said 'My sister', wiping his eyes with laughter.

Back on the dirt road to Makuri, Benjamin and the other three roared and laughed and tossed their spent bottles out of the window to shatter on the road. A group of guinea fowl dashed in front of us: big, hen-like birds with feathers of mottled grey, they looked like leggy tea-pots running across the dirt. 'Yey! Woo!' screamed Benjamin, spotting them. 'Speed up man! Kill them!' When I didn't, but braked instead, Benjamin turned in his seat, snarling 'Why didn't you kill them? *Agh* . . .' Then his head rolled forward, his eyes closed and he began snoring.

By the time we made Makuri all four passengers were catatonic, but they woke up as the vehicle stopped. As they stumbled out, I heard shouting and looked around to see old man /Kaece advancing on us, his goateed face distorted, an accusing finger pointing at Benjamin's chest. Behind him clustered Makuri's women, looking fierce. One, a particularly pretty girl whom I recognised as the one that had been sharing Benjamin's hut the first time I met him, began wailing, and flopped down as if the wind had been knocked out of her. Benjamin, taking it all in, grinned vacantly.

Royal's wife, who seemed less drunk than the others, explained: 'Benjamin had two kids by this girl, then he ran away. /Kaece told him never to come back here. Now here he is, with a new woman . . . I told him it wasn't a good idea to come, but he would not listen.' The sound of someone crying nearby interrupted her: Benjamin's new girl, the huge Ovambo, stood keening, tears running down her big cheeks. '*Ai*, this is too much for me! Benjamin has too many women!'

The Casanova in question was now laughing openly. Incensed, /Kaece strode forward and struck him, yelling at the top of his lungs. 'He says we cannot stay. We must go. Out, away from here,' translated Royal's wife. Benjamin disengaged himself from the old man and staggered over to us. 'Rru, there's a small problem. I don't know why, but /Kaece won't let me stay. You must drive me to my grandmother's village, then come and fetch me tomorrow . . .'

'How far?' I asked, avoiding /Kaece's glare.

'Ten, maybe fifteen kilometres . . . you must drive us there and then . . .'

I opened my mouth to protest, but Benjamin saved me the trouble. At that moment he staggered backwards, eyes rolling up in his head, and toppled sideways, sprawling unconscious in the sand. 'Listen,' I said to the air, 'I'm going back to camp to cook. If you want to eat, come in an hour.' And I got into the car and drove back to the big tree.

Greg and Tracy already had dinner underway, and had thought to cook for several people. We consumed a bottle of warm Chardonnay quickly and in silence. As the light around us dimmed and the evening cooings and singings began out in the wild, I related the craziness of the past few hours.

Just as dinner was about ready, Royal's wife and the Ovambo girl materialised out of the darkness. I regarded them sourly, but Tracy was more gracious, inviting them to sit and serving up two plates of pasta. Once the first couple of spoonfuls were down, Royal's wife, now completely sober, said: 'I'm really sorry. The men . . .' and she shrugged. The Ovambo girl, who still seemed tipsy, kept silent for the moment, wolfing down her food. I asked after Benjamin and Royal. Still unconscious, came the reply, but apparently things had calmed down in the village. /Kaece had relented, and decided to let them stay. What would the men eat, I asked? The girls shrugged: 'Someone will feed them when they wake.'

Greg and Tracy introduced themselves and coaxed the girls into telling something more about themselves. Royal's wife, it turned out, was a teacher in Tsumkwe, and Benjamin's girl a nurse. She was, she said, only half Ovambo, with a quarter Bushman and a quarter white on her mother's side. 'She brought me up Bushman, wild,' said the girl, laughing, 'but I was so big, they could not find enough food for me in the bush – Ay! I was trouble.' Their men were not working, it turned out: Benjamin did not go to Baraka any more, said his tall girl, and Royal, though a qualified teacher, was currently unemployed. The girls were supporting them. They sighed: but that was just how things were in Tsumkwe. It was hard to have come from that traditional life, and now to live 'as whites', said Royal's wife shyly. 'You end up caught between cultures.'

Later, after coffee, I walked the girls back through the bush to the village. We could hear, as we had the night before, the sighing breaths and ripping of branch and foliage that meant elephants were nearby. 'You must be careful when you go back,' said the girls. 'You do not want to meet an elephant in the dark, no . . . he will take you.'

We found /Kaece, Benjamin and Royal sitting round a low fire with some men of the village, laughing and joking. All seemed forgiven and forgotten. I nodded greetings and took a place by the fireside, marvelling, not for the first time, at the Bushmen's capacity to forgive, and to put wrongs behind them so quickly.

Benjamin asked me: 'So Rru, you have come back to Makuri.

I want to know and the people also want to know. What has brought you back here?'

I told them how I had wanted to see if their tourism project had ever got off the ground, and how I was also writing a book, trying to get a picture of life right across the Kalahari. I told them of the Xhomani's land claim, and Dawid and Izak's injunction to be their bird, to go out, spread the word, find information.

There were murmurs from around the fire. Then /Kaece spoke, Benjamin translating: 'He says he wants to tell you that the Nyae Nyae Foundation people are no good. They are taking the decisions for all the *nyores* [villages] in the area. They are not listening to the people. He is not happy about the money that has come from the government for the game conservancy. It is not coming here. And the tourists now, they are going to other villages. No one is looking after Makuri.'

'I hear him,' I replied. 'But all the same, aren't the people glad at least, that they've won the battle for the game conservancy, that the Herero and their cattle are gone, that the things that were threatening you have gone away?'

But /Kaece only responded with another litany of complaint, a vitriolic torrent. These Nyae Nyae people, they were crooks. And the tourists, they weren't coming because people were saying bad things about Makuri. And this government money, where was it?

Soon afterwards I made my excuses – it had been a taxing day – said goodnight and wandered away into the darkness in the direction of the camp. Several times I had to stop dead, when a tell-tale sighing snort sounded from a thicket to my front. Once, just in time, I glimpsed a trunk and flapping ear close, too close, and froze, heart racing, until it felt safe to creep around the other way. In all, the short journey back took over half-an-hour, but I made it safely to the big tree, and the glowing, dying fire beneath it. Greg and Tracy were already asleep and, very soon, so was I.

Next day, back among the concrete shacks on the edge of Tsumkwe, Benjamin asked me, 'So, Rru, when will you come again? I still have many important things to tell you.'

'I don't know,' I answered, not wanting to lie. 'I don't know if I will be back.'

'Also me – I don't know if I'll be here next time,' said Benjamin. 'Maybe I'll go to Windhoek . . .'

Standing there in the hot, bright sunlight I realised that, almost certainly, this would be the last time I would see Benjamin, my first Bushman friend, the one who had drawn me into the story, and whom I now wasn't sure was still my friend, or whether I even liked him any more. We embraced, but it felt empty.

Nigel was drinking tea as usual in his hot, messy living room and listening to Elgar. 'Hi, guys,' he said, 'how was Makuri?'

I gave him the story.

'I could have told you,' said Nigel sympathetically. 'But I thought it'd be better if you found out for yourself. *Ja*, Makuri seems to be going downhill, I don't know why. And Benjamin: there've been all sorts of problems with him.' He recited a list of offences: stealing one of the Nyae Nyae Foundation's vehicles and driving someone off the road, injuring them. Drunk again, he had punched an American Peace Corps girl, stationed at Baraka, over some imagined slight; he had taken and wrecked another vehicle – 'And those are just the highlights,' said Nigel, 'The problem is that Benjamin thinks he's indispensable. And he is, in a way – he's without doubt the finest translator in the whole area. But he's basically made himself unemployable, and he doesn't want to go back to the traditional life. So he sits and drinks. *Ja* man, it's sad. I don't know what else to say.'

Hours later, back on the tar road with another two hundred-plus kilometres to make before nightfall, we pulled over to relieve ourselves. Another car drew up behind ours and one of the women from the Nyae Nyae Foundation offices in Windhoek, presumably on her way to Baraka, stepped out. Surprised to see me she asked how I had found things there. I told her the same story I had told Nigel.

'Ah well,' she said with a rueful grin, 'I suppose that's the process of empowerment, isn't it? The reality is that soon they won't need us any more, and they know it. They've got the land, they're getting the skills to run it and now they're letting us know they want us to go. It's sad, but people don't often say "Thanks awfully chaps, for everything you've done, now would you mind if we took over, now that we feel ready?" No, they say "Fuck you." Our presence now is just a reminder of the days of disempowerment and they're champing at the bit to get on with things themselves and just be left alone. I suppose it's a measure of success.'

The Tsodilo Hills, which lay *en route* between Nyae Nyae and Ghanzi, the town where I was to meet Bulanda and go in search of Besa, rose above the bush in three isolated massifs called the Male, Female and Child. The hills are sacred to the !Kung Bushmen, who believe that the first men descended from heaven to earth here. Their yellow stones are covered in ancient rock paintings. As a child, reading Laurens van der Post's account of his sojourn in these hills, I had longed to visit them. According to him, they were a sanctuary where no man hunted. When one of his party violated the taboo by shooting a steenbok, he wrote that all their camera equipment had mysteriously broken down. My cousin Michael had also travelled here and had told me that the old traditions remained strong. He had even come across one old man who still made his arrow-heads from giraffe bone, rather than steel.

When we reached the three hills, after hours battling through the worst sand road I had yet driven in the Kalahari, we found no Bushmen at all, only the thatched, stockaded homesteads of the Hambukushu – a black, livestock-owning tribe. Cattle, goats, sheep and the occasional horse stood about in the shade of the tall trees, flicking their tails at the flies. Seeing a hand-painted sign nailed to a tree, pointing to a 'New Tourist Camp', we followed it and came onto a clearing in the middle of which stood a large safari tent, surrounded by a few plastic tables and chairs, all shaded by large thorn trees. A young BaTswana sat reading in one of the plastic chairs. Seeing us drive in, he closed his book and got up to greet us.

He was pleased to see us – no visitors had come through there for over a week, he said – and gave us cold beers in return for a little conversation. It seemed that the !Kung had all been moved away. The Botswana Museum, he told us, had had the hills declared a national monument and the inhabitants had been cleared out, for fear that they might destroy the rock paintings that their forefathers (and probably they too, sometimes) had created. He sipped his beer. The Bushmen now lived six kilometres away, in a new settlement.

'So there are no Bushmen in the hills at all?' asked Greg.

'That's right,' said the man. 'But the Hambukushu and all their livestock are allowed to stay. Crazy. Tourists come here wanting to see who did the paintings. I've told this to the museum and ministry of tourism people dozens of times, but they don't listen. But the Bushmen can fill you in better. One of the official museum guides is a !Kung and speaks English. If you overnight in one of the caves here, he'll probably find you in the morning and take you out. Let him tell you about it all.'

I woke the next day, just as the dawn was blushing the eastern treetops pink. Not long after, as Greg and Tracy began to rouse themselves, a small, yellow-skinned man came walking up out of the trees. His name was Nau, he said, accepting a cigarette from Greg. He was a guide. He sat, patiently smoking more cigarettes while we made ready, then led us up onto the Female Hill, pointing out gallery after gallery of red-daubed animals – rhinos, giraffes, elephants, all crudely depicted as if they had been painted by very young children.

At the top of the hill, where the air was sweet with the bubblegum scent of fallen marula fruits, we came upon the summit plateau. Leading us through the trees and rocks to a sudden vibrant patch of green grass, Nau squatted down and mimed sucking water up with a reed straw.

'A sip-well!'* I said, recognising his motion. 'Do the Bushmen here still know how to do that?'

'My grandfather and great-grandfathers did, when they lived here, hunted here.'

---

*Underground water reached by digging down through sandy ground to a moist patch and then sucking out the water by means of a hollow reed filled with fine, dry grass, which acts as a filter.

'Hunted? You mean the hills weren't a sanctuary? I thought hunting wasn't allowed,' I said, thinking of the van der Post book.

'No, the hunting here was very good, especially for kudu,' said Nau. 'My grandparents used to drive them off the cliffs.'

'So how do you feel now, working for the museum that moved your people away?' It was fatuous, but I had to ask.

He looked at me blankly: 'I have a wife, a child. It is work.'

Later, Greg and Tracy having elected to stay back at the cave, Nau took me to the new Bushman village. It was tiny, and thick with flies from the Hambukushu-owned cattle and goats which lay about on the village edge (as did a handful of their young men, gathered under a tree, watching us as we drove in). Sitting in a circle in the shade of a big thorn tree were several women, young and old, and about a dozen children, dressed in the usual mix of rags and skins. In the centre sat a wizened ancient man, dressed only in a *xai*. He looked up as we approached.

Sitting down before him, I told the old man, cringing at how pompous it sounded, about my role as Izak and Dawid's bird – to tell them about the land claim and the NGOs and the pressure now being put on the Kalahari governments, the efforts being made to end the long cycle of dispossession. 'I know nothing of this,' said the old man. 'But tell these people that we sit here in a place that is not a place and look at our home in the hills. Tell them to come and help us before I die.'

That night the forest was ablaze with moonlight. Greg, Tracy and I went walking in it, enraptured, washed in silver. At dawn, we packed up and chugged off in the morning cool. By the Hambukushu village south of the Female Hill, we were waved down by a man dressed in heavy jacket and trousers, and carrying a suitcase. Was he Hambukushu, we asked, when he had climbed in and settled himself? No – he was a Xhosa and far from his native South Africa. What was he doing here in the deep Kalahari?

'Actually,' replied the man, in a deep, musical bass, 'I have been with the Bushmen.'

His youngest brother, so he told us, had gone to college in Gaberone, Botswana's capital, and while there had begun to hear voices in his head. A friend had brought him here to the Tsodilo Bushmen, whose leader, said our passenger, was known even in that far city as a healer. On hearing the news he had hitchhiked a thousand kilometres north to see his brother. I remembered the young black men whom we had seen at the Bushman village, whom I had assumed were Hambukushu youths hanging around the !Kung women. But no, said the man, they were boys come for healing.

We made Maun late that afternoon and camped by its dry river. In the cool morning I put Greg and Tracy on a southbound bus, then headed west for Ghanzi where I was to meet Bulanda, for the last and most crucial part of this Kalahari journey. It was just past five o'clock when I drove into the dusty little town and parked outside the Danish-run Bushman craft shop where Bulanda had, in the letters we had exchanged, told me she was working. She was standing outside the gate, looking pretty and amused.

'You're late,' she said, smiling, as I got out of the car and walked over. 'I was expecting you weeks ago.'

12

The Leopard Man

Bulanda had found out where Besa was living. It was a remote place called Groot Laagte, about a hundred kilometres northwest of Ghanzi. A road of sorts led out there, but after that, warned Bulanda, there was nothing. If Besa was not in the actual settlement itself we might be in trouble, for the bush was thick thereabouts, and trackless. We should leave the following day soon after dawn, she told me, as we walked over to the First People office to negotiate a leave of absence from her husband Roy Sesarna, the organisation's chief. He agreed that Bulanda could go, provided I paid a translator's fee.

That night I slept out at the Hardbattle ranches. Neither Tom nor Andrea was there (nor Karnells, who was on walkabout somewhere near the Central Kalahari Game Reserve), but old mother Xwa was in residence, sitting huge and regal outside her hut with Katherine, a younger daughter by a Nama man, who, as luck would have it, spoke English. This young woman told Xwa that I planned to go in search of Besa next day, and at this the old woman smiled broadly – it was the first time I had ever seen her look animated – and spoke, looking directly at me, which was unnerving. 'Yes,' said the daughter, translating, 'My mother says that if you find him you must bring him here. My mother is still in too much pain from losing her son John. She has been talking about sending somebody to find Besa. You must bring him here.'

Later that evening, under the winking Kalahari stars, Katherine told me more about Besa. Though a BaKoko, he was actually a blood relative of some of the Nharo of the Hardbattle ranches. He had even lived there at one time, and had for a while been a kind of mentor to John Hardbattle, inducting him into the beginnings of the healer's path until John's organisation, First People of the Kalahari, began to take up too much of his time. Katherine had met Besa several times, she said, had been present at some of his healings. Even the one where he tried to cure John Hardbattle of his stomach cancer.

When word had reached the ranches that John was dangerously ill in Germany, Besa had come south from Groot Laagte and had told the Nharo that John had been ill-wished by BaTswana witch doctors in the pay of certain government officials. So he had called all the people in to help him in a great healing. He would leave his body and fly abroad, he had said, to the hospital in Germany where John lay, and heal him at least enough so that he could get home. Then, when Besa could actually lay his hands on John, he could set about finding out exactly who had put the bad magic on him, and lift it.

So, Katherine told me, they had all gathered to make a big chorus, and when Besa had gone into his trance, he had fallen down unconscious. Katherine and the others had then seen coloured lights go shooting up from his body into the heavens. She had seen this happen, she repeated, with her own eyes. As Besa had instructed them, they had danced on all night, so that his body, emptied of its spirit, might not die before he returned, so that the cord that kept body and spirit together might not break. At dawn they had seen three lights fall into the bush some distance away and, a moment or two later, Besa had come round, saying that he had been successful and that John – whom he now knew to have a terrible cancer of the stomach – was ready to fly home.

Some days later, the news had come that John would indeed be flying home. Besa set himself to rest, garnering his strength for the coming healing. But, said Katherine, when John's plane had touched down in Johannesburg, he had suffered a relapse, having been exhausted by the journey. He was hospitalised there and then and the doctors had decided to operate right away. John died while in recovery.* Besa was still mourning, said Katherine, for he had been

---

*Perhaps because of time and distance, Katherine had the exact circumstances of her half-brother's death a little jumbled. He died in fact from lymphatic cancer. However, Besa did indeed try to heal him long-distance.

sure that, had John returned home to Ghanzi, he could have lifted the illness from him. Yes, said the young woman, Besa was truly a great healer.

Groot Laagte, when Bulanda and I reached it early the following afternoon after a long morning of sand-rut driving, might have been the shanty outskirts of any African town. Despite being surrounded by wild, virgin bush, the place was a tip: a few shabby, rundown government buildings, rubbish everywhere, barren patches of baking hot sand, some trucks standing about, and in between them straggling collections of traditional and not so traditional huts in various stages of disrepair. Pot-bellied smiling kids, non-smiling, shambling drunks, dogs, hobbled donkeys – that was Groot Laagte, the place where we were to find Besa.

We got directions from the settlement's main store, run by a young half-BaKoko, half-Bantu woman whom Bulanda knew. She sent us east along a track which, every few yards, would fork confusingly, splintering gradually into a maze of sub-tracks. But Bulanda seemed confident and finally we came to a small clearing in the bush, right at the farthest eastern edge of the settlement. In the middle of this clearing stood a seringa tree, slender and delicate, surmounted by a rounded dome of leaves around which buzzed large, droning beetles with shiny yellow and black wing-cases. Under the tree sat a small man of perhaps sixty.

We stopped and got out. The man, who had been seated with his legs tucked neatly up beneath him, rose to his feet. He was tiny, dressed in ragged things that had once been a pair of trousers, bare-chested. But he was strong, that was clear. Above a compact torso the colour of honey was a high-cheekboned face, smooth, almost Asian-looking, but with round, predator's eyes, like a leopard's.

'Besa?' asked Bulanda.

The man nodded, and sat down again under his tree. I looked briefly around. His home was just over there in the sand, a square enclosure of thin poles bound together with grass and rags. No roof. You could see through the poles to some kind of sleeping bundle of skins and cloths. We sat down in front of the little man, cross-legged, like children. His small, round eyes were inscrutable; his mouth a stoic line. He listened as Bulanda spoke, introducing me, explaining why I was there.

We sat a while in silence, waiting for a reply, the yellow-and-black beetles droning in the slender tree against which Besa leant his back. People appeared out of the bushes around us. A tall, lanky woman, with a lantern-jawed KhoiSan face under a dirty headscarf, dressed in an old cotton shift, now the colour of sand, her bare feet cracked and dry, came and sat down next to Besa, head cocked towards us. Some other women and girls, and a snot-nosed kid or two came and sat down: I nodded, they nodded. Still Besa didn't answer, so I began to speak, pausing every few moments so that Bulanda could translate.

I had come to ask him something, I said. But now that the man was here in front of me I could not think what. Until now, all my energy had been focused on just getting to the man and I realised that I had not thought about it at all, merely acted on a deep, gut drive to get there. I had thought I had wanted to know about shape-shifting, but for some reason that seemed completely unimportant now. So I told him my story, beginning at the beginning, with my mother and the childhood stories, of the years of not managing to get to the Kalahari, of the meeting with Benjamin at Makuri, of the meetings with the Xhomani, the land claim, the book, the mantis, the mouse and the bird, the cheetahs, the mouse and the owl: all of it. I spoke of the shape-changing stories which, for some reason I couldn't explain, seemed to lie at the heart of things, which led me here, to him, under this tree.

He looked at me, silent a long time. The others looked too. Then he spoke, his voice somehow both high and deep, both rich and thin, reedy like a flute. 'I know nothing of this shape-changing thing,' he said.

Of course, I thought, that would be his answer. I looked down at my cheap running shoes. The soles were cracked. I would have to replace them soon. I got up, hearing myself laugh, feeling the smile. 'Well,' I said, through Bulanda. 'Thank you anyway. Thank you for your time, for listening to my story. I understand; at least, I think I do. Goodbye.' And I walked towards the vehicle.

'Stop,' said the man. 'Stop,' translated Bulanda.

I stopped, turned round.

'Sit', he said. 'I will tell you of these things.'

Much later, when I recalled Besa's words (for this time I did not play the journalist, or the anthropologist, but sat and listened without scribbling, keeping my eyes on his), they came back in disconnected snatches, like words from a remembered dream.

If he wanted to heal, he said, he would fly abroad as a bird. He would find the spirit of the sick one, lying down, resting in the sunlit bush. He would hop onto their back, lightly so as not to disturb them, and perch there, singing, until he had sung the sickness out of them. The person would feel the light bird's presence on their back and smile. And when he felt that smile, Besa could go back to his own body and rest. Sometimes he would 'climb the rope' to another place, to a shadow land where the spirits of those who had caused sickness wandered, blundering about in the darkness of their own creation. When he found them he would confront them, demand the truth, an admission of wrongdoing from their spirit to his, and in their utterance of that wrong, their bad work would be undone.

And sometimes, if he needed to, he could send his spirit out on mischief. Not to kill, which was forbidden, though there were times when he had wanted to. He became a lion or a leopard: a lion to hunt, maybe to run off someone's cattle. Leopard was better, quicker, smarter. When he went abroad like this no lights would fly from his body; he would simply go, making sure nobody but those closest to him knew that he had gone. When he came back he would be tired beyond measure.

'Now', he said. 'Tell me again why you have come.'

'This story I am going to tell, this Bushman story, I cannot tell it alone. I need a blessing. Do I have your blessing?'

'I can do better than that,' said Besa. 'Tonight I will trance for you.'

An hour later, Besa and his wife, Katerina, Bulanda and I were all on our way south to the Hardbattle ranches. It was early evening by the time old Xwa's homestead came into view. The place sat on top of a low hill, overlooking a wide, dry riverbed shaded by tall camel-thorns standing apart from each other like trees in a park. Xwa's people had a foot in two worlds: half Bushman, half something else, something from the white rancher from England who had married the matriarch, something from each of her other husbands – Nama, Herero, BaKgalagadi. She lived in a one-room concrete house that looked newly-built (Andrea and Tom were obviously trying to look after their old mother); another, half-finished structure stood next to it, and opposite that a large, sagging army tent surrounded by more traditional-looking shelters made from conically piled branches, with bows and game bags hanging from the trees around them. There was a lowing of cattle from the riverbed. Bulanda shivered as she looked down there and said, 'It is full of ghosts here. The ghosts of her men.'

'*Hmph*,' said the old woman by way of welcome as I walked shyly into her compound with Besa and Bulanda at my side. The little healer sat down next to the wooden chair from which she overflowed and began chatting away, for all the world like a schoolboy talking to his aunt. Bulanda and I slipped out quietly while they talked and went into the bush, along with a few able-bodied youngsters, to collect firewood.

When dark fell, we had the flames crackling and snapping merrily outside Xwa's house. She sat on the ground now, the apex of the small circle of people, a rock of silence amid the fireside chatter, the laughter and smoking and coughing. I sat silent too, understanding none of the talk, looking up at the stars. There was the Southern Cross, which the Bushmen called the giraffe's head. And Orion, which the Ju'/Hoansi said were three zebras that a hunter had shot at and missed. His arrow was another star just below them. The mistake had cost the hunter dear, for now every night the zebras galloped off towards the dawn horizon while he, 'the hungry star', plodded wearily after.

Looking back into the circle I saw that Besa was standing upright in the firelight, a little bronze god, his mouth open. He was singing in his strange, reedy voice and then suddenly he had sung himself straight into trance on one pure, high note that shot upwards into the warm night-wind, fell back a moment into his chest, then exploded back outwards, straight from his taught-veined neck to the stars. No one else was singing, or clapping. No chorus, no dancers; just Besa, alone, singing to the stars. The note rang out again, and then, first with one foot and then the other, he launched himself, slowly, like a swimmer gingerly entering cold water, into the dance.

He held his note, let it fall, then whipped it into a series of high yelps like a coyote or a jackal and danced over to Xwa, putting his small strong hands on her head. She accepted it without expression, as I had seen her do before, while his song changed to a mutter, a babble, a deep, guttural growl, and finally, unexpectedly, a short, ear-splitting shriek that snapped him upright. He grunted through his nose like a gemsbok, then resumed the flute-like song. And danced over to me.

His palms curled around my head. His voice rose again to a choirboy's pitch, echoing off the cathedral vault of stars and back again to become a bubbling, happy sound deep in his belly. Besa was holding my head and laughing. Then whooping for joy. I opened my eyes, sneaking a look. Tears were running down his face, as if he'd been told a joke that just doubled him up. Up went the voice again, his hands, very tender, clasping the top of my skull. He squatted down, pressed his head to my chest, to my back. He was shaking, so that as he touched me, I shook too. But there was another feeling behind it, something like a gentle electric current, or a pulse. Besa reeled off, circled the fire, then came back and laid his hands on me again, laughing so joyfully that an image came to mind of a parent rejoicing for some good thing a child had done, or some bad thing the child had escaped. He removed his hands, executed a few steps of a happy jig, then put his hands back on a third time. He started to shout. Words into the night, words I did not understand. When at last he danced away, back to old mother Xwa, Bulanda leant across and whispered: 'Leopards. He was saying "leopards" –

I don't know why, but he keeps saying it when he touches you.'

Perhaps a minute later – startling us all – a leopard coughed just outside the circle of the firelight: a noise somewhere between a rough growl and a dog's bark. As one, the village dogs rose up, barking maniacally, and dashed off in the direction of the noise. The 'cough' came again, this time echoed by another from the opposite side of the fire: two leopards. The dogs came rushing back, afraid, all their hackles up. Laughing, Besa danced over to me and put his hands on once again, pulsing his slow, calm current through my skull, into my brain, down my spine, and out in tingling throbs to the fingers, legs and toes; a subtle, heart-felt pleasure, almost too good, too delicate to bear. Half of me wanted to break from his grip, the other half, to open the top of my skull like a lid and let him pour in anything he wanted, even himself, a little man tipped up, two legs kicking from the hole in my skull.

For perhaps two hours he danced on tirelessly like this, laughing, laying his hands and his head upon me while, out in the midnight bush, the leopards coughed and the dogs growled and howled from rage and fear. At some point, the people around the fire took up a clapping chant. All the while that warm, pleasant current buzzed gently through me, felt dimly at the farthest edge of sensation. Then, without warning, Besa staggered and fell face first to the ground, unconscious. The dance was over.

His lanky wife went to revive him, helped him to the fire, and handed him a bone pipe stuffed with rough tobacco. Besa looked as though he were about to die, all vitality drained out of him. I, on the other hand, felt brimful of peace, contentment, quiet euphoria. I went over to where he lay in a foetal ball, drained, empty, old and wrinkled-looking, yet with his eyes open. I touched his back, rubbing his shoulders, wondering if they were sore. He flinched as if I had stabbed him, looked at me as if wounded, and hid his head in his arms. I let him be, went back to my place, lay back in the sand and looked up at the stars. I could not remember the last time I felt this good – no tiredness, no anxiety, no aggravating tension in my shoulders, no little nagging voice telling me I was no good. The mood seemed the same around the fire. People started to laugh, to joke. 'Hey Bulanda,' they teased, 'Why don't you give your white boyfriend some loving?' She translated, embarrassed but laughing. Soon after, we were all asleep.

There was leopard spoor all around the settlement when we woke next morning. And lion spoor not far along the road. We took our time driving over the slow, rutted tracks. A quiet euphoria lay over us still. Besa was withdrawn, as before, though no longer quite so drained-looking. As the hours passed, he seemed to recover, to the point of laughing and joking a little with his wife in the back seat. I kept silent, leaving them alone until we were perhaps twenty minutes out of Groot Laagte. A question had been bubbling, unspoken, on the tip of my tongue for some time. Had the healing worked, I asked? Bulanda translated my question. From the back seat there came a thick, high–low, thin–rich laugh.

'Oh yes,' came the reply. 'Oh yes. I went up there. I spoke to the old man. He says go on. Go on as you are.'

And the leopards. What had they meant? He did not say. But I had a feeling that if I kept my eyes open, then sometime I would know.

Back in Ghanzi, Bulanda and I stopped at the First People office and there ran into the organisation's new co-ordinator, who had just arrived from Europe. A kindly-looking Dane, he and an account- ant had been sent out along with the donor money to take up the administrative reins. It was a surprise to me – Bulanda had said nothing of his coming. Perhaps she thought it unimportant – another European come to tell the Bushmen what to do. Still, it was clear that First People needed some kind of direction. When I brought Bulanda back to the house that she and Roy Sesarna shared on the edge of Ghanzi – a one-room wattle-and-daub squatter's hut, built on ground they were occupying illegally – Bulanda showed me the organisation's files. A pile of documents heaped any old how into a trunk; jumbled, disordered, scribbled on, a mess.

But a mess that would bear fruit in the end, I was sure, just as the Xhomani's mess would, for all their violence, drinking and squabbling, just as the dispossessed Ganakwe of the Central Kalahari would, and the divided villagers at Kwaayi, the smiling, trusting congregation at Khekhenye, and as the Ju'/Hoansi at Nyae Nyae already had. Despite the centuries of genocide, of the collapse and loss of everything that supported them, these people were after all *still here*. The calm I felt from Besa's hands remained with me, causing something inside to purr. I sensed movement here, a change, a beginning of the end of the Age of Wrongs in the land of my forefathers.

I slept that night on the ground outside Bulanda and Roy's hut, hugging a long axe in case one of the shambling, arguing, shouting drunks who passed the low fence from time to time should notice me. But the peaceful feeling conquered my fear, made me sleep quiet and untroubled. Bulanda saw me off on the road south after a breakfast of mealie pap and coffee. I must be careful not to pick up any hitch-hikers, she told me – without a trace of irony – as sometimes they turned into snakes and attacked those who had given them a ride. It was true, she said, many people in Botswana had died like that.

Somewhere to the south, on a lonely stretch of bush road, a huge kudu bull – the largest and most regal I had ever seen – jumped out in front of me. Instead of running off, he stopped and regarded me, stamping his hooves and pacing, a knight and charger rolled into one. I stopped the car and watched him until, having looked his fill, he turned and sailed over the roadside wire in one effortless, elegant bound. Three full days of driving later, I reached Welkom, where Belinda and Dawid were waiting. Throughout that drive the quiet, unfamiliar happiness left over from Besa's hands stayed with me.

Back inside the Red House, I told Dawid and the people where I had been, and what I had felt and seen. As I related each incident, each situation, the Xhomani sat in total silence. It was unnerving, to be listened to like that, to have their full, complete attention. Thin plumes of smoke drifted up from the small hearth around which we sat, a tight circle, Belinda translating, red firelight glowing on the watching faces. Even the children were quiet. Only some minutes after the story was finished did the people begin to talk among themselves, whispering and muttering in small voices. Dawid sat, looking down, brow wrinkled, lost in thought. Belinda leant across and whispered, 'Time to go, I think.'

We got up. I was puzzled now. Had I unwittingly done something wrong? I looked at Dawid, but he seemed hardly to notice us. The people began to drift away. Dawid looked up, nodding distractedly as if to dismiss us. 'Tomorrow,' he said. 'Tomorrow we will talk. Come as soon as you can. We will talk.'

So Belinda and I went back to her house inside the National Park and there, in the black, welcome darkness, I slept.

13

Dawid Makes a Request

'OK,' said Belinda, coming in at noon while I was still bleary-eyed. 'I managed to slip out to Welkom quickly mid-morning. Dawid says he's got a lot to tell us to do with what you said last night. But he says it can't be at Welkom. So what we're going to do, is you, me, Themba, Erica, Cor and any of the other students that want to come, we're going to take Dawid and Sanna up into the park to spend the night in the management's private camp. And he'll tell us what he has to tell us there.'

'Dawid in the park, are you crazy?'

'*Ja*,' affirmed Belinda, eyes twinkling.

'But Dries, Henriette, *oom* Maarten – all the managers I mean, won't they go through the roof when they find out? Won't you get fired?'

'Already fixed. I'm management too, remember? Or sort of, anyway. And management have the right to take friends – any friends – up to the staff camp if they want to. So I thought we'd go as a big group of friends: the students, Themba, Cor and them, and someone else, Werner, this German guy who turned up while you were gone, and who's bought a tourist lodge, the Molopo, south of the park. He says he's interested in the Bushmen and wants to help. And Dawid and Sanna will come too – just part of a group of friends. I went and told Dries and he OK'd it. Sure, he gave me a funny look, and told me I'd better be careful to keep my nose clean. But we've got his blessing, and none of the other management can say anything. Well, they can, but they can't do anything.' She grinned. 'And you know what's the coolest thing of all? Your cousin Steven Smith, Steven Smith of the Mier, is lending us his truck to do it in!' Belinda snapped her fingers with delight and did a little dance.

'You're amazing.'

'I know.'

I paused, taking it in, then asked: 'When did Dawid last spend a night inside the park?'

'Twenty-five years ago, he told me,' Belinda laughed a great belly-laugh. 'Can you believe it Ru? We're going to take Dawid to spend a night back in the park for the first time since he was kicked out, and he's going to stay right in the management's private rest camp! I'm off at four. Get your sleeping bag and stuff ready and I'll come pick you up – the others are going in a couple of other vehicles. You and me'll pick up Dawid and Sanna, then all meet back here to be out of the gate and into the park two hours before sunset. Can you go down to the store and pick up some supplies? Here's a list.'

'But hold on,' I said, worried. 'You're sure this isn't just going to cause trouble for you and for the Bushmen? I mean, aren't the other managers going to resent this? Aren't they going to want to get even in some way later on?'

Belinda looked at me fixedly. 'Listen, of course they will. They'll try and do something – afterwards – that'll make sure I never do it again. You see, they're so fearful of Bushmen being in control, and they regard the park and this camp as their own private domain. You know what'll really get them about this trip? The thought that now they'll have to sleep on beds that Bushmen have slept on. Me – well – they can just about handle me sleeping there.'

Belinda burst into tears. 'Oh Ru, it makes me so angry! You just don't understand how it works in this country. They're not going to kill Dawid Kruiper! Never while I'm here!' And the next moment she was gone.

Some hours later we were driving on the park's northern road, following the dry Nossob riverbed along the Botswana/South Africa border, with Dawid and Sanna in Steven's car, and the others up front in Erica's vehicle. Dawid had still said nothing since the previous night. He sat between the front seats, wedged between Belinda and me, looking out of the window at the familiar landscape long unseen. Sanna sat in the back.

Then, abruptly, he spoke. 'There,' he said, pointing to a small limestone outcropping on the Botswana side of the riverbed. 'You see there? If you dig under there, you'll find water. But you have to suck it up from the ground with a hollow grass.'

A little further on he said: 'And there, that's where Regopstaan tried to plant some vegetables. But the springboks came and ate them all up. And over there, those little holes in the riverbank – the girls used to play doll's house in them with little people made of clay. *Ja Mama*,' he went on, looking around. 'This is the Xhomani's land. Dawid's land. You know my dream for it – that when we get this land back, all the people will come and I will show them. Show them the animals, the plants, how to live in the desert, how to find water, medicines. Let them come here, the broken ones, all the people that need healing. Let them come here to Dawid's land.'

Something small and brown flashed across the road in front of us, trailing a long thin tail behind: a mouse. And a short distance further up the track, in the branches of a huge old camel-thorn, sat the great, horned owl we had seen before, staring with its dark-moon eyes. I stopped the car. In front of us, the other car's dust cloud moved on and away, leaving us under the owl-tree.

'You see the patterns?' Dawid pointed up at the great bird. 'Nature will tell you everything if you open yourself up to it. This one, the mouse crossing left to right like that, the owl in daylight – work and wisdom – a pattern of strength. *Ja-nee*; there are some things I need to say.' He turned his head to look at Belinda. 'You,' he said. 'You are the person who brings in the love, the loving people.' He gestured to me and up the road in front to the people in the other car. 'If a mountain were to rise in front of you Belinda, or a wall, I would open it and let you through, and close it behind you again so that nobody could hunt you, nobody harm you. You are the one who brings the love.'

Belinda, looking back at the old man, began to cry. 'Oh God, Dawid, all I've ever wanted was a family. What did I have growing up? Church and beatings and an angry God and an angry father with a strap. I just want . . . a father.'

Dawid turned in his seat and took Belinda in his arms, while Sanna looked on from the back seat, nodding approval. He held the young woman, his wrinkled eyes closed, stroking her short, clipped hair, while she spilled her tears on his shoulder.

I drove on. A few minutes later, Belinda dried her eyes, sniffing, and pointed to a track that wound off to the left, uphill into the dunes, away from the riverbed. 'There,' she said. We turned, watched by an old wildebeest bull and an elderly springbok ram, long since ejected from their herds by younger males, now looking out for each other. With the setting sun shining full and blinding into our eyes, we crested a final dune and dipped into a wide, natural bowl filled with yellow grasses, and pulled up behind the first car.

The others were already unloading their gear and taking it into a large open-sided thatched structure, inside which was a rough table and some cots with mattresses. The sides, open to the air, were protected by strong wire mesh that reached from the ground to the eaves. The breeze could blow through, but no animal could wander in.

As we got out of the car, Dawid hobbling stiffly, Belinda called everyone together and we stood in a circle. I looked around at the faces, a strangely disparate group of people drawn together this night: a Xhosa, a Brit, a German, two white Afrikaners (Cor and Erica), a coloured woman and two Xhomani Bushmen.

'I'd just like to say a few words before we get into things tonight,' said Belinda. 'This is a great honour, to be with Dawid and Sanna while they sleep a night in the park, the place where they were born, for the first time in so many years.'

Dawid laughed, coughing to hide his embarrassment, and looked around him. 'Welcome,' he said in Afrikaans, 'Welcome to Dawid's land. There will be a place for you here always, always a place for the friends, for the people that come with their hearts open.' Next to him, small and youthful-looking, her head in a neatly wrapped scarf, Sanna beamed.

Then, as the sun set, it was down to business – getting a fire going, putting the sleeping bags inside the shelter, cutting into steaks a springbok haunch that Werner, the German that Belinda had adopted, had brought from his new Molopo property as a gesture of goodwill. It was happy work, chopping the onions, squash and other vegetables ready for the *braai*, sorting peel and end-bits carefully into bags to be stored inside, so as not to tempt creatures out of the night. We fell to eating as the moon rose. When we put the plates down, out came the pipe – a little one of bone, made by Bukse, with two pictures carved on it: a jackal riding a lion, and a hunter with an antelope's head, poised with his bow.

Dawid cleared his throat, and at once we were an audience. The night was warm, the grass smelled sweet and our bellies were full. We were ready for a story. 'You know,' he said. 'In the old days this place, where we're sitting now, used to be the hunting ground of a pride of lions that were especially fierce . . .'

'No way!' came Belinda's voice. 'They're still here then – everyone in the park talks about the fierce lions that live near here, that's why they put up the wire cage!'

'*Ja*, well,' said Dawid, nodding. 'That would be so. Lion families keep their territories from generation to generation. Like Bushmen. The ones who live here today will be the grandchildren of the ones we knew. So we must be careful tonight to have the wind at our backs.' He shifted his bottom in the sand and looked behind him, as if expecting to see a lion stealthily creeping there. '*Ja*, like I said, I know this place well. Back when I used to work here as a ranger – me and Jakob both did, you know.' Dawid settled into his story, the stars glowing above him and the fire crackling below. 'Some bigwigs from Pretoria had come to visit the park, and *oubaas* Leriche brought them out here, to this very place, to camp. He wanted to impress these men, who were something in government. So he brought Jakob and me and some others to cook and put up the tents and serve the food.

'Well, the whites are all drinking beer and talking *kak* and laughing, and old Jakob's there, working the *braai*, when all of a sudden he feels something isn't right. But he just stands quiet, going on with his work while the big white men sit and drink and laugh. That is being a Bushman, feeling the danger before it strikes. Well, he knew it was a lion coming. So he just *braaied* and waited, feeling the lion come closer and closer, wondering what to do.

'Then he heard it, a low growl. The sound a lion makes just before it charges. And old Jakob, he leaps! Right over the *braai*, right into the middle of all the white men, and grabs a stick from the fire and sure enough there, right where he was standing, is the lioness! Man! They shat themselves!'

Dawid laughed and, as always, had to recover from a coughing fit before beginning again, changing tack. *'Jasus!* We used to see things. I remember once on those dunes just over there' – he pointed to the low dark rise behind us – 'I saw a big spotted hyena try to sneak up on a mother ostrich and her chicks. He was just creeping along, trying to pretend like he wasn't there. And then, while the mother was looking off over there, he runs in fast to snatch a chick. Well, the mother hears him and spins around. And man, when the hyena saw that, you should have seen him try to stop! Tried to reverse in mid-run! He curls into a ball just as the mother ostrich comes running in and kicks him: like that, like a football, clear up the side of the dune, then again – *Bliksem* – down the other side. That hyena, he shat like those white men at the fire did! Left a stream of shit all the way down the dune! And then the mama ostrich, she nods her head once, like this, like a woman who's just won an argument, and walks back to her children.'

More laughing and coughing. *'Ja,* the things we got up to. Vetpiet; him and me, man, we used to have some times. Once, while I was still a ranger, *oubaas* Leriche took us out hunting poachers. We used to do it a lot in those days, especially after those *skelms* on the Botswana side. The best bit, though, was going to court afterwards to convict them. I used to love it, the court. *Jasus!* I would lie, man! If they had killed one gemsbok I would say they had killed five. I would just sit there and lie, just to get those *skelms* stuffed into jail. Anyway, one day me and Vetpiet and *oubaas* Leriche were out, and we came up on these two men on donkeys. One had a gun, another had a kerrie. Old Leriche jumps out of the vehicle and grabs the bridle of the front one, the one with the kerrie, who swings, but the *baas* ducks and the man misses and the swing takes him clear off his donkey, but with a foot still caught in the stirrup, so he's got him. Leriche shouts to Vetpiet, who jumps from the back of the vehicle. That's when I hear the click of a rifle bolt, and I see the man on the other donkey pointing his gun straight at Vetpiet. "*Bloed vir bloed*!" he shouts – Blood for blood. Nobody moves, nobody can move. And then I say, quietly, "*Hou*: Hold, halt."

'I got out of the vehicle, slow, and walked over slowly, like this, one step at a time, looking straight at the man. And slowly, I take the weapon from his hands. Still we stand there, no one knowing what to do. Then Vetpiet says: "Let them go, we'll settle this in court."

'So, with no one hurt, we let them go their way, without the gun, which old Leriche took to use as evidence. We backtracked along their spoor and found the gemsbok they'd killed. So we had everything we needed for a conviction. Well, when the time came for it to go to court, the *baas*, Vetpiet and the rest of the rangers had to go to a far area of the park. So the *baas*, he tells me I must now be the one to go as a witness and testify, and then, at the next court date, he'll go and settle the conviction. He was so sure of everything – we had all the evidence we could need – that he thought it would be safe with just me going.

'So there I am in the courtroom. Like I told you, I love courts. There I sit, ready to say anything I have to. And in walk the men from that day. And the magistrate tells me to tell him everything that happened. So I tell them the story just as I told it to you. And when I finished, the magistrate asked me how I can be sure it was these men.

'I say, "What? Are you telling me it was two ghosts I saw there in the veld? In daylight? With the *baas* and Vetpiet there too, and a dead gemsbok at the end of their spoor?" And this magistrate, he doesn't like this cheeky Bushman talking to him like that. He asks me if I was even sure that, even if it was these men, there was a bullet in the rifle. How can I prove my accusation?

'And then I thought, you think you're clever, but Dawid Kruiper's head is quicker than yours. So I ask him if I can see the gun. They bring it up to the witness stand, let me handle it. And then I ram

207

the bolt home and point the gun right at him. Right at the magistrate! For a moment, no one in the room moves, then they all move together, the policemen rush in and grab the weapon, *Donner* [hitting] me! *Jas!* I let the gun go, put my hands up and shout above all their shouting: "Who cares if there's a bullet in the barrel! When a man points a gun at you, it's your life. And you remember!"

'Well, the poachers got their sentences, and I got a contempt of court. But the magistrate, he was a friend of the *oubaas*, so I didn't go to jail. But oh boy, I was in trouble when I got back . . .'

Dawid fell silent. Clearly he was not finished yet. He took another pull at the pipe. 'I left the park soon after that,' he said, looking into the now dying fire. 'Working all month for fifty rand on land that was ours anyway. Well, even if we'd wanted to, the park wouldn't let us stay.'

Some of the group had already drifted away to find their sleeping bags. Only Belinda, Themba, Cor and I still sat by the dying fire, waiting for the old man to finish his roundabout story. Out from beyond the dunes came the shrill chorus of a jackal choir. First one voice, then the whole pack together. 'Hear that?' Dawid cocked his head towards the noise, 'That one's found something to eat, and he's telling the others to come. Ah jackals, they are small, but clever. They help each other.'

Then, out of the blue, Dawid looked straight at me across the fire and said, 'So Rroo, Rupi, Rupe-man, my friend. Have you a title for this book?'

The question took me unawares. It had, in truth, been much on my mind lately. I told Dawid so, and he replied, 'Well, as you know there is healing here, in this Kalahari. This book, this story, must have such a name that anyone from any place could see it and, before they even open the pages, feel some of the power of this land. You know, long ago I had a dream. I saw a man who would come and heal us, we broken Bushmen. Since that dream I have often heard of a healer, a powerful one, up in the Ghanzi area, and I have often wondered, is that him? Well, I think this man Besa is the healer from my dream. We down here, we are fighting for this land. If we win, then all the little people across the Kalahari will begin to win. You know the prophecies. But we are broken. I too used to be a healer, but I lost my strength long ago, with all the drink and the fights and all the bad things that happened to us. Look at us, even if they give us the land, how can we look after it when we are as we are, when I, the leader, am as I am? We, I, need to get strong again. I the leader need to find my healing power again. I think that this man Besa is the healer that can give me back my power. You must take us up there, Rupe-man. Soon.'

He stopped talking, eyes still on mine, waiting for an answer. 'OK,' I heard myself say, 'OK, in September, we'll go then. I need three months to raise the money. I've spent all I have now. But I'll get the money. September – three months is the soonest I can raise it. But we'll go, I promise.'

There was silence around the fire. I got up and left the circle, seeking my sleeping bag in the dark of the thatched shelter.

In the red dawn, as we drove back to Twee Rivieren, Dawid asked me to let the other car go on ahead and to take a different way back, along the road which followed the Aub riverbed. He had something to show us there.

We drove over the intervening dunelands between the Nossob and the Aub. Sparse yellowed grasses waved in the wind. Above them arced the great blue, studded with small, flat-bottomed clouds, white boats cruising on an ever-changing sea of air. Far up, visible even through the dusty windscreen, thin silhouettes of vultures circled in and out of the rays of the morning sun. A pair of delicate little steenbok, standing at the roadside, watched us pass. We reached the west bank of the Aub and followed the track southwards, down along the wide riverbed road.

Soon after, we came to a waterhole, an artificial one put in by the National Park to attract game to the roadside where the tourists could see them. Most southern African parks are studded with such waterholes, which are actually boreholes powered by small windmills. No longer do the herbivores need to rely on *tsamma* melons to get them through the dry season.

Dawid made us stop. 'See the water coming up from the ground here? In these past years, since we left the Aub and the Nossob, I have noticed some things. People have brought me into the park a few times to visit. And I have noticed that it is dry, much drier than it was when Bushmen danced in the land. There was no drought then, only the dry season and the rains. Now, since they have put these boreholes in, it seems there is always drought. When the little people danced here, there were no boreholes, but the land drank from the sky.'

Twisting in his car seat, he pointed to the roadside dunes: 'Just over there, over that dune, that's where I was born. Regopstaan had a little *kraal* where he looked after Leriche's cattle, and the cattle of some of the BaTswana. Soon after that they put the fences up and said we could no longer hunt. But if we looked after ourselves in other ways then, they said, we were no longer Bushmen. And so we had to leave. And now, what am I, this little old man that was born behind the dune there? Am I still a Bushman?'

We drove on, the morning growing in the sky to our left. '*Ja*,' said Dawid, 'These past few years things have been really changing. Down at Kagga Kama, you know, one of the reasons we've stayed so long is because the ancestral spirits are very, very strong there. They cursed the place. Bushmen were killed there, far back, long ago, maybe two hundred years. Rape, murder, bad things happened in that place. Our job is to bring those troubled spirits, our ancestors, back from there and release them into the Kalahari, where the Bushmen live still. Where there is still peace.

'It's as if all the bad things that happened there – even the bad things that we ourselves have done there – are a test for us, to test our faith, our strength. We used to dance in the big cave there, the one with the old Bushmen paintings, the ones painted by the Bushmen who were killed there in the first days of the Boers. That's where the voices are loudest. We would dance there and try to get above our bad feelings, our bad blood. One day, during one of our dances, the ancestors sent an arrow of death. We saw it in the dance and Pien, my youngest son, fell down in the grip of that death. It was another test: we had to dance all night, right until morning, to bring him back. And in that dance, Sanna and my daughter Oulet had a vision, that the cave crumbled in on top of them all, and when they looked down, the rubble was covered with huge scorpions. When a vision comes to a woman, its truth is strong, and when they heard it, everyone rushed from the cave. Only I had to stay and not run from the bad thing, but keep dancing, to bring Pien back and take the power from that bad spirit.'

We drove slowly down the empty road. 'You know I am always talking. This old man's mouth is always working, no? And sometimes it seems I am talking to no purpose. Well, listen. These tests, this life we lead here, has drained me. That's why we need to go to this healer you have met, that I have dreamt of, to bring us back to ourselves, to restore our power. Now, when I heard your story, Rru, of where you had been, I was shocked. Me, Dawid, this old Bushman was shocked. This Besa, said my heart, this is the man we need. And now you have promised to take me, and that is good. But there is still one thing more I need to know, something that is missing.'

'Ask away,' I said, wondering what was coming.

'I need to know why you are writing this book, Rru, why you came to us so that we would choose you to tell our story. What was it that brought you here? Not just money for a story, not just to see how things were, not just politics. Something else must have sent you here.'

Dawid looked over, expectantly, as did Sanna and Belinda, and it occurred to me with a slight shock that I had, indeed, never told Dawid my story. Until now I had played the journalist, the man come to chronicle the political process, yet we had strayed far from that. I had not wanted to be exposed, I realised. And now, under Dawid's gentle but unwavering eye, I felt afraid. Might he laugh at me, judge me?

So I told him, starting with the earliest days, with my mother's stories, the artifacts in the house, the tales of all the white African relatives, the feeling of displacement, the growing fascination with these Bushmen whom I had come to feel lay at the root of everything in the place where my family came from. Dawid held up a hand for me to stop.

'Your mother, you say?' he said, his brow furrowed. 'So the

mother had the vision before the son? So she is the one who sent you here, who kept the Bushmen alive in her heart in that far place you come from, while we were dying here in the Kalahari. Who sent a son out here to tell their story. Well then, in September when we go to see Besa, your mother must come too. Your mother must be there, for the vision lies with her.'

My time was running out again. In three days I would have to be back in distant Johannesburg, boarding a flight to the USA. That afternoon, feeling buoyed along by the momentum of recent events, I went over to Steven Smith's house, partly to return his truck, partly to ask if he had talked with his father Piet Smith, the Mier leader and my newfound cousin. After greeting me and asking after my journey, Steven replied that he had talked to the old man. A meeting had been arranged. We could go the following day if I liked: 'But I have to warn you, my Dad's words were: If he's for the Bushmen then I don't like him.'

I wasn't exactly surprised. 'But,' I replied, 'Surely he should see me if he wants to put the Mier's side of the story. I mean, everyone's painting the Mier as the bad guys. Here's an opportunity to tell it from their point of view.'

Steven smiled. The next afternoon, he told me, there was going to be a Mier meeting at a place called Loubos, this side of Rietfontein. But I mustn't expect the old man to be friendly, and I should know a bit more about the Mier. 'You see,' he said, the tamarind tree in his front yard casting dark shadows across his face. 'The Mier, most of them, have no title to their farms. You know that. My father for instance, he has title to one farm out of several. If the Bushmen win their land claim he could lose almost everything.'

'But what about the compensation?'

'It's not so simple. The compensation isn't in land, it's in money. But the farmers would only get what the farms were worth about twenty years ago. How will they buy other land with such money? Where will they go?'

'But I've always been told that the Mier were getting compensation in land too.'

Steven shook his head. 'Well, that's not what the Mier think. And there's also dissent within the Mier community itself. Some of them want to take the money, want the Bushman land claim to go through – mostly the guys who have no land of their own and graze their stock on the common lands, which are always overgrazed. It's not easy to understand the situation in Mier – there are about five organisations all wanting something different. Some follow the National Party, some the ANC, some are allied to each other, some hate each other. My dad has a lot of influence, sure. But he's not the only one. Plus there's another complication. The Mier are filing their own land claim against the park, remember? All this will have to be sorted out before anything to do with the Bushmen can go ahead.'

'Tell me,' I asked, after a moment. 'How much of all this is just about pride?'

Steven smiled, the ends of his thin, droopy moustache lifting. 'A lot,' he admitted, 'A whole lot. Listen, there's so much mistrust here. Look at the whole Northern Cape history: Basters, Griquas, Korannas, Mier, Boers, all fighting for the same land for a hundred years or longer.' The smile faded. 'I can tell you. It's a really sad history. There's no trust. People don't know how to. They've never learned how to. Here, if you trusted your neighbour, your neighbour would only *naai* [fuck] you. Maybe worse. No trust, I'm telling you. Not here among the park management with all their colour and class bullshit, not within the Mier, not among the Bushmen even . . .'

I nodded. He spoke truthfully, but only one side of the truth. 'But surely, at the end of the day it all comes down to economics? I mean, there's money to be made here for everyone, isn't there? The Mier mostly don't have money. I've been told the park's about bankrupt, and the Bushmen have nothing. But it's not like there's too many people and not enough land – more the other way round. What if the Mier gave the Bushmen a cut from some of the profits from livestock? What if the park, Mier and Bushmen all shared their resources, got a proper economy going? Is it really impossible for all three parties to get together, decide how to allocate land, how much money to draw from each other's operations; you know – work together?'

Steven's smile returned, this time as a broad, ironic grin. 'You know, even me, at some of the meetings in Mier, I have suggested something like this. I've said that politically we are on the losing side here. Can't we work together, get involved in tourism? And my father, do you know what he said to me? "How can you, one of the family, say this? I can't believe my ears. I am a farmer and that is that."

'But you know,' he went on, his voice thoughtful. 'He sounds so strong, my father. But the stress from all this, the uncertainty, the land claim, the bad press, everything, his MP duties, it's all getting too much for him. While you were off travelling, he had a collapse, fell down one day and when he woke up, couldn't speak. He was hospitalised, lying there with tubes coming out of him, and the doctors couldn't say what was wrong with him. I think all this is killing him. So, don't expect him to welcome you with open arms, OK?'

That same evening Belinda and I went down to the Red House. By now everyone there had heard of, and approved, Dawid's decision to go up to see Besa in September, even those living in the huts along the road. And to bring my mother; that was the key, Dawid impressed this upon me once again, the others nodding.

I reiterated my promise. But now that the euphoria of the previous night had worn off a little, I began to wonder how I was going to manage it. I had assumed that my mother – now sixty years old – would agree to go. But would she? Then there was the money: my publishers had told me that they had given out all they could until they saw some sample chapters – and I had hardly written anything, being so busy writing freelance stuff to fund the trips and keep the bills paid at home. I was already far into debt from the last two trips. Assuming I could raise the money, what if we went all the way up to Groot Laagte and found Besa gone? Bulanda had told me that he didn't always stay there, that sometimes he disappeared back into the bush for weeks at a time. There was so much that was uncertain, difficult.

Then Bukse, who had come in to the Red House from the roadside, and who had sat unusually silent until now, cleared his throat from the shadows. He was a little drunk, but quietly so. 'Listen Rru,' he said. 'I will give you something to take away with you, to keep you strong. When you come back from the Mier tomorrow, I will give it to you.'

It was a long journey to Loubos. The road, at times, was barely distinguishable from the rolling dunes through which it ran. And out there, even though fences straggled along the roadside, there was game. One little group of springbok who had been about to cross the road ducked away as we roared up, turning as one, like a school of fish. We passed them, and they were gone, swallowed by the red immensity around us.

Loubos, when we finally arrived, proved to be no more than a collection of rough concrete, tin-roofed houses, some terribly run down, others fairly prosperous-looking. There were some wooden stockyards and a long concrete shed, inside which the Mier meeting was in progress. The surrounding area was flat, close to a dry riverbed, in which several clunking windmills pumped up water for the desolate village. A few sparsely leaved trees grew from the bare earth. Those people not inside the big shed-like building milled around in their shade.

As we walked through the crowd, it seemed that South Africa's entire colonial history was being presented to me. Every conceivable blood type was there: KhoiSan, European, black, here and there even a hint of Malay.* One woman with dazzling green eyes, who looked almost Irish, with freckles across her fine nose, had an Afro of tight, dark curls that were reddish as if hennaed. Others looked Spanish. Still others looked like Bushmen, only bigger, more

---

*Back in the early days of Dutch rule at the Cape, slaves and exiles were imported from Dutch Batavia (now part of Indonesia) to boost the working population of the new African colony. These people interbred with the Khoi, creating a class of coloureds known as Cape Malay. To this day, many Cape Malays still practise Islam and look more to that culture than to Africa for their heritage. Although the Mier and other coloureds of the Northern Cape live far away from the centre of Cape Malay culture, some of this blood has seeped into every area of coloured South Africa and Namibia.

confident, better fed. Their clothes were good, and their trucks, all parked neatly in a line, were for the most part newish models. This, I realised, was the Mier aristocracy.

Piet Smith, when he finally appeared, was every inch the master of this feudal world. When he came out of the building, the crowd parted to let him through, and the men he stopped to talk to seemed, through their body language, to defer to this stocky man of medium height, with a bank-manager's hair-cut and dark suit. The face, when at last it came level with mine, was absolutely without warmth. Piet Smith was not thinking 'family' as he looked at me. His nose was red with burst veins and had a small rug of coarse black hair on it. His handshake was limp, moist, not reassuring. 'I hear you want to talk,' he said.

We went over to the stock fences, where we would have some privacy, Steven following to make up for my bad Afrikaans. A little daunted, I began reeling off the questions I had prepared: Had the Mier ever really got their story across to the media? Was there perhaps room for compromise? Did he think that the Mier and Bushmen could live alongside each other as neighbours, rather than rivals? Could they not figure out a way to benefit each other?

He interrupted me, holding up a finger. 'You come here to talk for the Bushmen, but now you listen to me.' And he launched into a litany of complaint and refutation. Amazingly, he claimed that the Mier had come to this region long before the Bushmen: the first Bushmen, he told me, had only showed up in these parts when he was already of school age. Now they were saying it was their land? Well, they were liars, and drunks, and *skelms*, trouble-makers, ungrateful for all the opportunities the Mier had given them: jobs, schools, the church. 'And they aren't even real Bushmen any more,' he said, taking up the old charge. 'They are just like us, *bruin mense* [brown people], poor coloureds who intermarried with the Bushmen that showed up here in the forties, and now want to cash in. This land was never taken from Bushmen. How can they claim what isn't theirs?

'*Ja*, they can have farms if they want them. We Mier are generous people. But it is for them to come to us, we are the *baases* here.

They can apply, like anyone else, to the Mier Council and put their names down for a place. Then, if a farmer dies and his son doesn't want to carry on, maybe they can come in line for a farm.' He nodded, encouraging himself. 'And I tell you this, if the government takes any land away from me, they must compensate me with at least half as much again in value. For they are making me leave *my* ancestral home!'

With that, he turned and walked away, back to the crowd still gathered around the big shed. Steven shrugged: 'Told you. Listen, come back to the house, it's not far. He'll have calmed down a bit, later.'

The Smiths had the largest house in that dryland settlement, a suburban ranch-style affair with arches and French windows looking out at the poorer houses and the parched, rubbish-strewn common where thin, ribby horses and donkeys grazed. Steven's neat, hair-sprayed, hen-like mother, unsure how to deal with me, served tea and biscuits in the airy cool of the living room, the white curtains billowing in the draught while we waited for the old man to come back. When he did, he looked amused to see me still there. He sat down, drank some tea and began again.

'You ask me what I will do if Mandela gives away my people's land to the Bushmen? If Mandela takes my land I'll cut my own throat! I tell you: it will happen only over my dead body!' His voice rose to a shout, ringing off the cool white walls. 'A reporter from some Swedish newspaper came to bother me with these same questions a week ago, while I was lying there in hospital. Lying there with tubes coming out of me! Even there you people won't let me rest! I say to you what I said to him. Any bloody Bushman who comes on my land telling me it's his; that Bushman I will shoot.'

He mimed picking up a rifle and shooting some distant target. 'It will be war, you understand? War! And then, when the shooting has started, what will you do with this war that you have caused? Yes, you. Will you then run away, safe back to your own country?'

I looked into the shrewd eyes and glimpsed a flicker of humour. Somewhere behind the bluster, I realised, was another Piet Smith, watching all this from afar, playing with me. 'Well,' I answered at length, 'tell me when the war begins and I'll come back with the cameras.'

But he wasn't to be so easily thrown off: 'Why don't they take the white people's land? Why must the coloureds always be called on to pay for everything? Well, no more, no longer. Not while Piet Smith is alive! Your Bushmen – do you want twenty people to benefit while 5,000 Mier find themselves without homes! I'm telling you, man, we can fight this thing with our own land claim! We'll tie it up for years, I promise you. These Bushmen think they are clever . . .'

I waited while he rumbled to a halt, then, half-heartedly, changed the subject to family, knowing that this too meant nothing at all to him. You can't choose your relatives, after all. I would record his words, I assured him, but now could I take a picture for my mother?

Back at the Red House my leave-taking of Dawid was brief. I knew what I had to do. We shared a pipe, looking out across the night-time dunes towards Regopstaan's grave. From there, Belinda and I went down to Bukse's fire, to receive the gift he had promised me. There were two parts to it. The first was a small bow, made of gemsbok horn, and three reed arrows; two tipped with steel and one with bone. 'Ostrich bone,' he said, making me feel the carved head. 'There are no giraffe here, but the thigh-bone of an ostrich is also good for arrowheads – strong and light.'

In the dim light of the much-waned moon, I looked at Bukse's face and saw a different man from the drunken, raving one who complained endlessly about Dawid, jealous of his older brother's power. Now that he was sober I saw him as he was: lithe, compact and powerful. Not unlike Besa, but with a finer nose, and eyes that slanted up at the corners. Bukse was handsome.

'Here,' he said, picking up the second object, 'Here is something else; for luck.' It was a small container, also fashioned from ostrich-bone, from a hollowed-out section of femur. On it were carved pictures of a jackal riding a lion, and a hunter shifting shape, transforming into a gemsbok. Inside was something precious: a dark, crumbly powder that Bukse called 'poison root'. 'If you are in the veld and a snake bites you, or you take a wound that goes *vrot* [rotten], you sprinkle this stuff onto it and it will draw out the bad. And, look, it also makes fire.' Bukse put the little container onto the ground and produced, from his torn trouser pocket, a flint and a broken piece of metal file. Striking these together, he sent a red, glowing dot into the dark powder which immediately began, coal-like, to glow. Tearing up some dry grasses, Bukse twisted them into a tight wad and put them to the glow, blowing on it as he did so. A wisp of smoke came snaking up. Then he quickly whipped the grasses out, replacing the cap over the glow so as to deprive it of air, and put the smoking grasses on the ground, blowing them into a small flame that grew larger. Some twigs helped make a little blaze, the flames licking at them eagerly. 'Wherever you go when you travel, you are safe with this luck. And this bow; when you are back in America, look at them and think of us here in the red sands, and remember what you have promised.'

In the cold dawn, Belinda drove me to Upington, from where she had managed to arrange a lift for me back to Johannesburg. We drove southwards from the park gate, picking up speed as we passed the dark huddle of Jakob and Leana's hut.

Late the following afternoon, back in Johannesburg's wide-awake, hustling streets, the experiences of this astonishing trip tucked themselves away, becoming dormant among the press of people and buildings. The aeroplane was better: peaceful and silent.

The next night I spoke to my mother. Of course she would go, she said. Of course. When did we fly?

It took the full three months to earn the money, cold-calling editors, lining up freelance work on anything, any idea I could think of that would earn the cash necessary to finance the trip. Mark, a radio producer friend who had broadcast a piece I had made on the situation at Nyae Nyae two years before, offered to come along and help share costs. Meanwhile, Belinda told our plans to any tourist that evinced even a slight interest in the Bushmen. Donations came in from here and there. Belinda and I ran up terrific phone bills calling each other back and forth with updates. Dawid even hobbled into the park a couple of times to use the telephone and wake me up at 6 a.m. in Colorado, where Kristin and I had moved, to cackle into the phone: '*Ay* Rroo, this is your old drunken Bushman here. You busy writing? Busy working? You'd better be or I'll give you such a smack when I see you . . .' and the line would go dead, crackling and cackling with laughter and static.

Airline tickets were booked, and in the first week of September 1998, I arrived back in Welkom, a few days ahead of my mother Polly and Mark, to plot with Dawid and Belinda just how we were going to do this thing.

14

Bushman Politics

I had arrived in advance of the others so as to have time to prepare the ground and make the travel arrangements, as well as to find out how many of the Xhomani were going to come with us. My mother was to fly into Johannesburg by herself, and after visiting some relatives there, would make her way to cousin Gert Loxton's at Keimos, as would Mark, the radio producer who was going to travel and split costs with us. No sooner had I arrived than I discovered our departure to see Besa would have to wait a week. There was to be, of all things, an election at Welkom.

Matters had moved on politically for the Bushmen. At the prompting of Petrus Vaalbooi (an urban, literate Xhomani from the town of Rietfontein whom the South African San Institute (SASI) seemed to have adopted over Dawid as the new spokesman), and on the advice of Roger Chennels, the land claim had been opened up to include people from outside the Kruiper clan. Anyone who could prove a Bushman bloodline could now be part of the claim. SASI had spent the past months actively seeking out people of Bushman descent in the townships and farms of the Northern Cape. About three hundred had come forward claiming Xhomani or other South African Bushman bloodlines. Some – including three sisters from Upington who had, it turned out, been born under the tree that now shaded chief warden Dries Engelbrecht's front yard – were direct relatives of the late Regopstaan, and still spoke the Xhomani language. But many others seemed to have almost no Bushman blood and there were mutterings, when I arrived at Welkom, about people jumping on the bandwagon and a coming conflict between the original clan and these newcomers.

But this did make for greater numerical – and thus political – strength. Combined with the fact that the urban Bushman Petrus Vaalbooi (or 'Vaalie' as Dawid called him) was becoming so vocal, it had meant that South Africa's newspapers and TV news crews had begun to follow the land claim more closely. The issue had entered the media spotlight once more.

Roger Chennels and the SASI people were astute enough, however, to see the dangers inherent in this opening up of the land claim. It was in order to address this that SASI had suggested that elections be held, to create a committee of both 'moderns' (Vaalie's lot) and 'traditionals' (the Xhomani) who would decide how to campaign further for the claim and who would manage the land once it had been won. So, as Belinda told me immediately upon my arrival, she and I were to drive straight down to Kagga Kama and fetch the people there so that they could attend the election, and ensure that the 'traditionals' would be represented in full strength. Izak, the Kagga Kama leader, had put up money for the hire of a vehicle. But it meant a drive of a thousand kilometres in two days, much of it on bad dirt roads. Having just spent almost twenty-four hours flying from the USA, I hardly felt up to it. But there was no choice.

Belinda, too, was clearly exhausted, and looked as if she'd hardly slept during the three months I'd been away. The double life she had been leading between the Bushmen and the park was clearly taking its toll. The physical change in her was alarming. She had lost weight dramatically and her skin looked unnaturally pale and stretched too taut, eyes sunk too deep. She had a wild look to her, and began talking incessantly from the moment she picked me up in Upington.

That afternoon, as we drove the long red-dune miles to Welkom, she filled me in on the events of the past three months. The hostility towards her from the park management, said Belinda, had upped in intensity ever since the night we had taken Dawid into the park. Her faxes had been intercepted and her phone calls listened to. Dries, the park warden, had begun calling her into his office almost daily, citing an endless succession of small breaches in regulations – things that never came to anything, but were meant to intimidate, she thought. There had been subtle racial slurs, even a rumour spread that she was a lesbian. One of the more Christian managers had besieged her with entreaties to turn away from these demons that the Bushmen danced with.

The situation had been exacerbated by the more mischievous Bushmen indulging in some blatant manager-baiting. Sillikat and Rikki had taken to coming into the park drunk and talking with the tourists in the rest camp, forcing park staff to come and throw them out. Elsie had stormed into Henriette's office one day and called her a liar, a promise breaker, making the blonde woman cry. Kabuis and his wife Betty had taken to spending days and evenings in Belinda's (and therefore the park's) house, taking showers and watching TV, which had incensed the other residents of the managers' compound. Belinda had eventually been ostracised by the white management, isolated in the place she lived and worked.

The Bushmen had stood by her, however. Jakob had taken her onto the dunes one day, and, as Rikki had done when Steven Smith had been trying to catch Belinda out with *dagga*, many months before, had given her a piece of bitter bark and told her to think about the two managers who were most hostile to her, then spit out the chewed bark and think only good thoughts. Within two months, he promised, the two men would have left. Amazingly, it had turned out just so; they both left for jobs at some new, swanky private game reserve near Johannesburg.

On another evening, she said, after an unusually hard rain, she had walked outside the park gate to the dry riverbed, where the Nossob and Aub joined their empty courses, and had found the Xhomani all dancing there together. A dance about her, it turned out. Bukse had taken her aside and told her that he'd had a vision of her the night before as a 'guardian spirit' of the Xhomani, had seen her float up above the riverbed and then metamorphose into a strange, white shape. That morning, he said, he had found a bone in the riverbed that was exactly the same shape as the 'thing' she had turned into. He had fashioned it into a pendant for her and called it Aub, after the river, and put strong magic into it to protect her. That was why they were dancing – to dance the magic into the bone. The clan had then taken her to the Red House and painted her face with the markings of a female springbok. That night, all the men – Kabuis, Bukse, Sillikat, Rikki and some others – had danced again, to see who would be the springbok's man, and ended up by falling down in mock exhaustion. 'You're too strong, too strong for us,' they had whimpered, joking, from the ground.

These events had brought her much closer to the Xhomani. But she had made ugly discoveries too. She had come to realise, for instance, the sadistic extent to which the men of Welkom beat their wives when drunk. Jakob was the worst, she said, but they all did it. So she had told the Welkom women to stand up for themselves, fight back, make the men think twice about hitting them. And a couple of nights later the women had indeed attacked their men – with kerries, gemsbok horns, pots and pans, and beaten them out of the village. The men, especially Jakob and Bukse, had been furious.

Listening as she drove, I felt a twinge of misgiving. Was it her place to put the women up to violence, whatever the reasons? Her eyes glittered a little too brightly as she talked about it.

There had also been rapes, she went on, not within the clan, but by outsiders. Two of the coloured park rangers had taken Elsie onto the dunes one night, got her drunk and forced her. One of the older women, a shy, frail cousin of Dawid's (the same elderly lady I had met at Kagga Kama with Cait) had been gang-raped by some local coloured men. But no charges were ever pressed because, said Belinda, the Bushmen were too afraid.

The worst of it, though, had been sexual crimes within the clan – not rape, but selling the women for liquor and for dope. She had found out that the women of Welkom were being routinely sold to local coloureds and blacks by their own men. Some of the Bushmen said that Dawid had been ordering it for a long time past now, especially using Betty for the purpose. Others pointed the finger elsewhere.

Belinda told me she had finally decided to take matters into her own hands. During the time I had been gone a new CEO had been appointed to the National Parks Board in Pretoria, Mvuro Msimang, a Xhosa who had announced that local communities would be the first priority for all new National Park strategies. Belinda had taken a risk and rung this man Msimang and arranged a meeting with him. She had taken a few days off and booked a flight at her own expense. The night before leaving, old Antas had given her a gift: a little tin, inside which was some animal fat, or grease, and sitting in that, a single South African cent, a penny, promising that the talisman would bring her all the money she needed.

She had arrived in Johannesburg, told her relatives there why she had come, and they had given her enough money not only to pay back the ticket but also to hire a car. She had driven up to Pretoria to see the new CEO and, to her great delight, found him a willing and sympathetic ear. He had assured her that he meant to do everything in his power to see that justice was done.

So back she had come, full of hope, to face whatever chaos awaited her in the Kalahari. And chaos there had been in plenty. The animosity between Dawid and Petrus Vaalbooi was growing hotter by the month. The people at Welkom were worried that Dawid's authority would be usurped – along with the land – if they won the claim. As yet, the idea of an election to decide the leadership question had not been thought of. Meanwhile a man called Harry had begun appearing at the SASI meetings. No one seemed to know who he was exactly, only that he also lived in Rietfontein but seemed to support Dawid. This man Harry was calling himself the 'prophet for the Bushmen', and exhorting them all to remember the old prophecies, the traditions. He had targeted Petrus particularly, said Belinda, and so created another conflict.

Meanwhile, just as Steven had warned me they would, the Mier had now also laid their own claim to a large section of the park which they said had been taken from them back in the 1960s. Until this had been fully examined, the National Parks Board lawyer was refusing to move any further on the Xhomani claim.

At Welkom, the emotional ups and downs created by all this, said Belinda, had been causing a greater degree of conflict and fighting than ever. Bukse was still defying Dawid's authority at every turn. Jakob and Rikki were throwing violent tantrums every few days and, for some reason, no doubt a private quarrel, Sillikat had informed the police that Dawid and Jakob had rustled a sheep from one of the neighbouring farms, and now there was a court case pending.

Next morning, Dawid, Belinda, Izak and I drove south to Kagga Kama. By contrast with Belinda's tales of Bushman craziness, the trip down was peaceful and full of humour. At a filling station in Upington, Dawid made us buy him a copy of *Hustler* and, as we drove southwards over the dry, rocky Karoo, he and Izak carefully perused every page. Sneaking a look back in the rear-view, I saw Dawid's and Izak's rapt, giggling faces. I said, 'Hey Dawid, haven't you seen porn before?'

He looked up, frowning like a professor interrupted from deep study, then gave a wide, yellow-toothed grin. 'Oh *ja*, didn't I ever tell you about my time in Germany? It was after the indigenous peoples' conference in Geneva. Michael Daiber⋆ took me to a sex show. There was a big blonde woman, just like this one here. Bouncing up and down on someone! I never knew white women did it like that! Always so beautiful, so composed, and there this one was, grunting away like a baboon!' His laughter thickened to coughing, a great, chest-heaving fit of it while Izak looked out of the window, trying to control his smirk.

Sometime in the late afternoon, on the rough mountain track that led in to Kagga Kama, Izak said, a propos of nothing, '*Ay* Ru, you have travelled since the last time we saw you. It is like I said that first time. You are the bird, the one that takes and brings the message.'

I was flattered but I didn't agree. Not this time. Another picture had sprung to mind. 'No man,' I said, 'You know what we are, Belinda and me? We're two little donkeys, and you and Dawid are the ones sitting up on the buckboard, driving.' Dawid roused from his light sleep, chuckled. '*Ja Mama*, that's right: Giddy up!'

That night, in Kagga Kama, we slept all huddled together under a shared bundle of blankets in the back room of Izak's and Lys's stone hut. Sometime in the night it rained hard, and the battered tin roof dripped cold water onto any part of the body that fell outside

⋆An anthropologist who worked with the Xhomani in the early 1990s.

226

the covers. But at dawn the rainstorm blew itself out. The sun appeared, rising warm and splendid over the mountains, and the people sang and laughed as they got together their bundles, ready for the trip. It took time for them to do this, however. While we waited, Belinda and I let some of the Kagga Kama children lead us down to the graves of the three Xhomani who had been killed, a few years before, when the vehicle carrying them down here from Welkom had flipped over and crashed. They lay in a neat row, three sandy coffin-shaped mounds with wilted flowers and little bottles of water placed on top. 'This is so the spirits can come and drink when they're thirsty,' said the children, pointing at the bottles. 'When they drink it down to here,' they indicated a certain level on the glass, 'we fill it for them again, and then they're happy.'

Before leaving, we ate a meal of *braaied* meat, laid on by Izak and Lys, who wanted Belinda and I to be strong and alert on the drive. Then all those coming north to attend the elections packed themselves, sardine-like, into the van. As we drove slowly down the mountain track, Izak turned to Dawid and said: 'You know, come December we're going to need to organise some more vehicles to take our stuff up to the Kalahari.'

'What d'you mean?' Belinda butted in, her pale, tired face alight. 'Do you mean you're going to leave Kagga Kama?'

'*Ja,*' nodded Izak. 'By the end of the year there will be no Bushmen here. We want to come home, Dawid, to the red sands, to the Kalahari. See how the rain has gone north?' he pointed up beyond the mountains, in the direction we were going. 'The work here is done, the old curse almost gone. The times of big rain for the Kalahari are coming again. Bushmen must follow the rain.'

We drove all day, and overnighted in Upington. The following morning, as we turned onto the Nossob riverbed road, the last stretch to Welkom and the park, someone shouted from the back: 'It's him, up there – Regopstaan, there in the sky! Can't you see him?' The man who spoke was Hendrik, the well-built, muscular young man who had danced the gemsbok dance for Chris, Cait and me, the first time at Kagga Kama. He shouted again. 'There, up there, sitting in the blue, feet pointing towards the south. Can't you see him?'

Next day I turned around and went south again, to meet my mother and Mark at Gert Loxton's and bring them back to Welkom. '*Ja*, go,' said Dawid. 'Bring her to us. The time has come for us to meet her. Go and fetch her, so the healing can begin.'

It seemed the most natural thing in the world to walk into Gert's farmhouse and see my mother, Polly, small and blonde, sitting on the back porch, her bespectacled face illuminated by a shaft of dry South African sunshine, to hear her speaking Afrikaans with Gert and the people on the farm, to see her put on a wide-brimmed sun hat and go down to the livestock pens with Cynthia to feed the lambs. This, clearly, was her natural context, her home. Why had she stayed away so long?

Mark arrived in the evening, excited by the bits of Africa he had seen on his way down to meet us. We passed two quiet, good days at Gert and Cynthia's. We drank wine, explored the farm, talked with Gert. Despite the bad memory of his humiliation by the park officials back in the apartheid days, he said he intended to come up with us and meet Dawid and these Bushmen who were fighting for land.

Belinda had booked a chalet for them at Twee Rivieren, so they could attend the elections. They would drive up in the evening after Polly, Mark and I had already arrived. As the three of us drove north in Mark's small car, the red sand miles flying by, I kept thinking: Christ, it's really going to happen. I'm going to see the Bushmen with my mother.

At Belinda's house, it was a meeting of two glittering women. Two generations of South African women coming together across the old colour bar that no longer separated those who wished to cross it. My mother looked at Belinda and thought (or so her diary read): '*A woman who definitely runs with wolves. Beautiful, golden and delicate like a steenbokkie.*'

'So you've brought her,' said Dawid, as we arrived at the Red House, smiling so broadly that the smile seemed to radiate out into the air around him and make that smile too. 'The woman that kept us alive while all the time we were dying here in the Kalahari.'

Dawid took both my mother's hands in his own and beamed at her. '*Mama, mama, dankie mama. Ons is bly Mama!* [. . . We are glad, Mama]' Then the people hugged and kissed her, with Sillikat, Kabuis and Rikki squeezing in for their hugs too.

'*A fairylike people,*' my mother later wrote. '*Like twigs and flowers, sweet-smelling, thin, thin silky skin taut over bones. High cheekboned triangular faces, little diamond eyes looking intently into yours.*'

Gert and Cynthia, having followed the directions we had given them, arrived just in time to see their sixty-year-old white cousin submerged in Bushmen.

We *braaied* at Belinda's that night, eating meat from the park shop and tinned sardines donated by Izak and Lys. Everybody came: Roger Chennels, the Afrikaner student Erica, the Xhosa student Themba, the coloured student Eleanor, Gert and Cynthia, my Mier cousin Steven Smith, even a journalist from *National Geographic*, come out to write a piece on how the Bushmen were coping with today's world, of which the morrow's elections were a part. It was a relaxed, informal meeting of worlds and personalities. Only cousin Steven was not as warm as he had been the last time, though he had good reason. The child his wife Henna had been heavily pregnant with three months before, had been still-born. He came to the *braai*, had some meat and beer, met my mother, Gert and Cynthia, but went away soon, to be alone with his grief.

When everyone had gone to bed, my mother, Belinda, Mark and I climbed the fence behind the house and walked up the towering dune beyond to lay out our sleeping bags on sand turned blue by the night. The worry about lions, snakes, scorpions faded as the intense, cool delight of soft sand, pale grasses, stars and the fresh night wind washed over us.

Next day, we found Welkom transformed. A great marquee had been erected in front of the Red House, attached to its open entrance with ropes, making a stage of the inside of the dune-like building. Hundreds had come. People with every type of face, from pure Bushman to near white or black. Dressed in rags, or designer gear, or (in Jakob's case) in nothing but a *xai*. They had come from the veld, from sheep farms, from shanties, suburbs, the poorer edges of cities. They had come from Upington, from Rietfontein, from Loubos, from Cape Town, even from Johannesburg. They were the fruits of SASI's search for the remnants of the Bushmen that had once populated all of South Africa. There were teachers, professionals, labourers, housewives, paupers, pensioners, children, teenagers in Reeboks and Adidas, teenagers in torn shorts with sores on their legs. Some three hundred in all made it a day of pride. But, apart from Belinda and the student Eleanor, nobody from the park was present.

Outside the Red House, with its strange, canvas extension, a music box pumped out African jive, and people danced around and around in a stamping Bushman circle. One old, old man hobbled and wobbled along in the dance, leaning on his stick, a toothless smile gaping from under the shadow of his wide-brimmed hat, a huge green coat enveloping his bent old body. In front of him, cloud-like and billowing, a woman with a mild case of Down's syndrome and a tall *doek* on her head. When the ancient man left the dance, I tried out my Afrikaans on him, asking who he was, where he had come from.

'Heinrich,' he told me, his voice a mere whisper. 'Heinrich Jongbos.' He was ninety years old, from Upington, but born in Keimoes.

'Keimoes?' I asked. Did he know of the Loxtons?

'Ah, of course,' replied the ancient. 'My father worked for them, he was a Bushman on their farm.' And with that he hobbled away, disappearing into the crowd to greet friends.

I looked around for Gert and Cynthia, whom I had seen arriving, wanting to point the old man out to them. But they too had been swallowed by the throng. In the meantime there was much to distract the eye. Mark, with his headphones, DAT machine and microphone primed and ready, was speaking to Harry, a tall, mixed-race man in a porcupine quill headband. He was here, Harry said to the proffered mike, to make sure that in this new political time the Bushmen did not forget their traditions, did not forget their god.

Roger Chennels, the lawyer, also made a statement. 'The San movement is irrevocable. They will *definitely* get their land, *definitely* get their rights in the park. We will be looking for a ratification sometime next year, 1999. It will turn back the tide of history in southern Africa.'

The crowd was called into the marquee and the pre-election speeches began. First on was Petrus Vaalbooi, attired to look half modern, half traditional, a headband of coloured beadwork above his glasses and tie somehow giving him instant credibility. Here, I thought, is a politician. Belinda translated for me. 'Keep the heart open,' Petrus was urging. 'We are here to speak, not to compete.' After him came another man in suit and tie, who took the microphone in his fist like a rock singer and began to rant and shriek. 'From Rietfontein,' whispered Belinda. 'One of Vaalie's lot.' The rant, which was about Jesus, seemed to last for ever. Finally Dawid, in ragged shorts and no shoes, stepped up to the mike. He spoke succinctly: keep the tradition, he said. That was the most important thing. Without it there was nothing.

The 'lost' Bushmen, those who had come forward in the past months to claim their heritage, also made speeches. One spare old man from the Upington townships gave his in the Xhomani language, which he had not used since he was a boy. 'People had said that there were no Bushmen left, but Dawid took the message that this was wrong to the world. He found the friends of the Bushmen, those who could help. And because of this, the Bushmen now have a future. Thank you.'

An ancient lady, one of the three sisters who had been born in what was now Dries Engelbrecht's front garden, also spoke in the Xhomani tongue: 'To live in denial of one's ancestors – this was the greatest pain. We were buried by the white man, by the Boer, but Dawid came and dug us out of the sand. For so long I had no one, just my two sisters, surviving in the white man's world. My heart is like a flower today. The time has come for truth.'

When she had finished, it was time for politics. Petrus Vaalbooi stepped up to the mike once more, took a deep breath and, just as the Jesus man had, let out a great shout. A long, fierce-sounding monologue followed, like a preacher's harangue. The veins in his neck bulged, beads of sweat sprang onto his caramel forehead and began to trickle down over the coloured headband, misting up his glasses. He shouted so loud it made one wince to listen. He too was talking about the pain of denial, the long years of waiting. But one couldn't help feeling that he was milking it. He started crying, stopped, blew his nose, looked down at his notes and began to shout again. Dawid had begged him, he said, as the powerful one, the one who understood politics, to help him, had begged him to motivate the community. 'The people have no jobs, no status, no pension, no security, no future. I am come like the rain to help put this right.'

Then Harry, the half-white, half-Bushman in the porcupine-quill headband, stood up to take his turn. He looked straight at Vaalbooi, who avoided the other's gaze, toying idly with a pencil. 'Today I see two flashes of light, and both come from God. The first light is the tradition; the second is the Western way. This is a way that should never have come. Don't listen to false prophets. Go as God leads. Nature will guide you. You do not need money. Everything is the Bushmen – you are the sand, the honest spirit leads where there are no tears. Now here is a warning: do not leave this place today and back-bite, work against each other. The Bushmen do not live through politics. Do not let us lose God.'

There was silence. Into it stepped Roger, the lawyer, smiling. 'Regopstaan's spirit is here today. He asks: where do you go? What do you want? These elections – why are they important? The Bushmen are riding a bus. Dawid is not the only driver, but he's at the wheel. Let us all help and make sure the bus goes in the right direction. But whoever you elect remember that Dawid still steers.' Soon, promised the lawyer, the Xhomani would have their ground, some of it inside the park, some of it outside. What was crucial now was to choose the people who would run it, to elect the committee to do so in front of the whole people, so that nothing should be hidden.

Finally the Bushmen, the half-Bushmen, the quarter and one-eighth Bushmen, all cast their votes. Dawid was publicly acknowledged, by 100 per cent vote, as traditional leader. Petrus took off his headband and there before the crowd, 'crowned' Dawid with it, like an archbishop conferring power on a king. Petrus Vaalbooi was elected chairman.

As for the committee, only four of the traditional Xhomani were elected: Oulet (Dawid's daughter); Hendrik (he who had danced the traditional dance that first time at Kagga Kama and who had seen Regopstaan sitting in the sky); Lys (Izak's wife); and another from Kagga Kama. The rest were all from Vaalbooi's 'modern' faction from Rietfontein, outnumbering the 'traditionals' by two.

And that concluded an historic event – Western politics done Bushman-style for the first time in the New South Africa. The air was heavy with a sense of the struggles to come. Harry stalked off into the veld, looking angry. The crowd, muttering and talking, were fed with a *braai* laid on by SASI.

As this was the Kalahari, however, the day was not without its element of farce. While everyone was eating their *braaivleis*, a tour bus loaded with white, old-age pensioners from the town of Upington came chugging up over the sand and parked right outside the marquee, disgorging a score or so of vague-looking grannies and granddads who came tottering over, asking if there were any crafts for sale, and if these were real Bushmen. Someone eventually found the driver and told him that now was not the time. Apologising, he rounded up his blue-rinsed flock, put them back in the bus and started the engine, only to find the vehicle was stuck in the sand. So all the Bushmen put down their paper plates of *braaied* goat and *roesterkoek* (ash bread) and heaved the bus out.

Gert and Cynthia appeared – it was time for them to be getting on home, they said, but a most interesting visit. They shook hands with the Bushmen and drove away southward. Watching them go, I realised I had forgotten to tell them about the ancient man whose father had been a Bushman on their farms. I had been too tired to remember. They had seemed tired too. Everyone was tired. A *zol* went round, and after that it was time to leave.

But there were two more things still to be done before we could head out to find Besa. Mark and Belinda had to drive the Kagga Kama lot back home, another thousand kilometres in a day and a night. While they did this, Polly and I were to take Jakob and Dawid into court in Upington to sort out the issue of the stolen goat, the strange quarrel between them and Sillikat which Belinda had told me about when I first arrived. The four of us smoked a bowl of *dagga* (my mother was taking well to the habit, I noticed) and crashed out, only to rise before dawn, drive out to Welkom and load the Bushmen into vehicles once more.

It was something to see Dawid and Jakob work the magistrate. The story about the goat – who had killed it and exactly why – seemed to change with each telling, and there were barely concealed smirks around the courtroom. But Dawid's anger at Sillikat and Elsie was clear. There seemed to be so many divisions within the clan. And the power struggle with the Rietfontein Bushmen also loomed large on the horizon. Dawid had been right about the Xhomani's need to heal. On the road north back to Welkom, we saw eland, springbok and gemsbok thronging by the roadside fences. 'See?' said Dawid. 'Animals showing themselves in the open. A good omen. Yes.'

The day after the court date was to be a day of rest – at least for Polly and me – before the trip north to Besa. Belinda and Mark were not yet back from Kagga Kama, so for once it was a peaceful morning with nowhere to go, nothing to do. A chance to rest before the coming adventure. Polly climbed the dune behind Belinda's house and sat there painting. I drank tea, went for a short walk, watching the ground squirrels dart and rush about, and then stretched out on Belinda's makeshift couch and opened my book to read.

Almost immediately the front door banged open, and in marched Betty and Elsie, singing. They carried branches of green, sprouting bushes that had put out delicate new leaves in expectation of the coming rains, and also a little container of yellow pollen.

'Smell here! Smell this! Smell here!'

My mother, hearing the noise, had come back in from the dune. Betty reached out for her with thin arms, and pulled my mother's small blonde head down to sniff where she had dabbed some of the pollen. I smelled it too – aromatic, sweet, untainted by the small amount of alcohol sweating through their skin.

'This is our scent – *lavental-saun*. And this,' they said, presenting a plant in an old Pringles tin to my mother, 'This is for you!'

Surprised and delighted, she thanked them, took the plant, then went to Belinda's kitchen to find a container so that she could put it in water.

'No!' giggled Elsie and Betty. 'Not water, silly. You put it in sand, look.' They took the tin out to the dune behind the house – the same dune, they told us, where Dawid's middle son Toppies had been born before their expulsion from the park – and dug into it with their hands. They scooped up handfuls of sand into the cylindrical tin and placed the plant inside. 'It grows in the sand. Like us. You see, we don't need the Europeans at all. We don't need scent – this is our scent. We don't need soap – this is our soap, we use the plants. We want a fire? We have sticks and grass. There now, this plant, it will sit in the sand and wait for the rain, you do not need to give it water from a tap.'

There was a sound of male voices. Kabuis and Sillikat came over smiling, singing a song of their own making. They and their women began, gently, to pluck at my mother's shirt. 'Take it off take it off! You must sit here on the dune with us.' Elsie took off her own shirt, revealing small brown breasts. Betty did the same. They sat down in the mango-coloured sand, pulling my mother down with them.

'Rru, Rru, come and take our picture! Like this! All together!'

Their hands were all over my mother. Off came her shirt, then her bra. At first she tried to hide her white nakedness, then she relaxed. Erica, the Afrikaans student and friend of Belinda's, appeared. They made her sit down too. 'Take it off take it off!' She wouldn't, but snuggled up to them all the same, giggling. Kabuis sat down beside the women, took my mother's bare foot and washed it gently with sand. He showed her a dark, flat mole on her foot, then pointed to two similar ones in his and Elsie's insteps. 'We are like you and Rru. You are also spotted here – and here and here.' He pointed to my mother's moles and freckles, sharply exposed by the harsh, metallic glare of the sun.

I did as they bid, snapping my mother, laughing, delighted, almost naked in the sand with the four Bushmen. Then I offered to drive them back to Welkom, these happy, drunken people who had made my mother feel loved. I was grateful to them.

235

But back at the Red House, there was trouble. Everyone was drunk. Dawid, Sanna, all of them. Belinda had just been here, he told me, and it had been decided that just he and Sanna would come north to find Besa. We must leave next day. So now, he chuckled, before gathering strength he must indulge in some weakness.

'OK,' I said, 'See you tomorrow, we'll all get some good rest.' But, suddenly adamant that they had to come back to the park and see 'their *Belindy*', Betty, Kabuis, Sillikat and Elsie refused to get out of the car. Somehow they had become even more drunk than before – they must have had another bottle stashed away somewhere. They had to see Belinda with their own eyes, they said, to make sure she was safe back from the road. I was really tired by now, and lost my patience. 'Come on guys, get out of the car,' I said.

Dawid came hobbling up, shouting: 'Don't you hear what Rru is saying? Get out of the car, now!'

They pulled the doors shut, Betty locking hers.

'OUT!' screamed Dawid, furious now. He reached in the passenger side window, unlocked Betty's door, wrenched it open, grabbed her arm and started to pull her out. She slammed the door shut again, closing it on his arm. He roared. A swaying, liquor-smelling crowd gathered from the huts.

Sillikat got out and drew me to one side, speaking conspiratorially: 'You see, you are my brother. You know what's in my heart . . .' I didn't know the half of it, he said. Dawid was not even the rightful leader. And they were all against him and Elsie.

I shook him off. Betty and Elsie were out of the car now, screaming at everyone and making a scene. Accusations flew back and forth, then there was a flurry of activity around Betty. The people closed in on her in a pack. There were blows. She fell in the dust awkwardly, twisting her hip and spine. She didn't get up, but lay there crying. Then I saw Kabuis trying to get to his wife. Blows were rained on him too, mostly by Oulet, surprising because she was so small. Elsie, sobbing, took off towards the coloured village, yelling that she was going to call the police. Sillikat tugged at my elbow: 'You see, my friend, they are all against me . . .'

Oulet detached herself from the mêlée, ran off to the Red House,

236

and came back wielding a gemsbok-horn with a jagged lump of skull still attached to the bottom end. I rushed in, grabbing her bare-breasted form around the middle in a makeshift tackle. For someone so very small and slight, Oulet was surprisingly strong. It was all I could do to hold her. Someone else grabbed her too, and we wrestled Oulet down onto the sand together, prising the weapon from her hand. She squirmed loose, furious, spitting like a cat. She screamed at me, 'Get in your car, go!'

I did. Sillikat had climbed in too. 'Take me down the road,' he pleaded. 'I can't stay here, they'll kill me this night.' So I drove him down to his roadside hut, where he collapsed into a snoring heap inside the grass shelter.

Back at Belinda's house, I was greeted by the sound of women's singing as I walked up to the front door. Belinda and my mother were singing a song from my childhood, *Bobejaan klim die berg* ('The Baboon Climbed up the Mountain'). Their voices flowed together beautifully. I tiptoed through the kitchen to the back porch beyond. Mark was recording them, headphones on, microphone out. He put his fingers to his lips and smiled.

When all the songs they knew had been sung, Polly and Belinda told me that everything was now ready for the next day's departure. Mark and Belinda had stopped in Upington and collected the vehicle on their way back from Kagga Kama. We loaded the supplies before we turned in. Eight hours later, in the windless, cold pre-dawn, we picked up Dawid and Sanna. Dawid had money – eight hundred rand – which he insisted we put towards the expenses of the trip. Around him, the people pressed in to say goodbye. They were calm now. Old Antas sang a blessing over us. Oulet was embarrassed when I looked at her, but hugged me goodbye nonetheless.

Dawid was wearing the headband of coloured beads that Petrus had 'crowned' him with. *'Ja,'* he said, grinning mischievously. 'It has old *Vaalie's* sweat in it. Clever sweat.'

And then we were off to see Besa, Mark and my mother in one car, Belinda, Sanna, Dawid with me in the Toyota. *Ou Mackai te Kiraha,* they sang, as we headed out over the wide desert pan towards Namibia and Botswana beyond.

15

Off to See a Wizard

Once over the Namibian border, Dawid insisted that we take a slow dirt road up the dry riverbed of the Aub, the same Aub that ran into the Kalahari Gemsbok National Park. He had come this way with his family many years before, in a donkey cart, to look for work when he'd first been kicked out of the park. He told us, 'In the time before the fences, our people used to travel freely up and down the whole length of the Aub. Many of our ancestors are buried all along this riverbed where the road goes. It is still thick with their spirits.'

The road turned out to be quite a good one, considering it wasn't tar. The kind of dirt you can do a hundred kilometres an hour on provided you drive with care. We began to leave the small car, in which Mark and Polly were travelling, behind. A little later, they overtook us, Polly at the wheel, driving faster than she should. I slowed, to allow some distance and to drop back out of the dust. That's when I saw them go into a spin.

Round went the car in a wide arc, rocking onto two wheels. As I slowed down, so as not to run into the back of them, I saw it leave the road backwards and come to a halt facing north, the way we were going, nose pointing into the road, tyres in the veld. We stopped. Everyone got out. Polly was beaming, almost euphoric from the adrenaline rush of her narrow escape. Mark was white-faced and quivering. He looked angry.

We examined the tracks left by the tyres as they skidded. This, said Dawid, was a reminder from God to go gently. Since the car had spun around and around but ended up safe, and facing the direction of travel, he decided 'our journey is blessed, but we must be careful'.

North we went, to Windhoek, where we returned Mark's hire car just as dark was falling. Then west towards Botswana. A few hours further on, we pulled off onto a secondary road and camped right there on the roadside gravel, too tired to go on. Next day we were up with the dawn and journeying westward, watching the bushveld give way to grassland, and finally, late that afternoon, we drove into Ghanzi.

Once there, however, we encountered a problem: we had no translator. Neither Bulanda nor her husband, Roy Sesarna, were in town. As far as we knew, Besa spoke only the Nharo and BaKoko Bushman tongues, and had no Nama or Afrikaans. If we found no one to translate for us, then the language barrier might scupper the whole trip, even assuming we found the man. So, with just a couple of hours of daylight left we made camp by the roadside again, deciding to head for the Hardbattle ranches next morning to see if someone there could help us.

While gathering firewood at the roadside I found a tiny chameleon clinging to the dry sticks in my hand. I had never seen one of these creatures in the Kalahari before. You expect to find chameleons in the lusher parts of Africa, not in the dry grasslands. The little reptile swivelled its movable, mechanical-looking eyes at us, and held still, pretending not to be there. Dawid beamed when I showed it to him. To come across a chameleon at this parched time of the year meant the imminence of rain.

All that night, though, the sky remained cloudless and as beautiful as I had ever seen it: light blue around the moon, rich, royal blue beyond, with stars glittering like diamond hearts, the two brightest aligned directly along the route north to Groot Laagte. Along that northern horizon flashed faint and distant lightning. Sometime towards midnight, a long, green shooting star went streaking across the sky like a comet. Dawid could not have been happier: these were all auspicious signs, he said, as we turned in, Sanna silently brushing out the fire.

Yet there was nothing auspicious about the next day on the Hardbattle ranches. At Jakkalspits, both the homestead and the Bushman encampment were deserted but for a few old people and a

Herero overseer in a wide-brimmed felt hat, who told us that Andrea had gone away and left him in charge. A Herero left in charge of Bushmen, I thought, my prejudices rising; what could Andrea be thinking? He made us wait while he considered what to do with us.

As we sat there, sweating in the shade of the tamarind trees, a young girl appeared leading a gaggle of smaller children. I recognised her – one of the melon dancers who had come to lighten the mood after the trance dance at Buitsevango the year before. Twelve months had transformed her into a young woman. She and her cohorts joined us in the shaded area by the house, keeping us company, singing, dancing and prancing around like springbokkies, like songbirds in a wood. They danced the melon dance, using stones or wild fruits dropped from the trees. My mother sat down to draw them and they came rushing over, to check that she had drawn them all, before flying off again to settle not far away, aware of being watched, enjoying the attention.

Time passed and the heat rose. Dawid, Belinda, Mark and I walked out into the bush a short way to stretch our legs, but were soon defeated by the heat, and sat down in the shade of a thorn tree. 'Ja,' said Dawid. 'That spin on the road. It showed us we must go slowly, gently. The ancestors are making sure that we do just that.'

Mark then spoke up; he had been terribly scared by the near-miss, he admitted, and was furious with Polly for taking it so lightly, as if it were something frivolous. Belinda translated Mark's words for Dawid and he, looking thoughtful, reached into his little skin bag for *dagga* and newspaper and produced a *zol*. We smoked, silently, in the steadily mounting heat, feeling our own tension rise. When I lingered a little too long over the joint, Mark called me greedy. I snapped back at him in kind, and immediately regretted it. We said nothing more.

Back at the house we heard splashing. The tank, or pool, in front of the Jakkalspits homestead had been filled since I'd last been there. The girls, naked now, were cavorting in it, squealing, splashing and dunking each other. Mark stripped down and jumped in too, scaring the girls off into the shade. Then he sprawled out, cock and balls to the sky, arms spreadeagled as if to embrace the wide freedom of the blue. I watched him with irritation, went over, picked up his shorts and dropped them next to him, muttering about not causing offence, and showing respect. He was annoyed, but put them on.

Dawid joined Sanna where she sat in the shade, so still as to be almost invisible. The girls came fluttering over to him. The eldest one, now dressed again, held in her hand a small brown bird, alive but injured, with a bloody eye. She looked at Dawid, expecting him to do something, though there was no common language between them. Dawid took the bird gently in his knotted hand. 'Better to kill it,' he said quietly and pressed hard on its neck with his thumb-nail, before breaking the soft feathered spine with his teeth. The girl's eyes filled with tears as he held the corpse out to her. But the old man's eyes were twinkling: 'Now you can have a *braai*.' And he rubbed his belly comically and smacked his lips, so that the girl laughed, no longer grieving.

Some time later Titus, the Herero overseer, reappeared with a young boy in tow. The youngster would go with us, he said, take us down to where old mother Xwa was living – an hour's drive through the bush to the south – for nothing could be done without her say-so, and anyway most of the people were now living there. Perhaps we'd find the interpreter we needed at her homestead. So we started on the road again, taking all the children, who clapped their hands at the unexpected treat of a journey and clambered in to fill the spaces between us all.

We drew to a halt at Watering Sands, the bluff overlooking the dry riverbed where old mother Xwa had her settlement. Things had moved on since my last visit – there was now a group of small houses instead of the grass shelters and tents. In front of one of them – in the same place I had left her sitting three months before – sat old Xwa; huge and regal, her mouth a firm, authoritative line. If she was surprised to see us she did not show it.

'*Hmm*,' she said as Dawid explained in Nama why we had come. It was some time before she replied: 'Yes, you should find Besa, bring him here. There is a child sick here . . .' Dawid nodded at us, indicating that we should leave him, Sanna and the old woman to talk. So we left them there, these Bushman contemporaries from opposite ends of the Kalahari, and wandered down to the dry river-bank in the cool of early evening, following the sound of young peoples' voices. Under the tall trees was a small wooden *kraal* in which some donkeys and a few emaciated horses stood, flicking their ears at the youngsters who swirled and played around them. The eldest girl from Jakkalspits was there, surrounded by several admiring adolescent boys.

Inside the *kraal*, the younger children were playing with the donkeys, kneeling on their backs, lying on them, tumbling over them. The donkeys stood, patient, accepting all that was done to them, but the horses raised hooves and put back ears if the children approached. Mark decided to take one of the donkeys for a ride. I wondered if I should tell him not to – the bush hereabouts was dense, easy to get lost in, and big cats still prowled – then I saw a young boy hop on another donkey and go trotting after him, heels kicking as he disappeared into the dusk. Another day had passed and still we had not reached Groot Laagte, did not know whether Besa would be there, or if we would be able to talk to him when we eventually did.

As the sun set, the men of Watering Sands came in from the bush, where they had been out gathering wild foods. Some came on foot, slow and trudging, some on horse- or donkey-back. They recognised me, there were smiles, handshakes, hugs. We went back to where we had parked the vehicle and made a fire, just outside Xwa's yard. Dawid and Sanna were already there, their talk with the old woman done. Sanna was complaining of stomach pains. Dawid lay her down in the sand, as dark fell and the firelight began to flicker, and gently rubbed her belly with long, deep strokes from diaphragm to pubis.

Xwa had told them that Besa's nephew was expected there that night, and would be able to show us the way to Besa's place. His uncle had recently come back to Groot Laagte after a long walkabout in the bush. We would find him there for sure, and once we did, we must bring him back, so that *oom* Dawid and the sick baby could have their healings together. The old lady had told Dawid that it was better if the healings took place here, in the deep bush, away from Groot Laagte, which was full of prying eyes. More and more these days, she had told him, there was opposition to the old ways: many of the local Herero and BaTswana believed the Bushmen to be witches. Yet, she had laughed, 'They still come to us when they are sick, or in love, or unable to have a baby.'

Daylight revealed a flat tyre and a broken exhaust on our car. There was encouraging news from Xwa's yard, however. Besa's nephew had ridden in during the small hours and had agreed to go north with us, to help us find the healer. At this, Sanna said she wanted to stay behind and talk with the women here, for there would be less room in the vehicle now and besides, her stomach was still troubling her. So we set her up under a shady tree with blankets, food and water and unloaded our bags around her, so that we'd have room for all the people in our now very crowded vehicle. We set off, stopping at Jakkalspits, where Titus fixed our tyre. While we waited, Belinda told Polly that she wanted to shave her head, and handed her a pair of nail scissors. Belinda had hardly eaten the night before, or that morning and her eyes looked hollow. Polly took the scissors and, at Belinda's insistence, began to snip a tufty landscape on the back of her already cropped head. The tyre came back fixed when the hair-cut was only half done, so Belinda had to travel with the back of her head looking messy and mangy. Perversely, it seemed to satisfy her.

The road to Groot Laagte was as long and treacherous as ever, with stretches where you could make speed, only to plunge into sand so deep you needed the low range gears to get out. I had to concentrate hard as I drove, squinting in the glare, the vehicle jumping, lurching, skidding through the hot sand. Hours later, with the sun at its peak, we arrived at Groot Laagte.

The place was celebrating something. People dressed in brightly coloured rags were milling all over the sandy road, dancing to township jive blaring out from a ghettoblaster somewhere. They rushed up to the truck hooting and yelling as if we were some kind of sideshow arranged for their amusement. Wondering if it was wise,

I got out into the noise and clawing hands. I heard one of them asking me for money in Afrikaans, so at least we had a common language. Haltingly, I said who we were and why we had come.

But my words fell on deaf ears. I brushed away the grasping hands and made to get back into the vehicle, but just then an old man, thin like a stick insect, but with something commanding in his presence, came pushing through the crowd. He was an extraordinary sight; on his head was a wide-brimmed white fedora, like a pimp's, and he wore an ancient, rumpled, shiny suit over a white shirt and wide tie that was bright green, and splotched with even brighter green sunflowers, its style mid-1970s. On his face, sunglasses with flashing, polished silver rims, and blue lenses. And to top it all, a white vicar's collar, worn over the fat knot of the wide green tie. He introduced himself in Afrikaans as *oom* Spaggan, headman here in Groot Laagte. He gestured around him – this was a celebration he was throwing for the people at his own expense. He had bought an ox, had it slaughtered, and now they were *braai*-ing it over there. 'Everyone will have a full belly tonight,' he said, adding that he tried to do this for the people whenever he could. Then he asked: 'Who are you people?'

I told him, asking if he knew whether Besa was in the settlement. *Oom* Spaggan nodded briefly, and climbed into the truck, managing – incredibly – to squash himself into the little space that was left between Dawid, Belinda, my mother and Besa's nephew. 'Yes, Besa is around somewhere,' he said, twisting in the narrow space to shake Dawid's hand as if they were old acquaintances. 'But Besa didn't like crowds,' he went on. 'He'd been out in the bush today, might even stay there a few nights 'til things calmed down and the people stopped drinking.' We looked around the dusty, forlorn settlement, inching through thick sand and swaying knots of ragged people, past hobbled donkeys who would not move out of the way until you stopped and honked at them, skirting heaps of rubbish piled between the huts. We stopped at a few places, but none contained Besa.

We drove westward, out of the settlement, to a small group of huts set by themselves in the bush. Here, a Damara man from Namibia told us that he hadn't seen Besa for days, but he did have some nice *dagga* for sale, if we wanted to buy some. Dawid stopped and did so. The man was friendly, evidently a hunter in his spare time: the spiral horns and striped, grey hides of several kudu dangled from the thorn trees outside his hut. He liked living among Bushmen, he said, even troubled ones like these BaKoko here. They were more peaceful than his own people.

As we left, *oom* Spaggan directed us by winding, confusing trackways back to the tree at Groot Laagte's far eastern edge, where I had met Besa the last time. 'Best wait here,' said Spaggan. 'Maybe he'll come back.' He got out and walked away, back towards the noise of the party.

We sat in the shade under Besa's tree, smoking to pass the time. I realised how very tired I was, and how long this day might yet be. Lying there, I asked my mother how she liked the *dagga*. It wasn't exactly new for her, she had been a young woman in London in the 1960s, but never in her life had she smoked as she had these past few days. She smiled, saying in her clear, precise voice how entirely fitting it felt here in this world. It was all doing her a power of good, she said. She sat, beaming in the heat, looking neither tired nor anxious – as the rest of us were – but simply relaxed and happy.

People began drifting towards us. A young man came over, his presence making me realise that our other young man, Besa's nephew, had slipped away during one of our stops, no doubt to join the revels. The newcomer was sober, in rags like the rest, but still with something neatly put together about him. He lay down, propping himself up on one elbow and regarded us frankly, openly, without hostility. He asked Dawid, in Afrikaans: 'Why are you here?'

And Dawid told them, starting at the very beginning. He told them how his people used to roam the land in South Africa now known as the Kalahari Gemsbok National Park. He told them of old Mackai and Regopstaan and their prophecies. He spoke of Roger, of Cait, of Michael Daiber, of Kagga Kama, of being show-Bushmen for the tourists. He spoke of the land claim, and how Belinda had come, and me, and how my mother had dreamed of the Bushmen in the cold, damp air of England and kept them alive so that it could all come together here, at this tree. Of how he hoped that Besa would give him the strength he needed to go back and lead his people for the last stage of their fight, to hold on tight until they got the land. He quoted Regopstaan: *'and then the little people can dance and the little people across the Kalahari, around the world even, can also dance'*.

Listening to him, while Belinda translated softly into my ear, I allowed myself to think how very much rode on us finding Besa, on the healing taking place. For if Dawid's leadership failed, if the land claim collapsed for want of a leader to take it on, not only would the Xhomani disintegrate, but what hope would there be for the Bushmen scattered across the rest of the Kalahari: the Bushmen of Botswana's Central Kalahari Game Reserve who were facing the same eviction that the Xhomani had faced twenty-five years ago; the scattered bands up in the Tsodilo hills, where the old leader no longer visited his people's painted caves, no longer made the arrowheads from giraffe bone; those at Nyae Nyae, for whom eviction at the hands of cattle herders could still come, despite their land having been declared a game conservancy; the Namibian Bushmen already dispossessed like the Hai//Kom of Etosha, the Barakwena of Caprivi, the !Xoo of the Omaheke region where, I had heard, Afrikaner farmers and Herero cattle herders still made raids on the Bushman villages to snatch away children to work on their cattle posts? There were still so many obstacles to overcome: the Mier, the park, the snail-pace turning of South Africa's governmental wheels; the squabbles and fights among the Xhomani themselves, the alcohol, the violence. If the old man failed now, all could be lost for another generation.

But if the people here at Groot Laagte felt any such urgency, they didn't show it. Instead they thanked David for his words, got up and drifted away. Dawid rolled another *zol* and said, 'These people are losing their souls here.' He shook his head. 'Even here, with so much land, so much good veld full of food, full of animals, all open for them, they live crowded together like cattle, they live within fences, they drink. Why? It will not be like that when I have my land.'

Late that afternoon, *oom* Spaggan came back, his quiet demeanour

246

at odds with his loud, bizarre costume. He and Dawid talked softly. We would find Besa now, they said. We folded ourselves back into the vehicle, and drove out to the bush on the west side of Groot Laagte. The party was over now, and the crowd had thinned. Those still standing reeled about, semi-insensate. Dawid and Spaggan shook their heads. Spaggan explained that the government had given out to the Groot Laagte people some *tuins* ('gardens' in Afrikaans) – cleared areas of bush linked by a water pipe to a newly sunk borehole. Their hope was to turn some of the Bushmen into farmers, to get them to plant maize and prickly pears on these cultivated islands in the bush. Besa was among those who had taken a plot, he said.

We reached a fenced area, the bare thorns suddenly giving onto a wide expanse of sand and dust that had been hoed by hand into rough furrows. Making farmers out of Bushmen, said Dawid, tut-tutting. Why, with so much open veld hereabouts? 'These people,' he repeated, 'They are losing their souls.' He and Spaggan got out and began walking off into the cleared area.

So again we waited – we were getting good at it. I walked up and down along the new fence, Polly and Belinda stayed in the truck, silent. Mark joined me, headphones on and mike at the ready. Over the past few days, since we had been on the road, he had been steadily interviewing each member of our little party, asking them to explain why they were making this journey, what they hoped to achieve by it – sound bites for a radio piece on the land claim he intended making when he got home. Everyone, including Dawid, had given him clear, lucid interviews. But each time he had tried it with me I had found myself tongue-tied, and had put him off until another time. Now, at this moment of high suspense, my interview was worse than ever. He asked me, once again, to tell my story, explain my background, the purpose of the trip, all that hung on it. As before I fluffed it completely. What I knew in my head would not come out of my mouth. I said disconnected things, linked together with irrelevant details, spoke too slowly. Mark lost patience and we gave up and returned to the vehicle. For perhaps half an hour more we stood around in the heat, unable to find shade. Then, at last, two figures emerged from the dark thorns and began to cross the clearing. Then two more. It was them. *Oom* Spaggan walked ahead, alone, and behind him the tall, skinny form of Besa's wife Katerina. Behind her Dawid, head bent, talking softly with Besa.

16

The River of Spirits

'You!' said Besa, pointing, laughing and fixing me with his little, puckish eyes. His wife, Katerina, ran up and grabbed me. 'You! My little Besa, *klein Besa*, come back again!' She spoke in Afrikaans. Then she turned to my mother, seeming to know who she was, and said, 'My two Besas – *groot, ou Besa, klein, jong Besa.*' Despite the heat, Besa was wearing a long, thick, khaki-coloured coat that fell to his ankles, and a thick, shapeless cap on his head. Yet he was not sweating, as we non-Bushmen were in our shorts and T-shirts. He, Spaggan and Dawid were all grinning away like children at a feast. 'Besa has agreed to come,' said Dawid, relief showing on his old, grizzled face.

They squashed into the truck with us, and back in the centre of Groot Laagte we stopped to let Spaggan out. 'Good luck, stay well, heal well!', he shouted, waving. We drove on to Besa's tree: he needed to collect some things, he said. Once there, he told us that he would need a fee. I looked at Dawid, who nodded. I knew from my time at Khkekheye that this was standard custom: a fee, or gift, to seal the pact and open the heart of both healer and patient. Then Besa said we must also buy him alcohol. We all looked at each other. Dawid looked shocked. My heart sank.

'Yes', said Besa, almost aggressively. This time there must be alcohol: and he threw Dawid, especially, a challenging look, nodding emphatically as he did so.

I agreed, hoping I wasn't making a terrible mistake. Dawid still looked unsure as I drove Besa and his wife to a small shack nearby where liquor was sold. A fat BaTswana woman stood behind a rough wooden counter, bottles and cans arrayed on a shelf behind her.

Besa was precise: he and his wife wanted six beers and a half jack of brandy. With a twinge of conscience I handed over the money and back outside, Besa and his wife tossed down the brandy there and then. '*Ry*,' he said, making a shooing gesture with his hand, 'Let's go!'

We picked up the others and set off, with Mark at the wheel. Night was falling quickly around us, making it hard to follow the twisting tracks. Besa and Katerina started on their beers, shouting directions at us through the glass partition. Dawid's face clouded over and he swore under his breath. I could see his point. To travel so far, just for this, just for it all to end in booze. Still, we were committed now. We passed cooking fires, crawled around thorn-fences, almost hit a couple of sad-looking donkeys that couldn't get out of our way because their front feet were hobbled together so tightly. Besa and Katerina – now thoroughly drunk – hooted and cackled in the back.

It was sweaty and humid inside the vehicle and we drove around in circles, Besa and his wife chuckling away like chickens, sending us this way and that. Finally Mark pulled to a halt and said in a low, despairing voice: 'Just make up your minds and tell me quietly where to go.'

Belinda then took control and in five minutes we had found the road and were on our way south into the moonlight. Strange how the silver light had hardly illuminated the village, yet now that we were out on the main track, it rolled away clear and wide as if floodlit. To make more room, I climbed in the back with our two drunken passengers. Animals appeared on the road – a pair of jackal darting fleetly across, an owl swooping low, a mongoose who stopped to look, unafraid, as we bore down, only to zip aside when we were almost upon him.

Next to me, Besa and his wife began to sing. 'Two Besas, There are two, two Besas!' The old man hit and held a high note and, drunk as he was, went suddenly and absolutely rigid, like a man at the brink of orgasm, then convulsed, as if having a fit, flopping around the small space like a fish. I clutched him, holding his hard little body tight to make sure he didn't fall out of the back of the truck, which had been left open to give us air. His whole body was vibrating, literally humming like a string with breath and a strange, taut energy. It made my hands buzz to hold him.

'Two Besas!' whooped his wife, picking up the high note just as Besa's voice faltered, and the old man fell backwards against me, body twitching, mucus pouring from his nose and mouth, splashing us both. His hands reached back, fingers finding my chest, abdomen, stomach, and began to clutch at me. He sang as he did this, and there it was once again, that same feeling I had experienced at the fire outside old mother Xwa's, the same mild, persistent, gentle throb, the same quiet euphoria. I sank back, still holding him, and we lay like two spoons, like lovers, in the bouncing back of the truck while Katerina sang the song of the two Besas. His hands clutched and opened in steady rhythm on the skin underneath my T-shirt, as if he wanted to pull something out from my body. Then he propped up on one elbow and flung whatever it was he had extracted out into the night, whooping as he did so. He lay back against me once more, clutching and grabbing, his wife singing the song of the two Besas all the while.

Besa went suddenly limp against me, and the small current-in-my-body feeling stopped. I held him, unconscious, in my arms, and laid him down on the nest of blankets, staring at him in wonder. The healer lay curled in a foetal ball, like a child. I felt brimful of well-being, as if some pure, nectar-like love had been pumped through me, cleansing me and making me glow from within. Katerina ceased her song, letting her voice dwindle, smiling. The truck bucketed and swung onward. What did it mean, this private, intimate healing just for me? Would Besa have anything left for Dawid, for the sick child? I felt moved beyond speech, ready to cry and laugh together, not understanding but happy and light.

Then the truck stopped. Mark got out and opened the back. 'I can't drive any more today, I'm completely done in.'

'OK,' I said, 'OK, no problem. I'm fresh, fresher than I've been for days. Get in the back, I'll drive the rest of the way.' I climbed out onto white sand awash with warm moonlight. In the back, both Besa and his wife now lay sleeping. 'Did you hear anything of what just happened back here?'

Mark said he had heard singing, shouting but couldn't make it out, and anyway he had been concentrating on the road.

I got in the truck and started the engine, feeling distant from my own body. 'What was going on back there?' asked the others.

I explained, or tried to, but it sounded so wooden I broke off, and was saved by a movement at the side of the road. Eyes reflecting bright. A leopard, a small one, maybe a young female. We stopped and she walked into the middle of the road, looking right at us for three long seconds. Then she was gone.

It was past ten o'clock by the time we made it back to Xwa's homestead. People were asleep in their huts and Sanna was lying by herself beside a little fire of glowing ashes. As soon as I stopped the truck, out from the back sprang Besa, upright and alert as if he hadn't been drinking at all. Nodding emphatically at us, as if to say 'wait here', he walked right into old Xwa's yard, shouting to rouse the people there.

We stirred up the fire, put some water on to boil – we hadn't eaten since the morning and who knew how long the night would last? I was still dazed from the episode in the back of the truck, and everyone else was exhausted.

Belinda followed Besa into Xwa's yard to beg a three-legged pot big enough to cook a really large meal in, for it seemed expected that we would feed everybody once again. She came back with it and we poured in our full stash of pasta, packets of soup, and dried soya mince, making a giant stew. We put potatoes and onions in the ashes to bake. People were waking now; the women who would help make the song came bleary-eyed down to the fire. Xwa arrived with one of her many daughters, a young Nharo woman. She held the sick baby, which coughed and wheezed painfully in her arms. Children began to drift in too, worming their way between us to stare at the pot now bubbling away on the fire. One of the younger girls who had gone with us from Jakkalspits seemed to have adopted Polly, and was hanging close beside her. The night began to cool, then to chill. Belinda put her jacket around the little girl's shoulders. Besa and his wife reappeared. Dawid and Sanna watched silent, tired, from the edge of the firelight. When the food was ready, we dished it out in relays. Everyone ate. When the pot was empty, the women took up their clapping, their chant, and it began.

Besa got to his feet, stamping his rhythm, sucking the air in and out of his throat like an ostrich before letting go a series of the high, yodelling notes that would soon carry him into a trance and beyond. He danced in short, shuffling steps, laughing and talking to himself as he did so. Looking at his old face as he passed me, I realised that he had already entered his trance, but had gone in gently, softly, without fuss or drama. He was talking to unseen spirits, conversationally, not confrontationally, and was – it seemed – pleased with what they were telling him. His tone, as he shuffled his circle, was private, confiding, and he laughed often, as if at some joke, occasionally breaking back into those high, pure notes that seemed to be the strings on which he played himself when the trance was upon him. Briskly, with an almost business-like air, he began to lay hands on those gathered around the fire, his hands trembling with intensity. Round he came, touching us each in turn. But mostly he went back and forth to the baby. To Dawid he went only twice. When he touched me I felt nothing of the quiet pulse, just his hands shaking.

He took the infant in his arms, staggered with it into the fire circle. Hands reached out to steady him. The mucus poured from his mouth and nose in long, semi-liquid strings. He lifted the child to the stars, singing, offering it, then handed it back to its mother and danced on. To my mother he went three times, first to touch her lower abdomen and back, next to touch her chest and upper back, and lastly to play his shaking hands over her face and head, laughing the while. Several times he collapsed to the ground, but did not fall unconscious. He got up, danced on again, sometimes stepping right into the coals in his bare feet, which were not burned.

I looked over at Dawid. He was looking up at the healer from under his eyebrows. Whenever Besa danced close to him, Dawid would look away, occupying himself with some small task, such as scooping a little hollow in the sand beneath the fire and putting a stray potato in there to bake. On the two occasions that Besa touched him, Dawid submitted readily, eyes closed, letting the healer handle him as he would. But no sooner had the little man danced away again than Dawid's eyes were back on him, looking suspicious, unconvinced. Belinda's gaze, I saw, was more challenging still.

Besa staggered over to Mark, put his hands on his head and called out, true and clear '*Mark! Mark! Mark!*', then laughed uproariously. Finally, sometime near dawn, he collapsed for the last time and his wife left him lying where he had dropped. The people drifted away from the fire, and those of us who stayed curled up to sleep. Lightning flashed in sheets along the eastern and northern horizons, and sometimes there was a gust of wind that smelled of rain.

We took our leave of old Xwa in the cold dawn. Next to her crawled the infant granddaughter whom Besa had lifted to the heavens. The little girl stood upright on chubby legs, holding herself steady on her grandmother's fat arm, eyes bright as buttons, no longer coughing and wheezing as she had the night before.

Driving the long, sandy roads back to Groot Laagte, we saw steenbok after steenbok. I looked over at Dawid, but his face had been a closed book since morning. Belinda, sitting next to him, looked knowing, and perhaps a little angry. Back at Groot Laagte, Besa took me in a short but tight embrace, looked at me with the cat-like eyes that seemed to go right through whatever they fixed upon, and then released me. It was over.

We dropped Mark at Ghanzi from where he was to go on to Maun and the Okavango, the next leg of his personal adventure. As we drove away, leaving him at the bus stop, Dawid made his first joke of the day: 'He came and now he fucks off. That's what I'll call him: old Fuck-Off. Where's Fuck-Off today? Oh, he just fucked off.' He laughed and coughed. We headed west, towards Windhoek, from where, next day, Polly was to catch her plane home, and from where we would turn south, back to the park.

'What are you thinking?' I asked Belinda.

She was silent a moment, then said bitterly: 'Besa's a bullshitter. All last night while he was dancing I stared him right in the eye, challenging him. He wouldn't meet my eye. I looked at him and felt nothing. I felt nothing when he touched me . . .'

I looked over at Dawid, but he avoided the subject and began to talk about the Bushmen at Ghanzi and Groot Laagte. Their way, he told us, was not the way forward. When his land came there would be no big, sad settlements like that one, where people had the land all around them, yet could not or would not move freely. Bushmen in big groups lose their way, he said, lose their souls. Belinda nodded: 'Oom Dawid doesn't need healing. Besa knew it, he knew it . . .' Dawid neither agreed nor disagreed, but fell silent, watching the wide flat grasslands roll past the window.

As dusk fell we were still some hours east of the Namibian border. I pulled the truck off the road, drove it out of sight into a thorn thicket, and there we made camp. Sanna made little *rosterkoekies* (ash bread) on the coals. We must be careful here, said Dawid, for this was still lion country. He hobbled to his feet, and began to construct a little fence of fallen thorn branches around our sleeping place. Deep in the night two male ostrich passed close by the camp, booming softly and heaving sighs.

On the Namibian side of the border, Belinda made me stop so that she could go and sit in the back with Dawid and Sanna, leaving my mother and me alone together in the cab. As with Dawid, I was hesitant to ask my mother what she had made of the healing, feeling that now was too soon to talk. Instead we spoke of the sense of exile she so often felt in England, of the periodic depressions she had endured during my adolescent years, of the grief which had never left her for her lost parents, her lost country, her lost home.

When she was a little girl, she said, thrust into boarding school at the age of six, she had comforted herself at night by remembering every inch of the first house that she had inhabited with her parents before they had left for the war. Lying on the dormitory bed, she would go back to that house and visit every room, in her mind caressing each piece of furniture, living for the day she would return. But it never happened. She fell silent, watching the miles pass by outside the window.

Months later, she allowed me to read her diary from the journey. After that day's entry, she wrote that the experience of coming to the Kalahari, of spending time with the Bushmen, had been 'like a rebirth'.

What have I learned? Nee Mama, Ek is reg – I have all I need. To be still and quiet and let things happen. That sand is lovely to sleep in. Sand keeps you clean. Dagga is good for you Bushman-style, shared mindfully. In the desert you don't smell, hardly need to drink or eat or eliminate. The body lightens. You need very little. That what matters is God within. The pure heart. Loving kindness. Forgiveness. Restitution. Reciprocity.

We pulled over for a last *zol* near three small camel-thorns growing by the road. Dawid prepared it as usual, neatly tearing the newspaper, filling, rolling, licking, lighting, taking the first draw, passing it on. 'Mouth to mouth,' wrote my mother in her diary. 'Mind to mind.' Then, as we stood there in the bright sunlight, he pointed out the vegetation at our feet. That small, thin viney-looking thing growing out of the ground was a gemsbok cucumber. Late in the dry season, gemsbok would dig up the root with their forehooves, when everything else in the veld was burnt and barren. His grandfather, old Mackai, had taught him how to do this too, to make sure he could survive the times of hunger and thirst.

'The gemsbok cucumber root is very bitter,' said Dawid. 'Bite into it straightaway and drink the juice and it'll go right through you, taking the water inside you with it, and then you die. You must first cook it on a little fire until all the juices sweat, then you eat the pulp, drink the juice. And then you feel it, the water going into you, staying in you, first cramping your stomach and then going here, out to your arms, and here, to your legs, and here to your hot and muddled head. And then you can go on again.'

How strange and incongruous it seemed an hour later, to see the control tower of Windhoek International Airport come rising above the grasses and thorns. We drove in through the gates, parked, went into the snack bar, and ate plastic-tasting food. Then we took my mother to the security gate. 'I can hardly bear to leave,' she said. Belinda broke into the Afrikaans song, 'There in the old Kalahari', and did a little Bushman dance, laughing and snapping her fingers.

Polly went through the gate, waving. Later she wrote in her diary, 'What was starved in me is now fed.'

There was still enough daylight for us to travel some three hundred kilometres southwards, back onto the road that followed the Aub River. As afternoon reddened towards dusk, and we were starting to look out for a good place to camp, we came upon a strange thing lying on the road: a dead pelican, feathers white and yellow, lying on its back, its great wings outstretched as if in flight, yet hundreds of miles from the nearest ocean.

'Once again, we must keep our eyes open,' said Dawid. A little later, with the sunset in full swing, he told us to pull over. A short way along this road was a small town, Gochas. It was not good to camp too close to such places, where people wandered after dark in the veld, drunk and troublesome. We must camp here this night though, for Gochas had a meaning for the Xhomani that he wanted us to understand.

The place he chose was a small dip in the land, hidden from the road by a tall row of tamarinds. The ground beneath the trees was thick with fallen branches and sharp, broken sticks. While clearing them to make it smooth for sleeping we noticed a dozen or so small, letter-box-shaped holes in the ground: scorpion holes. Should we really camp here, I asked? Tonight said Dawid, no scorpions would bother us. There were other, more important things abroad, he could feel it in the air. Tonight the small creatures would not bother us.

We made a fire, cooked and shared a bottle of wine which I had stashed deep in my rucksack. When our *braai* was over and the wine finished, Dawid told us why the place was special. His people had been badly hurt here back when they had had to leave the park. He had been travelling in the donkey cart with a few relatives, among them an old woman. They had come into this town, Gochas, and had made camp on its outskirts, hoping to go in next day and see if there were any jobs to be had on the local ranches. That night, six drunk men from the town had cornered the old woman while she was out foraging for firewood, and raped her so violently that she had almost bled to death.

So Dawid and his people had had to stay on outside the town, eking out a living by begging, fending off more attacks, until the old woman recovered. Except she never really did recover, not properly, and had died not long after they moved on. That, said Dawid, was the beginning of the abuse of the women by outsiders that still continued, that was one of the most pressing reasons why they and *all* Bushmen needed land of their own, land they could retreat into, far away from prying eyes and grabbing hands. Strangely, however, one of the women, a cousin of Dawid's, had elected to stay behind in the town and had found a job there and a good local man to marry. He was pretty sure she still lived there now. Tomorrow we would try and see her before we drove on to the border and Welkom.

And now, said Dawid, suddenly beaming, Belinda and I must excuse him. He knew that he had not said much about the healing yet — we could talk properly about that tomorrow — but tonight he was feeling years younger. If we wouldn't mind sleeping in the back of the truck so that he and Sanna could be alone together . . . he turned to his wife and gave a low, throaty laugh whose meaning was unmistakable. In the firelight, Sanna glowed, looking down embarrassed. Belinda and I gave them their space, crawling off into the back of the truck as directed and crashing out on the blankets there, for in truth we were exhausted.

About five in the morning, just before dawn, the temperature suddenly plummeted and it became so cold so quickly that it woke me. I seemed to hear an eerie noise, something between a faint whistling — like wind caught among the stones of a canyon — and music. I looked up, out of the open tailgate of the truck, just in time to see something, or to sense something — in my semi-dream state I could not be sure which — pass by.

It was like a small white wind, an entity that turned, revolving as it moved, like a little whirlwind, only less distinct. As it passed, I shuddered involuntarily. When it was gone, the chill went out of the air and, puzzled, I lay back and slept until sunrise.

While Belinda and I were getting the fire together for coffee, she asked me if I had noticed anything strange right before dawn.

'You too?' I asked.

'*Ja*,' she said. 'It made me shiver to my soul.'

We drank our coffee, as Dawid and Sanna came awake. Once he had drained his mug, Dawid asked us: 'Did you two notice anything pass through our camp this morning early, before dawn?'

Yes, we told him. What was it?

'I think,' said Dawid, 'that was Death, or the soul of someone recently dead. I have been feeling it here since we found the pelican on the road yesterday – a strange sign, that. Remember that I told you that many of the ancestors are buried along this road? I think something was on its way to join them, or something sent out by them was on its way back. We will see – perhaps there has been a death, or a new beginning, back at Welkom.'

Half-an-hour later we were in the small town of Gochas. Dawid directed us into the poor, shanty-like houses that clustered along its northern edge and got out to ask the rapidly assembling crowd if anyone knew of a Bushman woman with the family name of Kruiper. The people here recognised him immediately as the Bushman who was leading his people back to what had once been theirs. They honoured him, Dawid standing among them like a quiet, diminutive king, nodding, bestowing his blessing, offering his thanks. Then the female cousin arrived. There were embraces and tears. 'Stay strong, Dawid,' she told him, cupping his wrinkled old face in her palm.

As we drove on, the day grew hot, the light hammered flat by heat. Sweat began to run into my eyes as I drove, making them sting. Dawid suggested we stop for a while and sit in the shade, until the sun passed. The place had a familiar feel, then I recognised it – it was where Polly had spun the car, on our way north. Dawid laughed. 'Yes,' he said. 'This is where we should talk, here where God told us to keep our eyes open, and to tread gently.'

'Now,' he said, once we were sitting in the shade of the trees, and looking me right in the eye. 'You want to know about the healing.'

'I do.'

'It *was* a healing,' he told me, in a tone that implied that this was but the first part of a more complicated message, and that he needed our full attention. 'What Besa showed me was that I have the strength here,' he thumped his old, wheezy chest with a bony fist. 'He showed me that it never left me, as I had thought. It took me a while to realise this, but that is what he has done.

'You know, this Besa is a truly powerful healer. You saw what he did with that child, what he did to you in the back of the car, even with the drink in him – for drink and healing do not mix unless you have a special purpose in mind. Besa is a man, like the rest of us. He has his weaknesses – he drinks, does wrong things, has followed the bad in order to know the good.

'That is what the drinking was for, to show me that he is weak too, but that his powers are the same as they ever were. That it was the same for me. That I should see his weak side and offer healing to him: that it was for *me* to heal *him*. That was his healing, to make me see that I still have the powers, the strength. So now I see the way forward clearly. I am old, tired, I feel death calling. I feel it hovering around me and a part of me wants to follow. I know now, though, that I can hold on as leader at least until the signing, until the land claim comes through. And I know now that it will. After that, I cannot say. But until then, at least, I will lead, do what I can for the others, pull them through to get their land, even though I am as weak, as stupid, as they.'

Dawid looked up at the hot sky – azure blue above the hard white haze. He seemed to be searching for more words. Sanna, Belinda and I watched him, silent, waiting. Then we heard a noise, a soft clopping of hooves on sand. A horse, loose, walking by itself, came slowly up the lonely road, swishing its tail. Dawid watched it disappear over the rise, before he spoke again. 'You know what Besa said to me when I met him in the veld, while all you were waiting? He looked at me and said: "You! I've been waiting for you for twenty-five years!" That is the time it has been since we left the park, lost our ground. Ah, Besa,' Dawid shook his grizzled head, still adorned with Petrus Vaalbooi's beaded headband. 'He is *slim* that one, clever. He told me that it is for us down here to show the other Bushmen the way, and that I will have to come back, and bring the younger men who will have to lead after me. All that he told me.' He fell silent, looking tired, as if considering the weight of the tasks before him.

'What about the leopard we saw,' I asked. 'It happened right after Besa had his hands on me in the truck. And, you know, the first time he laid hands on me and he called the leopards out of the bush, laughing. What was the meaning of that?'

At this Dawid lost his serious look and twinkled at me. 'That, Rupi, is your story, between you and Besa. Besa is a leopard – it is his animal, it is his spirit when he goes out. The leopard is strong but savage. It waits and watches, then springs. It does not give you warning, like the lion. You cannot negotiate with it. Almost never will it hunt you, but if it does, you have no hope. It will kill you slow, enjoying the play. But when this great, this independent power, is harnessed for something good, then see how the leopard can work! And you, Rru, you are a leopard too. That character is in you, the same as Besa. He has shown that to you.' He paused to laugh again, softly. 'You know already that you have other animals. Izak called you the bird. Others at Welkom have called you a porcupine – the bumbling one who muddles through only after much difficulty. What was it you called yourself and Belinda? The good little donkeys, harnessed to the Bushman cart? But you are also the leopard. You and Besa are the same kind. And now the leopard is harnessed alongside the donkeys, and *man*, see how he pulls!'

We drove the last hundred kilometres to Welkom in the golden hour. It had rained along this road since we had been away. Flowers, yellow and white, bobbed on the low bushes that had been black and bare when we had driven by them on our way northward a few days before. We reached Welkom just as it got dark. The people rushed around to greet us, some drunk, some not. Bukse was there, on leave from his new job as a tracker for a team of lion biologists in the park. He was dressed in clean, crisp khaki shorts and shirt. He embraced us all. Kabuis, also on leave from tracking in the park, came forward next, three tail feathers of a kori bustard sticking up in his hair. Joy seemed to ooze from him. But the greetings were quiet, not rambunctious.

When Dawid hobbled out of the vehicle, it was plain that the old man was very, very tired. After exchanging a word or two with

Bukse he told us that there had indeed been a death here, just the day before. Not one of the Bushmen but one of their friends in the coloured village. He must see to those who were grieving now. The little white wind had told the truth. 'Come and say goodbye to me tomorrow. You must go back and write now, tell our story. It will be a long, hard work. Come and see me tomorrow.'

We left him at the Red House and drove back along the road to the park. On the way, we stopped at the fires of Sillikat and Elsie, Jakob and Leana. Elsie kissed me full on the lips and I kissed her back. 'When you do that,' she told me, 'You make me feel beautiful.' Sillikat, sober for once and smiling, held my hand in a strong grip. Jakob and Leana were not so happy. While we had been away, he had beaten her badly, she told us. She had once again woken up to find his hands clasped around her neck, strangling her and had had to fight him off with the grandchild there, seeing it all. Yes, one day she would kill him in his sleep. Jakob sat silent. Truly, Dawid would have a hard time keeping the people together until the land claim could be settled. The old problems, the endless fights and squabbles, jealousies and intrigues would never go away. But if he could be strong, perhaps they could too.

Back at the park we found out that there had been all sorts of trouble there as well. Eleanor, the coloured student who had become Belinda's confidant, was waiting up for us and filled us in. That week, Dries and the other senior managers had called the coloured workers into his office one by one, trying to get stories out of them that would somehow incriminate Belinda. Did she smoke *dagga*? Was she stirring up discontent? They had wheedled, even intimidated, saying that there was an *element* in the park, an *element* that needed weeding out, and that anyone associated with that *element* could expect the worst. But the staff had refused to say a word, Eleanor reported proudly. More than that, they had said that they would file official complaints about the incident to head office, so now the managers were running around being nice to everyone. 'Basically it's business as usual,' said Eleanor, smiling wryly.

There had been incidents with the Bushmen too, said the receptionists. A few days before, Elsie had invaded the administration building and gone straight into the office of the senior warden, Maarten Engelbrecht (no relation of Dries). Elsie had dived under his desk, right by his feet, and sat there, looking up at him. He had told her to get out, she had ignored him, and eventually he had had to drag her out by her heels, sliding her along the linoleum while she shrieked and screamed, bringing everyone running from their offices. Once outside she had got up of her own accord, gathered up her dignity, and walked away, only to reappear moments later where Maarten stood talking the incident over with the other managers. 'Who am I?' Elsie had said to him. 'Do you even know who I am? I am Elsie. ELSIE.' And then she had taken his hand, shaken it and walked off. Later that afternoon, she had thrown a stone through one of the back windows of Dries Engelbrecht's house.

Rikki had gone also into Twee Rivieren. Taking advantage of a quiet moment when everyone was having lunch inside their houses, he had climbed the camp's 200ft radio tower. The staff, and some of the white managers, had gathered below, telling him to come down, that it was dangerous. 'In a minute,' he had replied. 'I'm just up here looking over my farm', and had waved his arm to the north, taking in the whole park with the gesture and leaning out crazily. He hadn't fallen. Instead, he'd climbed quietly down and walked back to Welkom, smiling and waving as he passed through the tourist camp site.

That night we bedded down on the dune but, hardly able to sleep, had sat up watching the shooting stars. Next day was to be another dawn start: I had to drop the vehicle off at the garage in Upington as early as possible in order to catch a bus to Johannesburg and home.

On the way out I stopped to say goodbye to Dawid. 'Go,' he told me. 'Don't wait around here like a bloody Bushman. You know what to do, go home and write, get working, what about this book, eh?' Sanna had a necklace for me, of camel-thorn seeds, raisin-bush wood and gemsbok horn. She put it around my neck and kissed me.

17

What Happened After

We shall mend the broken strings of the distant past, so that our dreams can take root.

With these words, on 21 March 1999, Thabo Mbeki, South Africa's president elect, signed the Xhomani land claim at the Molopo Lodge, some fifty kilometres south of the park. The Xhomani children linked hands and made an avenue for the glossy black government cars as they rolled in. The celebrations lasted two days, with a mock trance dance and all the people in traditional costume. A dead bat-eared fox was cast into the fire for luck and good fortune while the press cameras snapped and whirred.

On behalf of the Xhomani people, Dawid Kruiper and Petrus Vaalbooi formally accepted some 65,000 hectares of the Kalahari's red sands, most of it outside the park but 25,000 hectares inside the fence, on the clan's old hunting grounds. The Mier, amazingly, put up no fight at all: their land claim had also been honoured, matching exactly what the Bushmen had been given. The land inside the park could not be actually lived in, but the agreement allowed the Xhomani to visit their ancestral graves, hunt a little, gather a little and run their own tourism projects there. How exactly this was to be arranged was left unclear.

When the speeches were done, Dawid knelt down and picked up the sand in handfuls, laughing, letting the red grains spill through his fingers like dry water. A photograph of this was printed in next day's *Cape Times*, along with a smaller one of Dawid and Petrus sitting either side of the white-shirted, yellow-tied Mbeki as he put his pen to the historic paper. Yet, apart from Dawid and Petrus, the

Xhomani themselves were left strangely out of the limelight. No food was provided for them, no tent to shelter in, no speeches requested from them. The press noticed this too: reporters from the *Cape Times* wrote that:

> At times during the weekend's festivities, the needs of the people of the Kalahari appeared to play second fiddle to the whims of hordes of organisers, interested parties and journalists. If restoring the dignity of the claimants is indeed a key element of the land restitution process, was it right for people to be transported in three-tier cattle trucks to a ceremony celebrating the return of their land? Or to insist, when they are tired and have not been fed, that they dance around a fire in time for an advertised press call?

Apart from Belinda, no one from the park was present. She resigned her position soon afterwards and moved to Welkom where she and one of the younger Bushmen – Vetkat, the younger brother of Leana, Jakob's wife – married, having dreamed of each other. It was a traditional ceremony, with Rikki – who had stopped drinking, and who was beginning to perform small healing ceremonies again – joining their hands together on the red dunes.

Despite all these events, little changed fundamentally. Once the political fanfare surrounding the land claim had died down, months drifted by and still the Xhomani continued to sit by the side of the road as before. The reasons cited for this were bureaucratic delays over the transfer of documents; the farmers needing to let the lambing season pass before they could move their stock off the land. Then, in June, President Mbeki reshuffled the ministries and the Land Minister, Derek Hanekom, who along with the lawyer Roger Chennels had probably done more than anybody to see the land claim through, was fired. The Xhomani became frustrated, and there was a fresh upsurge in alcoholism and violence. By September they had taken possession of just one farm, Witdraai, opposite the Molopo Lodge, whose bottle store lay just a short walk over the dunes. Fights began to break out there regularly, both among the Xhomani themselves and with some of the district's poorer coloureds, who were jealous of the Bushmen's sudden switch in status from beggars to (on paper) landowners.

The clan began to scatter. Some, like Dawid and Sanna, Oulet, Rikki, Izak and Lys, settled at Witdraai. Others – Bukse, Antas and old Anna among them – stayed on at the Red House, saying that Regopstaan's dream had been for his people to go north, back into the park, not south, away from their home. The remainder, including Kabuis, Betty, Sillikat and Elsie, slept either at the Molopo Lodge or in huts along the road.

That same month Kabuis, gentlest of all the Xhomani, the one who spent most of his time working inside the park as a tracker, who still knew all the plants and animals, who protected Betty from the persecutions of the other women, who was not jealous of the sexual freedom she needed, was murdered. The killer entered the hut at night, struck a match and shone it in the face of each sleeper (Elsie, Sillikat and some others were sleeping there too). When he had identified Kabuis he stabbed him several times with a long, wide-bladed knife.

The killer – a local coloured man called Willem Gooi (whose family, I later learned, was notorious in the district as criminal and violent) – did not resist arrest. Later, in the police cells, he refused to say why he had done it or whether anyone had put him up to it. Fingers were pointed in all directions, but no evidence was found to support any motive from any quarter. A few weeks afterwards, Gooi was bailed out of jail by someone – the police would not say who.

In October Chris, the film-maker, and I flew back to the Kalahari. We were to take Rikki up to see Besa, to continue with the healings as we had planned the year before. We found the people drinking like fury – Dawid worst of all – and there was much discord. Bukse, Jakob, Sillikat and others were saying that Dawid had no right to be clan leader and that one of them should be given the role. On top of this the 'modern' Xhomani, under Petrus Vaalbooi, were trying to take control of the as yet unceded land. At a two-day meeting chaired by Roger Chennels, we saw that Dawid and the strife-torn 'traditionals' were being marginalised in the plans for what to do with the land when it came. At the end, Dawid had been assertive and pushed through an agreement to put aside two of the farms for those who wanted to live the traditional life. But that life, it seemed, was still strong. At Witdraai we saw the younger men going out daily into the dunes to hunt springbok and steenbok, whose skins were then stretched out over the huts to dry, whose meat was *braaiing* on the fires. At the Red House, Antas and the older people were coming in daily with food and medicinal plants from the veld. On the day we left for the road north to Besa we had to wait while Dawid finished healing three Xhosa men who had driven a thousand kilometres up from Cape Town just to see him.

When we finally reached Besa we found the old healer lying on his stomach, head down, dozing in the shade of a small, tattered-looking tree out in the drought-stricken bush to the west of Groot Laagte. He woke at the sound of our engine and looked up, saying nothing as we got out. I went over to him, nervous as I always was at our meetings, but then stopped, shocked. Besa looked terrible: gaunt, emaciated even, his face a skin-covered skull and his torn, soiled old clothes hanging limp about him. 'Ah, Klein Besa,' he said quietly, looking at me as I squatted down in the hot sand beside him. The others – Belinda, Chris, Vetkat, Rikki, Dawid and Sanna – came over. He took us all in calmly, evenly, waiting for us to speak.

Dawid broke the silence. 'How are you then, old Besa, eh? How goes it?' he said, with mock heartiness, taking Besa's fragile shoulder and giving it an affectionate shake.

'Look,' the healer replied, indicating his wasted body with arms that were no longer coiled with muscle but stick-thin.

Rikki came over and, at this, the old healer brightened visibly. 'Ah,' he said as Rikki, quivering with excitement, sat down behind him and took the older man's narrow, bony shoulders in a shy embrace from behind – an awkward gesture, but sincere. Besa twisted his head back and grinned, though a little weakly. 'You,' he said to Rikki, 'You.'

'My God,' said Belinda. 'Look at them, they could be father and son.' It was true; Besa's and Rikki's faces, when you saw them side by side like this, shared some striking similarities. The same deep-set, round, predator's eyes, the same high, wide cheekbones that suggested some kind of male cat, the same charismatic presence.

The story soon came out. Besa had been sick these past months, far too sick to do any healing or hunting. Consequently he had not been able to earn. He and his wife Katerina – even lankier-looking than usual from lack of food – were now looking after some BaTswana man's sheep and goats for a small return of milk and meat. He was recovering, Besa told us, but slowly. He did not know if he would be able to do anything for us this time. If we wanted anything from him we would have to provide food. He would have to eat, rest and think. Only then could he say whether or not a healing could be done.

It took him three days to decide. On that first afternoon we used the influence of *oom* Spaggan, Groot Laagte's head man, to find, buy and slaughter a goat for the healer. That took up most of the day, with much driving around before a Herero herder finally came forward with a beast for sale. At last, having eaten, Besa withdrew. For the rest of that hot day and all the next he lay in his hut, not speaking, hardly moving, while the rest of us found what patches of shade we could. Chris and I took the little tree, moving clockwise around it with the sun, minds deadened by the heat and suspense. Only late the following afternoon did Besa rouse himself. The healing could be done, he said, but he must call in another healer to help, and a really big chorus, for the song had to be as powerful as possible.

The healing that night was far different from any I had yet seen. At first, the chorus was merely made up of us, the extended family living at the huts, and Spaggan, who came wandering in from the village at sunset. Once dark had fallen, and the fire had been made up, Besa began to dance, singing by himself, until – without warning – he suddenly pitched backwards, blood pouring from his nose, twitching, shrieking and clutching at the air. Several onlookers leapt to his aid, caught him as he fell, laid him gently onto the ground. At that point a second dancer, a tall bearded man whom we had not seen arrive, stepped forward out of the darkness. He was not a Bushman. In fact, *oom* Spaggan told us later, this new healer was a

BaKgalagadi who had come to live among the Bushmen some years before, and who was reckoned even more powerful than Besa. He stepped out from the shadows like a dark spirit and danced over to Besa's fallen form. Singing over him, the bearded man knelt down and lifted Besa to his feet again, with his trance still intact. Then together, the two healers went one by one around our group, Besa singing a complicated pattern of high notes, the BaKgalagadi booming a deeper, bass harmony underneath.

Rikki, the person for whom the whole healing had been arranged, received the least attention of anyone. As he had done with Dawid the year before, Besa went just twice to lay hands on Rikki where he sat, bright-eyed amid the now growing circle of clappers and singers, which was beginning to swell as a quiet but steady stream of people from the village came wandering in out of the night. The rest of us received far more attention: Dawid and Sanna falling into a deeply meditative state, seeming to withdraw further into themselves with each touch from the healers' hands; Vetkat collapsing to the ground as soon as Besa's hands were upon him, to lie there, face-down, fingers fluttering and twitching, while the healers came to him time and time again to stroke, caress, sob, cry.

This time, when Besa touched me, I felt nothing beyond that touch. No quietly thrilling, strangely electrical pulse. Yet, as the dance went on, the old feeling of peace, of equanimity that Besa's hands always imparted came stealing over me until by halfway through the dance I was deeply relaxed. When I asked Chris his impressions afterwards, he said that he too had felt nothing beyond the touch of hands. But later he admitted that the healing stayed in his dreams for days.

When Besa collapsed face-down in the firelit dust some two hours after the dance had begun, I assumed that it was over. Instead, the other healer picked him up a second time, breathed into the slack, mucus-smeared mouth and brought him round. Besa stood, swaying a few moments and looking blearily around him, seeming surprised to find the chorus clapping and singing on as before. Then he snapped back into full, joyful consciousness and whooped – not an entranced, spirit-seeking whoop – but a breath of pure celebration. He took a high-stepping pace forward and, ignoring us now, began his own dance around the fire, eyes clear and bright, happy and laughing. The tall BaKgalagadi healer continued to go around the circle, laying on hands, booming deep in his throat, but Besa's job, it seemed, was done, and now he wanted to dance just for the fun of it.

The trance dance became a party, with more and more people drifting in out of the starlit night to sit or stand by the fire and swell the song, the rhythm, adding the weight of their presence to the dance. Looking up, away from Besa's frantically jigging figure, I saw that more than a hundred people had gathered: young and old, toddlers and grandmothers. The young men stripped off their shirts and began, one by one, to enter the dance, leg rattles swishing, each one dancing his own style, creating a symphony of muscle, rib and taught sinew in the flickering, tiger-striped firelight while their girlfriends cackled and whooped from the sidelines and the kids ran around the outskirts of the circle, playing tag. The night rang with sound.

A movement from the clapping circle caught my eye: Rikki quietly got up and sought out his sleeping place, away behind the dark bulk of the vehicle. I caught a glimpse of his face as he left. He was smiling.

Soon I went the same way, feeling that sudden deep tiredness that comes over one at the end of a long journey. I found my blankets and laid them out in a dark hollow of sand, not far from Rikki, but not so close as to intrude upon his privacy. I lay on my back in the warm-cool sand, the sounds of the party washing over me from the fire, whose sparks drifted up towards the innumerable, blazing Kalahari stars. The sense of peace, of well-being that Besa always imparted to me lay quiet in my heart. The Bushmen would be all right. The process had begun and the first battle was won. And I had been allowed to be a part of it.

Rikki was murdered on Christmas Day of that same year. They found his body, head staved in with a rock, lying in the veld near Askham, a small coloured community on the back side of the Witdraai dunes. As with Kabuis, no one could explain why Rikki had been killed. A sacrifice, said the people, mourning. He and Kabuis, blood sacrifices for the gift of land, and the good rains which had that year begun to fall. Now, they said, the pain could come out and the healing could begin, repeating this over and over like a mantra as they drank and mourned and watched the clouds gather over the dunes.

The rains that year were the longest and most intense in living memory, so strong that whole dunes were driven into the riverbeds, telephone poles battered over, and tall, centuries-old camel-thorns riven by lightning. The animals in the park bred and multiplied; the new springbok lambs filling the calm days between the storms with bleating, the grass growing high and green between the dunes.

In March 2000 – a full year after the signing of the land claim – the Aub River flowed for the first time in fifty years. Chris and I flew back out to see it, and drove with Dawid north into the park to where the riverbed road disappeared under a miraculous, cool, clear flow that stretched from bank to bank, submerging the grasses.

Dawid let out a long whistle: '*Jasus* man! Look at that. Soon the waters will rise and fish will come swimming down the river. Fish in the desert – the Bushman loves that. Well, you know that all this was predicted. Mackai's prophecy of the strangers coming. And Regopstaan, my father's – that when those strangers came, and we all danced, especially our children – the little people – then would we get our land back, and the long thirst would end. And now see, we are beginning to get back the land, the rivers are flowing, and the old days coming back.'

During those months several more farms were handed over, but the park gates remained closed. So we went on the road with Dawid one last time, eastward through the rainy Transvaal to Pretoria, so the old leader could ask Mvuro Msimang, the National Parks Board's CEO, when the last part of Regopstaan's dream would be fulfilled, and the people be allowed back inside their old hunting grounds.

'I thought we had reached an amicable agreement,' said the tall, besuited CEO, looking perplexed and buzzing his secretary to call in the executive responsible for the Northern Cape Region, Dick Parris. This man, his voice high and quavering at the sight of the camera, said it was not the park's place to seek the Bushmen out. It was for the Bushmen and SASI to advise the park when they were ready to negotiate their place in the new park. Then the National Parks Board would be happy to look at any proposal they might submit.

'*Jasus*, these guys!' laughed Dawid, as we drove away into the rain. '*Skelms*, all of them!'

At the time I thought his reaction unreasonable. The door seemed open after all, and the Parks Board attitude co-operative. But a year later as this book was being finished, the Bushmen were still waiting.

Nevertheless a new millennium has begun, and the Bushmen and their vast, golden land, are still here. There are still hunters going out across the dunes and grasslands, bows in hand, to follow the spoor as their forefathers did. There are still women moving patiently among the plants and trees, singing to themselves as they fill their hide or ragged cotton aprons with the produce of the veld. Each month, when the moon shines down on the earth, there are dances in which men talk to spirits and fly aloft on journeys of the soul. Living like that, as old Dawid would say:

So that the rains will come again, and the little people can dance. For when the little people of the Kalahari dance, then shall the little people around the world dance too.

Ou Mackai te Kiraha.
Ou Mackai te Kiraha.

Epilogue

So where is the story now? Although at the time of writing the Xhomani had taken control of several of the farms granted them under the land claim, the power struggle between Petrus Vaalbooi's 'moderns' and Dawid's 'traditionals' had now begun to rage in earnest. As Roger Chennels, the human rights lawyers, politely put it: 'Ensuring that they [the "traditonals"] get a fair slice of the resources and are not side-lined by their more worldy-wise colleagues is an ongoing source of conflict and debate.' But he added: 'It is considered that the community must experience the full extent of the conflict . . . so that a solution will emerge from their own process and not be imposed from without.'

There were many negative reports. Some claimed that the 'moderns' had, among other abuses, pocketed large sums of donor money. There were murmurs from government circles about an enquiry into missing funds. I was also told that the 'moderns' had shot out much of the game in order to make the land available for sheep and cattle, having paid the local police to provide the fire-power. Others saw the 'traditionals' as the problem, complaining that since the land claim they had simply descended into a worse drunken hell than ever, and were holding up the process of development.

As for the park, although no permanent settlement inside the fence was to be allowed, the authorities recognized the Xhomanis' ownership of 25,000 hectares in its southern section. Late in 2001, Roger Chennels wrote optimistically that 'a "joint-management" regime' for managing cultural and ecological agendas had been set up between the Xhomani and the park, controlled by a council of elders, and based on a system already worked out in Australia between aborigines and national parks. 'It seems safe to predict,' he wrote, 'that the agreement will be finalized by early 2002, and that a joyous "First Peoples" celebration, which aboriginal peoples worldwide will be invited to join, will be scheduled for August or September 2002.'

But at the time of writing – May 2002 – no such final agreement had yet appeared, and there was even debate among the Xhomani themselves as to whether they were actually ready for such a move, given their own internecine conflicts and continuing abuse of the bottle.

Meanwhile, up in Botswana, the government became more belligerent than ever in its attempts to evict the Bushmen from the Central Kalahari Game Reserve to make way for high-end tourism and diamond mining (under the aegis of Debswana, the 50/50 partnership between De Beers/Anglo-American and the Botswana government). In early 2002 the water supply to Molapo and the reserve's other villages was cut off. People were loaded onto trucks and moved out. By mid-2002 only a few families were still hanging on in the reserve, their hunting licenses revoked, eking out a living by gathering and on hand-outs and emergency water relief provided by the staff of First People of the Kalahari.

The British-based indigenous-rights group Survival International took up their cause, organizing vigils outside the Botswana High Commission in London (which ignited other protests in Paris and Milan). The First People of the Kalahari leadership took steps towards challenging their own government in the courts. A flurry of letters and petitions sought to shame Anglo American and De Beers into putting into practice their claim to adopt only beneficent policies towards indigenous peoples. There was even – in February 2002 – a meeting between WIMSA (the Working Group for Indigenous Minorities in Southern Africa) and the World Bank in Windhoek, Namibia, to discuss the issue – the first of several promised meetings. In addition to this, the European Union sent a proposal to the Botswana government offering to use EU funds to supply water, health and school services to the families remaining in the reserve.

Yet the situation did not improve. Summing up the attitude of the Botswana authorities, government minister Lt. Col Merafhe said (absurdly): 'We all aspire to Cadillacs. [The Bushmen] can no longer be allowed to commune with flora and fauna.'

So is there anything positive to say? Early in 2002 Roger Chennels' law firm won – on the Xhomanis' behalf – a vast 'intellectual property' claim against the pharmaceutical giant Pfizer (the company that launched Viagra). It turned out that the company had tried to patent as a slimming drug a Kalahari plant – Hoodia – used for millennia by Bushmen to suppress hunger and thirst. If ladies-who-lunch start buying this slimming drug the world over, this will bring almost unthinkably large sums of money to the Kalahari. How this will affect the Bushmen remains to be seen.

But when I got word of the victory, I could not help but remember Old Mackai and Regopstaan's prophecies. The rains had come, and the people were dancing on their own land – albeit with many, many problems – and now, with the land claims and the drug-company settlement behind them, perhaps a precedent had been set that might allow 'little people' elsewhere to begin that dance as well. Meanwhile, at Nyae Nyae in Namibia, the Ju'/Hoansi-run Game Conservancy continued to support the people in their traditional hunting and gathering life, and the community tourism projects there and at other locations in the Kalahari were slowly beginning to prosper. And the rains stayed good.

Belinda and Vetkat moved away from the madness and drinking to a wild farm called Blinkwater ('shining water') near the park fence. There Vetkat began to revive the tradition of Bushman painting, concentrating on the theme of healing and shape-shifting – and his first collection was purchased by the University of Pretoria. Meanwhile some of the elders began to pass on, among them old Antas, the gentlest of the Xhomani, who had healed Cait Andrews of her stomach cancer.

As for Dawid, he claimed that he was growing tired. Before making the journeys to see Besa, he had said that he would hang on, that he would be strong, only until the land claim was signed. In fact he had hung on several years beyond that. Now he began to take a back seat, letting the alcohol take him again, emerging to conduct healings from time to time, but otherwise appearing to give up on the role of leader. Others began to emerge in his stead – among them Isak and a younger man called Abraham, who had been very much in the background during the times I had visited the Xhomani. More and more the people began looking to these two for decisions about the future.

But Dawid was not finished yet. Late in 2001 my phone rang. It was him – one of his surprise, out-of-the-blue phone calls from the Kalahari. 'Rru,' he said, chuckling his naughty chuckle: 'Have you forgotten us? You'd better not or I'll *donner* you for sure the next time I see you.' He had dreamed another dream, he said. Of traveling to the USA to put the case of all of the Kalahari peoples to the media, and to meet there with other indigenous leaders and healers from the rest of the world. To remind us Westerners that we are the 'little people' too. 'E-hey Rru,' he laughed, his voice teasing: 'I hope you're feeling strong.' As this edition went to the printers we were busy raising the money to make his dream a reality.

And Besa? Besa is still at Groot Laagte. Still dancing; still healing.

A Note About the Cover

I was on my way to the Tsodilo Hills, hoping to see the famous rock paintings there and to meet the old Bushman leader who – my cousin Michael had told me – still made his arrow-heads from the thigh-bones of giraffes. The night before reaching the hills I dreamed – under the bright moon – that I had already arrived. The old Bushman leader and I were talking under a tree. Did he still make his arrow-heads from bone, I asked? No, he replied, his people had been moved away from the hills. And they were no longer allowed to hunt. So the old life was over and now he was just sitting in the sand, waiting to die.

Next day, upon reaching the hills, we found – as told in the book – that the Bushmen had indeed been moved away, and we made camp in one of their old caves. That night I dreamed again – this time a dream of flying. I flew out the cave mouth and up along a shaft of moonlight, swimming up it, laughing and laughing. Then I went soaring out over the whole Kalahari, which lay stretched out beneath me like a dry, moonlit ocean. This went on for what seemed like hours until, sometime near dawn, I returned like an owl to the cave.

That day, when I at last met the old Bushman leader I had come so far to see, I could have picked him out in a crowd. The same man from my dream – the very one. So I asked him, as closely as I could remember, the questions from that dream, which are those related in the text. His answers were, almost verbatim, those of the dream. Afterwards, on impulse, I told him of the two dreams. He simply smiled. Later, the young Bushman who was acting as my guide said, *a propos* of nothing: 'Maybe the ancestors are welcoming you.'

When the time came to write the book, I cut the story. There was already so much magic in it, and I was worried that anything that seemed too 'New-Agey' might undermine the urgent reality of the Bushmen's struggle for survival and identity.

Perhaps two days later I received a FedEx package from my publishers in London. It contained the image they wanted to use on the cover, and they wanted my approval. I pulled it out. It was the old leader from the Tsodilo Hills, the same one, the very same. But taken perhaps fifteen or twenty years before I had met him, when he *was* still making his arrow-heads from giraffe bone, and living the way his (and perhaps our) ancestors always had. I phoned the publishers immediately: 'Use it,' I said.